The TEACHINGS of the MASTERS of PERFECTION

Roy Eugene Davis

CSA Press, Publishers
Lake Rabun Road
Lakemont, Georgia
30552

Standard Book Number 0-87707-219-1

For information about Center for Spiritual Awareness or for information about book or study aids write: CSA, Lake Rabun Road, Lakemont, Georgia 30552

Printed and Manufactured in the United States of America

CONTENTS

Preface/7
How to Read This Book/10

PRELIMINARY ESSAYS
1   The Teachings of the Masters of Perfection/11
2   On Being Clear and Knowing Who We Are/21
3   A Natural Life in Harmony With Nature/29
4   An Overview: God *Is* All That Is/37
5   The Fourteen Spheres of World Manifestation/47

TEXT AND COMMENTARY ON THE YOGA SUTRAS
6   The Soul's Awakening and Turning to the Source/68
7   Kriya Yoga: The Path of Discipleship and Purification/82
8   Siddhis: The Powers of Perfection/111
9   Enlightenment and Final Liberation/165

EPILOGUE
The Emergence of the New Era and Cycles of Destiny/187

TEXT AND COMMENTARY ON SELF-KNOWLEDGE
The Wisdom Yoga of Shankaracharya/201

APPENDIX
Supplemental Notes to Chapters/238
Glossary of Sanskrit Words and Terms/295
The Realization of Spiritual Perfection/305
Guidelines to Personal Study and Meditation/311

PREFACE

This text has been prepared as a major source for sincere students of the enlightenment quest. It supersedes three of my former works* because of the more comprehensive examination of the theme. Except for some material used in the appendix, which I feel is useful to retain, the text is new and original.

The introductory essays were first distributed to our many students as a series of regular lessons. The commentary on the *Yoga Sutras* is the heart of the message and will require much careful study and analysis. The *Yoga Sutras* were first written as concise aphorisms over one thousand years ago and are considered to contain the essence of enlightenment systems practiced for thousands of years before that. The epilogue and the extensive material making up the appendix complete the work.

Readers of any faith and of any intentional spiritual discipline will find the information here shared to be most helpful. The preparation of the manuscript was extremely useful to me as an exercise in personal discipline and discernment. Indeed, I wrote this book for myself. I am pleased to be able to share it with you.

Roy Eugene Davis
1979

*The three books by the author which are no longer published are: *This Is Reality*, his initial commentary on the *Yoga Sutras*; *The Way of the Initiate*; and *The Path of Soul Liberation*.

*I salute the supreme teacher, the Truth,
whose nature is bliss, who is the giver
of the highest happiness, who is pure
wisdom, who is beyond all qualities and
infinite like the sky, who is beyond words,
who is one and eternal, pure and still,
who is beyond all change and phenomena
and who is the silent witness to all our
thoughts and emotions—I salute Truth,
the supreme teacher.*

—Ancient Vedic Hymn

Preliminary Essays

HOW TO READ THIS BOOK

In order to become familiar with the material it would be well to examine the text from beginning to end. Then, begin with the preface and read through completely. Wherever a word is found which is not completely clear to you, turn to the glossary and learn the precise definition. A few words and terms not found in the glossary will be explained in the body of the text.

After a careful reading of the material, begin again and study more slowly. Examine, with clear discernment and awakened intuition, the meaning of all that is shared. The section containing the commentary on the *Yoga Sutras* will be deserving of your attention for many years to come.

Many of the Sanskrit words and terms have entered into common usage and, usually, we have italicized them only when first used in the text.

Chapter One
The TEACHINGS of The
MASTERS of PERFECTION

The Divine Intelligence and Power has openly expressed for centuries through and *as* many enlightened souls. The work and teachings of such manifestations is our current theme and our title for the text is appropriate. Perfection refers to proficiency, a high degree of excellence, and the state of being perfect.

Levels of soul awareness can be minutely classified. An awakening soul, working through a human body, is said to be in material consciousness. When one is "born again" one begins to become aware of the true nature as a viewpoint of God. The stages are from simple consciousness to self-consciousness, then to super-consciousness, and, finally, to Self (Soul)-realization. When one is enlightened (Self-realized) while working through a body and still neutralizing mental impressions or karmic patterns, one is said to be free while embodied. When all mental impressions which formerly restricted are neutralized or transcended, one indeed experiences spiritual perfection. A person who is inwardly free, even while working out mental impressions due to prior causes, is a true master because such a one clearly comprehends the world-process as a play of creative energies; from the Godhead to the full outer expression of material manifestation. When such a soul becomes free from compulsory ties to any aspect of nature, that one is then known as a master of perfection. The Sanskrit word is *siddha*. The *siddhis* are the "powers of perfection" and are soul abilities which easily express when the mind is clear and the soul is fully conscious.

A master of perfection is not limited to any plane, dimension, realm, planet, or solar system. A master of perfection is truly a clear expression of God working within the realm of nature. Gross matter makes up our known material world. Subtle matter is the cause and support of gross forms. Behind the physical realm lies the realm of prana, the energy-life-force which enlivens nature. Behind the life-force realm lies the world of subtle electricities. Behind this realm is subtle-substance (*maya*), made up of: *Creative energy, light particles, time, and space.* On the other side (or the inside) of the realm of maya are the realms of light, the true "heavens." All of what we can perceive flows from the Godhead, the only outer expression of Pure Consciousness. The realm of Pure Consciousness is also referred to as the Void, the Absolute, and the Transcendental Field.

God and Souls Understood

That which is known as God is Supreme Consciousness endowed with electric attributes. The energy of God manifests as nature and the intelligence of God directs the natural order. Viewpoints of God which become identified with nature and animate forms are known as souls. A master of perfection is enlightened about the nature of God, souls, and the world-process. The body is the vehicle through which God (as soul) expresses in nature. "Know ye not that ye are the temple of God, and that the Spirit of God dwelleth in you?" (*1 Cor. 3:16*).

Souls are not born and they do not die. Souls identify with nature and forget, for a while, their true condition. Only the body or form changes, while souls change not in essence. When a soul is aware of its true nature, as a viewpoint of God, the idea of death is no longer relevant. "Verily, verily, I say unto you, if a man keep my saying (remain stable in the realization of his God nature), he shall never see death." (*John 8:51*)

A master of perfection is one through whom God's will and God's activity naturally flows. All power is given to such a liberated being; but it is the power of God that expresses, and a master of perfection has no self-will or ego-motivation in thought or action. This is why enlightened souls can only do the will of God and why they do not and cannot intervene in mankind's evolutionary process unless inwardly directed. There is a plan for the unfold-ment of the natural order, and God through Himself, as souls, does what needs to be done, on time and always appropriately. One who is not possessed of cosmic consciousness may wonder about the ways of God, but one who becomes possessed of under-standing clearly sees why events unfold as they do. We may ask, "Why does God not do away with war and poverty? Why does God not awaken more quickly as souls and create an enlightened world order?" The only answer can be for us to awaken to the level of God-realization and then see why things are as they are.

We shall explore, in the text before us, just how Consciousness expresses on all levels and just how we became involved with the grand process that is nature. We shall explore the possibilities before us of awakening to the ultimate realization of our true status as masters of perfection. For centuries, fully illumined souls have been working on this planet to quicken the evolutionary process. Not just a few masters of perfection, but thousands upon thousands of them have played their useful roles. Some have become known to history; most are not acknowledged because their roles were to work quietly, unencumbered by the misunder-standing masses.

The Methods and Teachings
of the Masters of Perfection

Who are the masters of perfection, the illumined souls who do God's will in the world? Where and how do they live? What are their responsibilities? What do they teach and how do they teach? Much glamorous fiction has been published about the presumed work of the masters. Few authentic accounts are available and, often, even in these works the authors leave out stories which might overly strain the reader's attempt to comprehend. One of the more complete accounts published in our current century is Paramahansa Yogananda's *Autobiography of a Yogi*. In this book my guru shared his understanding and introduced to the world the fact of certain illumined souls who have a specific mission to assist mankind in our current era. Yogananda told us that he could have written more than he did, but some things were too amazing to put in a book for the general public.

Once when Yoganandaji was living at his retreat house near Twenty Nine Palms, California, he told us the following story. He once was meditating and the thought came to mind that he would more intimately like to know about Sri Ramakrishna, the great saint who lived in India in the latter part of the last century. A disciple asked, "Did you succeed in communicating with him?" Yoganandaji replied, "Yes, Ramakrishna came to me in his subtle body and we sat together in meditation."

On other occasions my guru told us that the grounds of his retreats and ashrams were frequently visited by the saints whose bodies were so subtle that only the trained clairvoyant eye could behold them. This occurrence is understood by the masters of perfection. A *Siddha Ashram*, a dwelling place of a true master, is said to be so purified that the energies from the finer realms flow into the physical world at such places. Because of a master's purity and illumination, his immediate environment tends to be influenced by spiritual radiations. We are forever experiencing the interchange of radiation-influences. We are influenced by our environment and our environment is influenced by our mental condition and state of consciousness. When the inner eye is open we live simultaneously in this world and the rarefied world of God's reflection. This contact with inner and outer worlds is the major function of a master on this planet. Purifying energies flow into planetary consciousness through the presence and being of a true master.

In a larger sense, the purifying energy of God is also emerging today through millions of awakening souls. God expresses as the masters (conscious extensions of Himself) and God works through all souls in the direction of awakening to cosmic consciousness. There is the teaching of the *avatara*, the descent of God to earth in human form. There is also the understanding of the *universal avatara*; God resident in all human beings and coming into conscious expression through mass spiritual awakening. It is the Christ, the intelligence of God, awakening in every person which redeems the world. The Christ nature of each soul is identical to the Christ nature of God. When we inwardly know and affirm for another, "I behold the Christ in you," we actually awaken and call forth that aspect of God in another.

We are never alone in our quest for understanding. Our inner nature is already free and possessed of total knowledge, but, in many instances, this has to be allowed to come forth and take dominion over mental states and feelings. We can also attune our consciousness to the reality of God and experience conscious support, direction, and uplift. We can commune with the saints and masters of the ages and actually attract their spiritual energies into our lives. This very real matter of spiritual attunement is not always understood. Jesus referred to himself as the vine and to his disciples as the branches of that vine. Nourishment flows from the source of nourishment (God) through the masters to their disciples. Some rare souls can attune themselves directly to God always. We can each learn to do this through regular and correct meditation practice. However, even if one is not yet perfect in meditation practice, there is always the possibility of attunement with God through one of God's own expressions, a master of perfection.

A true master does not stand between a seeker and God. A true master *is* God appearing in human form. This is the mystical explanation of Jesus the Christ. That human form known as Jesus actually was Christ Consciousness *as* that life. When a soul is liberated it knows it is God *as* the viewpoint known as the soul. A liberated person does not think in terms of Soul and God but as God assuming the viewpoint known as the soul. All are viewpoints of God, but not all are conscious of this.

A master is conscious that he does nothing personally. A master knows that whatever is done by him is done by God *as* the personality and form others behold. Virtue flows out from a master's being, though his eyes, his touch, his thought, and his quiet presence. This *virtue* is the vitality of God flowing to meet whatever need is presented when, as a result of attunement and responsiveness, the person in need is open to receive.

Some masters live in seclusion and do their work behind the social scene, either teaching special people who will go forth to teach others or teaching prepared disciples who are working out their personal salvation. Always the spiritual radiations of the masters infuse the mental atmosphere of the planet and beneficially influence the evolutionary process. Some great masters remain "on earth" for hundreds of years even after they withdraw from the physical form. Through them the energy of God enters the universe. Other masters remain for hundreds, even thousands of years in physical form. They either renew the body through advanced methods, or they remain "ever youthful" in appearance because they work from the level of understanding by which this is possible. God is superior to the worlds and a realized soul is superior to the mind and body through which it expresses.

Some of the masters awakened to the realization of their true nature after having been involved with sense identification. That is, they came into this world partially unaware and then, usually after incarnations, experienced enlightenment. A few masters have never known delusion; they have always been conscious and came into this realm from spheres of light, without need and without being in bondage to externals. These latter masters are the true *mortal-immortals* who roam the manifest worlds as gods. And, just as there are masters of perfection on the physical planes, so there are masters whose mission it is to work on the inner planes, assisting those on the astral planes to higher stages of realization. Wherever there are souls in need of encouragement, wherever there is need for evolutionary influence, there will be the pure viewpoints of God known as the masters.

According to this teaching tradition, some masters are actively working to improve the world condition, knowing that the cleansing process will continue for many thousands of years. While inwardly knowing their respective duties, some such souls outwardly work in such diverse areas of world service as statesmanship, the arts, commerce, education, science, and wherever they can best serve. World transcendence is not the goal of all conscious beings. Some are destined to leave this world for realms of light, but many are destined to remain involved with material manifestation and play out their role in harmony with the longer process. This world-changing process is known as *dharma*, the way of righteousness. Here is a key to understanding our role in life: are we participating with the "way of righteousness" or are we resisting this trend? Or are we just moving through life in a trance, with hardly any conscious awarness of what is taking place? The masters teach that our present participation in the world-process, if conscious, is a spiritual discipline which results in true understanding and the liberation of consciousness. This message is revealed with clarity in the early chapters of that epic-text, *The Bhagavad-Gita*. In the *Gita*, Arjuna (the seeking soul) is world-weary and wants to withdraw from participation. Krishna (the Divine Embodiment; the higher nature of each of us) instructs his disciple in the practical matter of facing life's challenges as a hero-spirit should, as a spiritual warrior who can unfold the soul's capacities by learning through experience that there is a higher solution to every human problem.

How many masters of perfection are on the planet at this time, in our current era? There are thousands of them, men and women who live consciously with clear understanding and total attunement to God's will. There are thousands more being trained for world service and additional thousands being born into the world. Babaji, for instance, the first in my line of gurus, works quietly and participates in the gradual cleansing of planetary consciousness. He is one of the *mortal-immortals* and has been embodied for thousands of years and will continue his mission on earth for thousands of years hence. Readers new to this teaching tradition may find this difficult to accept, but I assure one and all that it is true. All masters of perfection work in harmony with one another even though their outer teaching tradition may vary. Let us be ever mindful that wherever a master is playing a role, there God is doing what God intends for world good.

Is there a *hierarchy*, a system of persons or things in a graded order, a series of successive ranks of responsible cooperation, now regulating the unfolding process of man's experience? Does God work through channels of command? Are there lines of communication through which God's good will flows into perfect expression? Of course, there are. God does obviously flow into expression in a gradual and successive order and there are ranks (levels) of responsible interaction. But it is God who *is* everything and it is God who *does* everything. The spiritual hierarchy, then, is God manifesting as every agent of expression. The masters of perfection are some of the agents, but, when we understand the process, so are you and I. We are all God's viewpoints and our world is God's energy-manifesting. A careful examination of this grand process leads to cosmic conscious understanding.

Some fantasy stories about the masters of perfection and their respective roles in the play of events can seem almost-real, but there is something left to doubt in many of the stories. Spiritual fiction may play a role in introducing new seekers to the real process of world redemption, but it must be seen for what it is once one settles into a responsible program of discipline designed to clear mind and consciousness of all that is not useful. Some books have been published as factual information when, in truth, the author was but sharing "what might be" according to his own ability to grasp the truth. Books about the masters have been the result of an author claiming telepathic communication with "ascended masters" or through trance mediumship. These books always contain a mixture of truth and untruth because of the influence of the author's conditioned mind. I do not know of any master who gives any credence to "channeled" material. Masters often do work through people, but their method is through gentle telepathic encouragement, a more evidenced input of will-to-positive-action, or by verbal instruction.

Except in rare instances, one who is seeking on the path will be directed to the written word or to an instruction opportunity in the form of a qualified spiritual teacher. God is all there is. God is all that is. We may write of the masters of perfection and we may tell of wondrous happenings, but everything of which we write, if it be true, is an activity of God. God is not the cause of human happiness nor is God the cause of human unhappiness. God is working to unfold through and as all creation and through and as all life forms. When we live in harmony with the laws of nature we experience health and satisfaction. When we are educated relative to the principles of correct thinking and wise living, it is then up to each one of us to abide by the principles we know to be true. It is by this process that the masters of perfection realized their essential nature. It is by this process that each one of us can realize the truth.

The Simple and Direct Way

There is a simple and direct way to the realization of the truth about life. The way, so the masters teach, is to yearn for knowledge and to yearn for a personal conscious experience in God. Then we are to do what we know we should do to insure harmony in our lives. We are to rid ourselves of all that is not in accord with freedom of the soul. We are to decide how much time and attention to to give work, to social life, to family and to friends. We are to decide how much time and attention to give to study and meditation. We can so easily tell what is actually important to us by how we spend our time and how we order our thoughts. *Each person on the planet is now doing what is most important to him, from his present level of understanding.* If it is important for us to meditate, to study, to remain calm and centered, and to discover the truth about life, we will direct our attention to these matters.

It is of value, I feel, for us to examine the teachings of the masters of perfection. More important, however, is that we emulate their lives and awaken to the understanding of our changeless nature in this incarnation.

No true master will say that his way, as far as methods and systems recommended, is the only way for all souls. No true master will say that his is the most important teaching mission on the planet. A true master, while working through a personality, is fully aware that he but plays a role and that God alone is the operant influence. A true master will attract our attention and then turn our attention and our love to God.

There is only God to be known and the truth about how God expresses. God can be known to all souls and the truth is available to every seeker. The truth cannot be contained by any organization, group, or person. God cannot be contained by any organization, group, or person. When we are fully conscious we are aware that God is what God is, without a form or with countless forms.

Chapter Two
ON BEING CLEAR and
KNOWING WHO WE ARE

To be enlightened, to be liberated, is to be clear and fully aware of who and what we are. Who we really are is not what we think we are or who we feel we are. It is human nature to draw a comforting conclusion about the nature of self and then justify that conclusion through rationalization or through attempts to prove it. There are undoubtedly more clear people on the planet than is publicly known because a clear person does not really have a need to announce his or her enlightenment or prove a level of understanding. On the contrary, unless it is a person's destiny to "go public" for the purpose of educating others, the enlightenment is not complete. It is a natural tendency for some newly enlightened people to begin to share their lives with the world, but if there is a compulsion in this direction, the person is not yet spiritually mature. While it is certainly an inspiration to us to meet others who are clear, the important matter at hand is for us to be clear. So, let us examine the situation and look through appearances to that which is real.

We will examine the nature of the soul, the nature and function of the mind, and the possibility of our awakening from mechanical survival activities to the experience of truly living as we were meant to live. We will not become caught up in fantasy or mental traps. We will avoid preoccupation with theory and opinion, with methods, techniques, and ways. I am sure the reader is aware that many people now involved with metaphysical studies or consciousness expanding processes are no more clear now than before they began their involvement. One of the traps on the enlightenment path is that of preoccupation with systems and philosophies. When we take our social needs and our conditioned responses into the arena of metaphysical study we are remaining as we were, in understanding, and we have simply changed our involvement with life while continuing to live out of human consciousness.

The Nature of the Soul and
Our Relationship With the Mind

The soul, the spirit, the being is a viewpoint of God playing a role in time and space and involved with material creation. This, according to the masters of perfection, is the correct explanation of who and what we really are. Insight into this reality can, alone, result in the enlightenment experience. The soul does not require experience in order to grow or develop because the soul is already self-complete, as God is self-complete. The soul may be inclined to participate in the drama of life, but it does not need the experience. Reams of philosophical nonsense have been widely published purportedly dealing with soul destiny, soul evolvement, soul requirements, and on and on. This material is merely the result of unenlightened speculation. It may have value for the person who develops the philosophy and it may inspire and motivate the seeking reader, but, just the same, much of what is explained about the nature and destiny of the soul is simply not the truth. Again, *we are viewpoints of God, playing a role in time and space, involved with material creation.* With correct understanding our potential for expression is virtually unlimited, restricted only by natural law. Whatever is possible for an enlightened person to do, we can do. Whatever is possible for an enlightened person to know, we can know. There is no difference between the reality of my being, the reality of your being, or the reality of any other being, regardless of the roles people play. The being, the real nature of a spiritual master is identical with the real nature of the most impoverished and victimized person on the planet. The soul has the capacity to manipulate matter, cause effects, create situations and relationships, and then dissolve situations and relationships. We do these things all the time, usually unconsciously and without intent or purpose.

What is this mind with which and through which the soul

operates? Can it be understood, used creatively, and rendered free from complications? Here is what enlightenment masters teach about the mind: *The mind is a subtle or fine material medium with electrical characteristics, which can receive, store, and process information.* The mind is not unlike a computer, except the mind is more complex, has greater potential, and can be consciously used by the soul. Not all souls use the mind with full awareness. Instead, they allow the mind to be conditioned or programed and then they live out their lives according to directions, tendencies, and needs of the subconscious and deep unconscious levels of mind. Our mental field works in relationship with our brain and nervous system, just as our subtle vital body works in relationship with our physical body. The brain is the organ of the mind, and even when the soul departs the body, leaving the brain behind, it can take with it the mind. It is also possible for the soul to step aside and examine the mind, repair any malfunctioning aspects, and then use the cleared mind with conscious intent.

We have all said, "I can't make up my mind," "My mind is confused," or "My mind doesn't work right." At times, so involved are we with our confused mental states that we almost allow them to overwhelm our rational sense. In many instances the refusal to take command of the mind and its functioning is simply a denial of personal responsibility. If we affirm that we cannot maintain the ideal mental attitude or that we are confused and inept because of what is happening to us, we are playing the role of the victim instead of assuming the viewpoint and role of the master of circumstance.

A useful experiment for anyone is to sit in a quiet place and, without judgment or rationalization, observe the working of one's own mind. Observe how thoughts emerge to the conscious level, how thoughts are connected, the interior conversations, how attention flickers from subject to subject. Sometimes, during half-sleep one can hear what seems to be definite conversations between various people who are expressing personal opinions and manifesting various shadings of emotion. It all takes place within our own mind. Recall the rich variety of perception and experience available to us while dreaming! This, too, takes place entirely within the mental field.

The mind's major function is to enable the soul, working

through a body, to relate to the material universe. Through insight as well as through personal experience with the world and our response to it, we learn to adapt and see to the survival of the body. The urge of the mind to see to the survival of the body leads to many interesting problems in human behavior. We see people who play the helpless role in order to be assisted by others. We see people who experience one illness after another in order to receive attention or to avoid the responsibility for taking control of their lives. We see people who resist awakening because they are literally afraid that when they know the truth about themselves and about life, their little human games will be revealed as the meaningless and purposeless routines they are.

Many of the survival routines we acquire are learned during our early childhood years. We are not here blaming parents or anyone's environment, we are merely pointing to the obvious time in one's human experience when survival routines are impressed upon the mind. We all know people who are fully aware of their dominating behavior, their need for control over others, their need for approval, their need for things to be a certain way to allow them to feel secure. Even when they know better, these people will still persist in unhealthy, destructive, or selfish behavior because it makes their life work. We also know people who are not aware of why they do what they do or of why they feel as they do. Courage, independence, creativity, communication skills . . . these can be taught early in life to any aware person. We have but to draw out the innate capacities of the soul for health and knowledge to be experienced. But the self-awareness of the soul can be at times shut down, and a person can be educated into fear, dependency, mechanical behavior, and neurotic response to relationships. Not all souls are heavily conditioned by environment; some seem to come through the most oppressive and life-denying conditions possible and emerge radiant, self-reliant, and healthy-minded.

To blame the past, to blame others, to continue to regret or resent presumed causes for present problems is useless. The past cannot be retrieved, others cannot change what they did or did not do, so regret and resentment are evidence of self-pity. Harboring regret and resentment, if allowed to run its course, will result in further inability to function and even illness. Whatever our present attitudes or conditionings, they are with us now, in the present . . . they may have a connection with past experiences, but their roots are not in the past, they are in the present. We can change what is presently at hand with a single decision. In meta-physical-occult circles one sometimes hears talk of present-time problems being due to events, actions, or thoughts of the past: thus the idea, "this is my karma I must work out" that many people accept. Karma is the accumulation of impressions stored in the deeper layers of the mind, often related to emotion or feeling. It is true that desires tend to externalize and be fulfilled. Long forgotten desires can, at any appropriate time, mature. We fulfill our own prophecies about ourselves over and over. When good fortune occurs or misfortune surfaces we often exclaim, "I knew this would happen. I just knew it would!" We often talk ourselves into the near and distant future by the words we use and the mental pictures we entertain.

We have before us the beautiful opportunity of knowing the truth about ourselves and of entering into a conscious relationship with God. A life lived without awareness neutralizes the purpose of our being here. From many sides we are given the wrong advice. "It's a hard, cruel world," one will tell us. "You have to compete, struggle and beat out the other fellow," another will offer. Still another will confide: "The way to make it is to cut the corners and work the deals." Then we have that classic: "If you have food in your stomach and a roof over your head, you should be grateful." We are not denying the usefulness of food and shelter, but body needs should require but a fraction of our time and energy. And what about our relationships? Are our relationships with others open, mature, fair, and honest? Or do we live a lie? Perhaps we have settled for "making do" and "getting by" as our way to survive? Whose life are we living anyway? Are we doing what we do because we are certain it is what we should do? Or are we doing what we do because we are allowing others to fulfill their dreams through us? Do others contribute to our feelings of guilt or ineptitude? Do we lack courage? Are we afraid to examine life and draw our own conclusions? Just why do we do the things we do?

Do we always have to be right? Do we require agreement from others concerning our position? Or is it enough for us to inwardly know we are all right and be self-content? Can we allow others the freedom to be themselves, without our having to change them or control them? All of the foolish things we do are done because we are working through mental conditionings and not from the understanding of our real nature as a free spirit. How does one get free? The easiest way is to just be free! If this isn't experienced we then must settle down to a program of working at it. Not that working at it causes freedom, but it creates the environment in which, when the occasion is right for us, we can awaken to the conscious understanding of who we are and what life is all about. This awakening is the enlightenment experience and those who report on it tell us pretty much the same things. They tell of an incredible sense of well-being, of inner peace, of true foundationless happiness. They tell us that being consciously aware is, in itself, sufficient.

Enlightenment frees us from dependence upon things. This is what is meant by soul liberation. Liberation is not necessarily our removal from the time-space field of expression; it is understanding everything so completely that we can function in time and space, play our personal role, freely, easily, and without need for relative security trappings or feed-back to prove our knowing and sense of being. Many human problems are due to the need people have for reinforcement and support. "I will be happy if you say you love me" is one line we use. "I will be secure and peaceful if I can be assured that things will always remain the way they are" is another line. We even affirm that we will be happy when we have enough money, when we reach a goal or fulfill a dream. When we talk like this we are going at life from the wrong end. A conscious being, a free soul, can cause effects, easily set and reach goals, openly communicate, and is free of the need for praise or approval. An enlightened person may function effectively in an active environment or he may choose a more remote and quiet space for himself. There is no right or wrong about personal choice in the matter, for an enlightened person simply does what must be done. An enlightened person, a liberated person, is sane, healthy and natural. An enlightened person is functional, and, in time, people and things around an enlightened person also tend to function more efficiently.

Attention, Intention
and Specific Purpose in Life

How conscious are we when we perform? How aware are we, how attentive are we, as we move through the day? When we have a job to do, do we give it total attention, follow through to completion, and then move on to the next task at hand? Or do we perform in a half-conscious manner, starting and stopping, never quite finishing? Or are we weighed down by our responsibilities and overcome by pressing problems? With complete attention given to whatever is at hand we are in total communication. We are no longer mechanical, living from subconscious urgings; we are conscious! When we initiate an action, what is our intention regarding the outcome? Do we intend to succeed or are we *expecting* failure? Do we intend to communicate or do we anticipate communication problems? When we say we will do a thing, do we do it so that others can depend upon us? When we make an appointment, do we arrive on time or do we always arrive late? If we clearly intend to do a thing we will then follow through and do it. This will result in inner peace and order for ourselves and will improve our relationships with other people.

A life lived with purpose is always more satisfying. We are not referring to unenlightened motive but to conscious purpose. I once heard a person declare, "If I didn't really believe that what I am doing had meaning, my life would be empty!" Yes, conviction and a sense of meaning to life is useful. Far more useful is to consciously know that what we do is useful and serves a purpose. With enlightenment there is no question about the usefulness of one's life. Without enlightenment there will always be the nagging suspicion that things are not quite as they should be.

One often continues through life, with good intentions, experiencing problems common to the human condition and hoping for enlightenment, sometime. The key to awakening is to utilize the present opportunities to live consciously, with directed attention, clear intention, and specific purpose. One might ask of oneself, "How would I feel, think, act, and respond if I were now enlightened?" Insight will be experienced and then one can go ahead and feel, think, act, and respond in line with higher understanding.

Even after enlightenment some traces of conditioned memory may yet remain, but they will have little influence upon one's life. An enlightened person will easily be impervious to conditioned patterns and occasional moments of doubt or fear. In time the mental field will be cleansed of all unwanted and non-useful patterns and there will be a perfect integration of knowing, thinking, feeling, and activity. Areas of the mind which were formerly not accessible will be opened, energy formerly restricted and restrained will be released, clear knowing will replace beliefs and not-knowing. The happiness, serenity, inner peace, and perfect sense of balance promised to all who are invited to awaken to the truth, will be permanently experienced.

Chapter Three
A NATURAL LIFE in
HARMONY WITH NATURE

The intelligent person learns to cooperate with nature's laws in order to experience health and to live the vital life. In some instances failure to live in harmony with nature is due to lack of understanding. In other instances failure to live in harmony with nature is due to in-built conditionings and attitudes which drive one in the direction of failure and death. In the former instance what is required is education and motivation; in the latter instance what is required is spiritual awakening and a new, transformed, outlook on life. I am here emphasizing that it is within every conscious person's grasp to learn, from now on, how to live a natural life in harmony with nature. The natural life is not hard, it is not complicated; it assures the best personal environment for growth and unfoldment.

Let us clearly understand that it is a characteristic of life to thrive, to flourish, to express. Given the ideal environment, the life force that animates every living form will see to the completion of the destined pattern of that form. The vital life within us is intelligent. Unlike electricity, the vital life within us has purpose. The vital life within us, the soul force, is the very expression of the life of God. As we examine the whole of the life process we see everywhere that the process is supportive and nourishing in urge and tendency. We, therefore, need but learn to cooperate with what is already in motion. We need not think in terms of causing health, healthy relationships or prosperity, we only need to create the situation in which health, open relationships and prosperity can express.

It is never too late for one to be educated correctly. Even should education be neglected until an advanced age, the knowledge can enhance awareness and be retained for future use in subtle realms or a possible return to this plane in a new body. Such phrases as "You can't teach an old dog new tricks" and "It's too late to do any good now" never enter the mind of a rational being. Of course, it is more useful to us to be correctly educated at an early age, for then we can experience the richness of living for our remaining years through the present body. Children will, if given the opportunity, immediately respond to honest and truthful instruction. They learn best by example, as do we all. When parents, teachers and other authority figures provide the pattern for children, then the children flow into the divine plan with ease. And what do we teach the children? The truth, that which is so about whatever subject with which we deal. Children in an honest supportive environment can handle the truth, sometimes more easily than adults who have already been incorrectly educated and have an inner resistance to change, even for the better.

If we teach only about the material universe and a body-survival oriented philosophy we do students an injustice. We should teach the whole story, from the nature of consciousness right on through to the reality of God and man's real reason for being. As social creatures we are born, we grow up, we mature, we relate, we make our contribution to the world, and we withdraw from the world and return to God. This is the ideal pattern for one's life. There is no reason why the human community on planet earth cannot work together in the spirit of full support and mutual cooperation. Ego games, dishonesty, prejudice, false pride, and just plain fear of the unknown often contribute to mankind's problems. Correct education can clear the field for personal and universal health and fulfillment, as is the intention of the evolutionary move of God.

What is not presently the norm in teaching methods and principles in public schools can be supplemented at home and by private and personal means. We do not have to leave the education of our children or of ourselves to others. Human beings can be taught that it is all right to be here and it is all right to express, experience, examine, study, become creatively involved, and to learn just what life has to offer. What does life have to offer us?

The conscious experience of being total. Is this experience available to each and every one of us? Yes, it is! It is not only available but it will eventually be experienced by every soul. Some are trying hard to experience it. Others are not even dimly aware that the experience is possible. Many try to experience it and they fail. They fail because they are "trying" instead of experiencing. If one can do a thing, then one does it. If one can experience a thing, then one experiences it. Trying usually results in failure.

In the education process information is shared. Also shared is encouragement to experience, so that concepts are translated into feeling and knowing. Haven't we often said, "I know what is so, and I know what I should do but I can't seem to get it together" ... we affirm that we "can't" succeed, and this is what we experience, time after time. And we are all aware that not every living environment is fully supportive to natural living. We may live with people who not only are destruction-oriented but will only feel comfortable if others in their space are also into their attitudes and practices. The darkness does not like the light, and people who are trapped in their survival patterns, as useless as they might be, tend to feel threatened if one of their group is of a different bent. To run to the extreme, history records that more than one savior met with severe resistance when attempting to educate people in need of instruction. An enlightened person, however, (or even a wise person) does not do anything to threaten his environment; he, instead, sets the example and does what he can. He may even absent himself from the company of "unbelievers" in order to survive and do more useful work elsewhere.

One of the reasons for the sense of despair that many people have is that their education has consisted mostly upon how to get along in this world. Except in rare and isolated instances, during the formative years very few people are educated relative to life's major questions. What is God? How were the worlds formed? Why am I here? What is the purpose of it all? These questions, which reveal the yearning of the soul to know, are frequently answered with a curt, "No one knows" response. It is the natural urge of the soul to seek answers which are not only meaningful but also true. We all know, innately, that we came from somewhere and we are going somewhere. Where, then, are the answers to the most pressing questions which come to the surface of the mind? The answers are to be found in the great bibles of the world and from the lips of enlightened men and women. We must slake our thirst for truth at the fountain of living waters because we will never be satisfied with incorrect or shallow answers to important questions. The Christ nature of us, the intelligence of the soul, is now being born into full expression. It will prevail. A most marvelous happening is that, despite the often lack of useful education, so many people not only survive but awaken and cut through the veils of ignorance and experience that truth which awaits them. Here, once more, is evidence that the true urge of the soul is in the direction of knowing and in the direction of freedom. All power (influence) over the workings of heaven and earth are given to the enlightened people of the world. Enlightened people are but extensions of God, and it is God who has full power and full and unrestricted influence.

Seeing to Needs of Body, Mind and Other Practical Matters

Only a little self-examination will indicate that the physical body responds best to a natural food diet. We are not suggesting extremes, merely common sense in the choice of foods and their combinations and use. Vegetables, grains, fruits and seeds are nutritious and easily available. Dairy products can be added to the diet to make it more complete, if this is desired. Whether one selects a purely vegetarian diet or not is a personal matter. Food selection will not cause the enlightenment experience, but enlightenment may result in conscious choice and a move in the direction of natural foods being desired by the system. Internal and external cleansing of the body is essential, and enlightened people are naturally inclined to see to personal hygiene and a clean and orderly environment. Fresh air and sunlight contributes to health, as does regular and useful exercise of the body. If one has self-respect, one will do what is required to see to body needs, including seeing to a cheerful and optimistic mental attitude at all times. The body is the extension of the mind, and our inner realization filters through mind and influences body function. The intelligence of the soul will see to health of the body if restraints and restrictions are removed and if one flows in harmony with nature.

Regular and needed rest allows mind and body to recover from stress and trauma. We know how wonderfully therapeutic sleep is and how well we feel after sound sleep. Too much sleep will weaken the body just as too little will tear it down. In some circles there is a rejuvenation program which is known and practiced and it includes prolonged sleep. One retires into a quiet, darkened room and resolves to remain there for several days, even several weeks in extreme instances. The body is detoxified through a program of internal and external water cleansing as well as a careful diet. Food intake is minimal but is selected for its body restoring influence. Sometimes special herbs are used. The main ingredient in the program, however, is bed rest and sleep, interspersed with occasional light exercise to contribute to circulation of the blood and lymphatic fluids. Waking time is given totally to gentle prayer and quiet meditation. By providing an ideal environment for body restoration and by being restfully centered in soul awareness, the healing currents of life are able to repair the body, neutralize mental-emotional patterns containing pain, and to rejuvenate the entire system. There are stories of sages in India and Asia who use a similar program every few years and are able to remain in a condition which has been described as forever young. Such people do not live forever in the body, but as long as their earth experience has purpose, they enjoy a body which reaches the prime of life maturity level and remains constant until they consciously depart the body when their work here is done.

Regular meditation has long been known as a procedure which offers one the opportunity to daily experience deep conscious rest. Accumulated tension flows from the body during deep meditation. Even the nervous system is unstressed and consciousness is then able to freely express through the refined system. Stress symptoms, anxiety, emotional conflict, mental confusion, inadequate diet and air pollution place a severe challenge upon the body's natural tendency to be in health. This is why we recommend that one intentionally create the most ideal internal and external environment for the free expression of the soul's vital force.

This Matter of Vocation

A conscious person will, so the masters of perfection teach, be led to intentionally participate with nature's trend which is in the direction of life enhancement and life fulfillment. Therefore, the work that we do should ideally be chosen so that it offers us the opportunity to unfold spiritually while at the same time gives us the sphere of influence which will enable us to make a useful contribution to the welfare of others and to the planet itself. If one is trapped in a life situation which results in feelings of despair, frustration and resentment, one's attitudes can be changed or the life situation can be changed. We have the freedom of choice. In relationship to the work we do, let us think in terms of whether or not what we do is serving a useful purpose. This is a clue as to whether or not we are really involved with life in the highest and best way. Again, the work that we do can be performed with conscious intention. In this way it serves as a training opportunity so that we unfold spiritually even as we perform our duties. The conscious performance of work puts us in the stream of nature's evolutionary influence, and it results in improved powers of discernment and concentration. The improved powers of discernment and concentration can then be used to advantage during times of study, meditation and the contemplation of life's real meaning and purpose. The ideal is not to split our time into occasions of "spiritual practice" and material pursuit. The ideal is to be totally integrated so that every waking moment is an opportunity for consciously knowing that we are viewpoints of God expressing in this particular time-space situation.

In most social situations a conscious being will have to come to terms with money and things. Without being greedy and without being adverse to handling the things of this world, a conscious person makes wise use of money and things. He sees to his own comfort and welfare and also contributes to the comfort and welfare of other people. An enlightened person does not experience lack and limitation in his life. Such a person may elect a simple pattern of living, but this is a matter of personal choice. Whatever his occupation or activity an enlightened person will be so in tune with nature that there will always be a ready supply of whatever is required for creative living.

Relationships With Brothers
and Sisters on Our Planet Earth

A conscious person is an appropriate person. To be appropriate means that we always do what is correct at the time, taking into consideration the levels of understanding of those with whom we relate, and understanding the present need. A conscious person will be free from neurotic drives and compulsions and will be open-minded and fair in relationships. A conscious person does not use other people nor is he, himself, used by others. In relationships we have only to be supportive, honest and fair, and be able to allow others room to grow and unfold in their own way. If we have duties and obligations to members of our personal family circle, to neighbors, business associates and others, we can handle these duties and meet these obligations in an open and appropriate manner. There will be no need to dominate others just as there will be no inclination to be victimized by others. When we are conscious and healthy we influence other people in a positive and constructive manner. When we are conscious and healthy, because of the interaction of feeling and energy between people and things, we contribute quietly to the welfare of the world.

By setting the ideal example for others, we allow them to experience true education relative to how life can be. Now and then others who see our calm and happiness will inquire about how we remain steady in this experience. This can then be the opportunity to reasonably discuss and explain, to share information, and even books and meditation instruction. By awakening and then drawing forth the awareness of the soul nature in others, we render the most useful of all services. At times, a person who is new on the enlightenment path, may tend to conclude that it is a selfish path, but this is not true at all. As a result of self-understanding we are then able to contribute to the understanding of others. Indeed, we find that when we are sufficiently aware people will be drawn to us and we will then have the occasion to share our consciousness and our understanding. There is never a need to convert another or to force another to accept our views. Every person is consciously or unconsciously seeking enlightenment because enlightenment is the fulfillment of life's purpose. When I know who I am, then I clearly know who you really are. Working from this level of conscious knowing, I can then gently persuade you to awaken and see clearly, also.

It will not be sufficient for us to have a mental grasp of the principles of natural living while remaining in a life pattern of restriction and incompleteness. No, we must live the ideal life, then we will really know the truth and then we will be able to honestly share the truth that liberates. Remember, liberation does not mean freedom from this-plane involvement; it means freedom from restriction and freedom from dependence. The masters of perfection walk among us and they tell us, "I am here as an example to you, and the work I do is not a personal work at all. The work that I do is God's work. I am here to remind you of the essential truth and to encourage you to awaken and see clearly. What I have to share with you is free and without price. You can know the truth and experience freedom in God if you will only accept it." As we leave the old ways behind and accept the new and true way, the way of harmony with nature, total fulfillment is experienced.

Chapter Four
AN OVERVIEW:
GOD *IS* ALL THAT IS

Every world scripture declares the Spirit of God to be everlasting, complete, without beginning or end: one, indivisible Being. On this point all masters of perfection agree. Such masters also teach the way of conscious understanding of this truth. It is traditional for the masters to explain the overview, giving a grand mental picture of how Supreme Consciousness appears, through Self-involvement, as all that is perceived. Sometimes just to hear this explanation can result in an enlightenment experience. In every instance, once the explanation is given, the seeking soul knows unto what to aspire and to eventually realize. Because we are here sharing the teachings of the masters of perfection, we shall remain true to the traditional form of presentation.

It is taught that a primal force causes all movement and activity in the universe. This force issues forth from God. The Spirit of God is the origin and cause of this primal force, but the transcendental aspect of God is itself unmoved and changes not. It will be well to be reminded that, according to this teaching, there is no independent universe and there is no individual person in the universe save God. To understand this, we must understand that the universe is an outpicturing, an outer manifestation of God-energy, and souls are but viewpoints of Pure Consciousness. To one of restricted vision there seems to be creation apart from God and it seems that there are billions of souls, but what we perceive through the senses is not the total picture at all. In this portion of our study we shall go behind the scenes of relative appearances and gain insight into causes which result in effects.

Most of us inwardly believe and intuitively suspect there to be a subtle changeless Reality behind sense-perceived reality. In esoteric teachings it is common to refer to that which is real to sense perceptions as reality and that which changes not as Reality. The world is real in that it can be perceived, but it is also subject to change. Reality is not subject to change, and It is the cause of all that outwardly appears. It also sustains all that outwardly appears, but It changes not. When seers teach us to seek that which is Real, they are encouraging us to comprehend the ultimate truth.

The reason an unenlightened person is unable to comprehend the subtle side of nature is that such a person is perceiving through *organs of sense perception which themselves are products of nature.* We shall examine this curious subject as we continue our study. It is taught that it is impossible for one working through a mind to comprehend that which is beyond mind. One may by careful analysis and mathematical examination of the nature of Reality learn to understand how Consciousness plays all possible roles. However, it is only by moving attention through the spaces of the mind that one can truly discern the truth, that which is so. When we are conscious of our divine nature we are as gods. When we are identified with conditioned mind we are known as man. Hence the teachings of Jesus (*John 8:28*), "Then said Jesus unto them, 'When ye have lifted up the son of man, then shall ye know that I am he.' " Knowledge is natural to the soul when mental restrictions have been transcended or set aside. Without such transcendence a person will remain confused and baffled, forever attempting to compare insight with educated concepts or revelation with narrow-minded opinion.

Supreme Consciousness is the origin of all knowledge and the source of all power. The realization of Supreme Consciousness is certain to result in the soul's final and everlasting satisfaction. Paramahansa Yogananda often told us that everyone is seeking fulfillment in God, even when seeking outwardly through the senses. The urge to power is the soul's desire for omnipotence. The urge to knowledge is the soul's desire for omniscience. The urge to sensation is the soul's desire for the experience of the supreme joy of Self-realization. There is certainly nothing wrong with our being free in the known universe, with our inclination to acquire necessary information for a more responsible performance of duty or with a natural appreciation of life through the senses. What can blind the soul is the almost total outwardly directed attention which results in one's forgetting God and increasing the sense of separateness from the source.

The perfect masters teach that the primal force of God is the cause of world manifestation. What makes the world process conscious is the omniscient awareness of God. This force and this awareness which is everywhere present in the universe is evidence of the reality of God. Since God is omnipresent and conscious in every space and dimension of His own manifestation, then God is also aware of everything that transpires and God is attentive to even the most subtle yearning of the soul. We can walk with God and we can talk with God, for we are God's very own. We examine the nature of Consciousness, but we also understand that we have a relationship with God of a very intimate nature. From the overview God is each one of us, because God has assumed a point of view known as you and me. In the relative worlds, as long as we feel ourselves to be apart from God, we can pray to God, we can love God, we can expect support from God. And God will answer our prayers (the heart's sincere desire), God will respond with the nourishment we call love, and God will meet our every personal need, always on time and in the most appropriate manner.

We often say that we are made in the image and likeness of God. This is true. In the Old Testament of the Christian Bible (*Genesis 1:27*) we read: "So God created man in his own image, in the image of God created he him; male and female created he them." A soul identified with mind (*manas*) is man. But man is male and female because of polarity. When the positive polarity is dominant man is male. When the negative polarity is dominant man is female. These are but roles played according to how the electrical influences exercise dominance; the terms do not refer to any superior or inferior status in the evolutionary process. When man directs his energy and awareness to the source of life within, man can experience his true nature as a ray of God, existing as a wave on the ocean of cosmic consciousness.

God is the cause of world manifestation. Nature emerges from God as God's primal energy flows outward. The primal energy of God is referred to as Amen, Aum, Om, or as *Pranava* according to language differences. Om or Amen, when vocalized, is our attempt to duplicate the sound of the outflowing current as we hear it during meditation. The primal energy is the result of God's force manifesting. This outflowing energy changes in frequency to manifest further as the subtle substance from which all forms are made possible. But the outflowing force is somewhat influenced by a balancing aspect of God, the magnetic attracting current, and this is why there is so much feeling-energy evident in the Om current. The current flows into expression as the universe, yet there is an aspect of it that attracts the seeking soul back to the source.

There are four aspects to the current as it manifests, and these aspects must be understood by the person who is willing to comprehend the full nature of God *as* the world process. One aspect is the impression of change or *time*. Time seems to pass, but the average person's time-sense is the result of his attention moving from event to event. Yet some recent investigations suggest that time flows and that time is a reality in the manifest world. We hear of time passing and of time carrying events along as a river might carry whatever is in the river at the moment. We also hear of how time changes things for people, which may be seemingly so, because, when a person withdraws from events and then returns to a perception of them, events are different than formerly perceived. For centuries "the words of the Preacher, the son of David, king in Jerusalem" (*Ecclesiastes 3:1, 2*) have informed us of this matter of time and events. In the Old Testament: "To every thing there is a season, and a time to every purpose under the heaven; a time to be born, and a time to die; a time to plant, and a time to pluck up that which is planted."

One view of the world process is that the appearance of a real world is due to manifestation of consecutive events. Change is a certainty in our world experience. Even matter is not stable but is the result of a series of events which occur at a level we cannot perceive. A seeming solid object is not solid at all when we examine it at the sub-atomic level of appearing. If change were not built into the world process, the universe and all it contains would be "frozen" in time, but this is not the situation at all.

Another aspect of the manifesting current is *division* or space in which events occur. Space is not distance: it is that in which events unfold, persist for a duration, and then vanish from casual perception. Within our immediate space-environment there now

exist dimensions and planes of which we have little or no awareness. We turn on our radios or television sets and immediately
become aware of signals originating at a distance which are now
converted into sound and pictures. We speak here of our physical
world, but there are other worlds which are just as real which exist
right where we are. The astral realms are here, the causal realms
are here, the heavens are here, ready to be perceived when our
inner sight is perfected or when our moment comes to experience
them.

Just as the outflowing current results in time and space, it also,
finally, appears as particles of light. We have then the current itself,
time, space, and the building blocks of material creation which
condense into fine matter. This is the substance of all that is to
be formed. We, therefore, acknowledge the teachings of the masters
of perfection as found in *The Gospel According to St. John* (1:3),
"All things were made by Him; and without Him was not anything
made that was made." That which is an extension of a thing is
inseparable from that thing. The outflowing energy of God manifests as the world process, as nature, and the intelligence of God
directs the world-process. This is why we teach that *God is all that
is.*

The Cause of the Sense
of Illusion and Unknowing

With the outflowing of the creative current and the manifestation of time, space, and light particles, the stage is set for what is
to come. Consciousness (awareness) is innate to material manifestation and will emerge in due time. The basic particles which are
produced to form the fine substance of creation are referred to as
the *throne of Spirit*, the supporting medium onto which the light
of God shines to manifest the worlds. The Sanskrit word for this
supporting medium is *maya*, the *darkness*. From *The First Book of
Moses, called Genesis* (1:1, 2): "In the beginning God created the
heaven and the earth. And the earth was without form, and void;
and darkness was upon the face of the deep. And the Spirit of God
moved upon the face of the waters."

Maya is not illusion, but when we are identified with it we
experience the sense of illusion. That is, not comprehending the

total process of life, we see only a portion, and this gives rise to confusion due to lack of true knowledge. When man experiences true spiritual awakening, he then comprehends the nature of this fine medium of creation and is liberated from bondage due to lack of understanding. Every master of perfection has taught that suffering is due to lack of spiritual understanding. A little understanding of the nature of the physical world allows us to experience a degree of human satisfaction, but the enlightenment experience results in total release in God.

The Spirit of God shining on the sea of fine matter is further reflected as material creation. When the *Attracting Current* influences this fine matter, then consciousness is awakened in it. This Attracting Current is known as the Holy Spirit, and it is this that quickens life in matter. The Holy Spirit aspect of God results in viewpoints of God becoming involved with fine matter. These viewpoints are sometimes referred to as rays of God or extensions of God, and we refer to them as souls. Pure spiritual rays are called the Sons of God.

When souls become identified with fine matter, the subtle covering they assume becomes spiritualized as a result of the infusion of consciousness and life. A magnetic aura is produced, and, because of soul consciousness, this particularized unit becomes endowed with feeling and a sense of separate existence. This is known as Ego. Here the Son of God becomes known as the son of man because of what follows. The fine matter sheath of the soul, being magnetized, has two poles, one of which attracts it to its origin (Pure Consciousness) and one of which repels it from the source and in the direction of material creation. The positive pole results in the manifestation of an organ of perception known as the faculty of intelligence. The negative pole produces an organ of reception (taking in data from without) and enjoyment which is referred to as mind (*manas*). This is the subtle explanation given by the masters of perfection regarding the soul's movement into matter. In Vedic texts, the Son of God is known as *Atman* and the soul aspect is known as the *jiva*. These are but words from different cultures. The understanding of the masters is the same.

The Further Involvement of the Soul

The Spiritualized subtle sheath of the soul has five manifestations of aura electricities, according to the ancient texts. These five manifestations constitute the causal body (sheath) of the soul. Influenced by the electric attributes (positive, neutralizing, and negative), the result is the production of five organs of sense, five organs of action, and the five objects of the senses. (See diagram for explanation of this process.) The causal body of the soul is then made up of root-causes which make possible further effects in the material universe. World manifestation flows from the inside outward. The coverings or sheaths of the soul are formed of the substance which is characteristic of each succeeding level of manifestation.

The five inner organs of sense are smell, taste, sight, touch, and hearing and are rooted in the mind of man. For instance, when we dream (or even vividly imagine) we can fully experience sensation. We can smell, we can taste, we can see, we can feel by touch, and we can hear. We can experience satisfaction of desire during a dream experience or during a vivid occasion of conscious creative imagination. Sometimes when we are frustrated in our waking experience, we can have compensating dream experiences which result in the neutralizing of desire. When our attention flows in the direction of the source of life, during meditation, we can smell, taste, see, touch, and hear on subtle plane levels. The five aura-electricities are polarized and influenced by the electric attributes (positive, neutralizing, and negative), and the organs of the senses are the result of the influence of the positive attributes of the five electricities.

The neutralizing attributes of the five electricities result in the organs of action. These are excretion, generation, speech, motion through space (feet), and manual skill (hands). This produces the body (sheath) of life force or prana. When there is desire for enjoyment or fulfillment, it follows that there must be the capacity for neutralizing of desire through experience, thus the life-force body is produced.

The negative attributes of the five electricities appear as the outer objects of sense perception, that is, the physical world. We have mentioned the inner organs of sense; the external sense organs enable us to experience our environment.

These fifteen attributes with the two poles (mind and intelligence) constitute the fine material body of the Son of God. This is sometimes referred to as the spiritual body which the soul can use to move through subtle realms. When a fully liberated soul is identified with this body or covering, it can directly influence astral and physical realms by an act of will or with mild intention, because such a soul is working from the level of cause, knowing the astral and physical realms to be but effects.

Outflowing force further extends and results in the manifestation of the physical universe, as well as a physical body for the soul's use and expression. As a result of combinations of the five negative electricities, there is the production of gross matter in its five forms: solids; liquids; fire; gaseous substances; and fine matter known as ether. In his treatise on *Self-Knowledge* Shankara wrote (*verse 11*): "The physical body, the medium through which the soul experiences pleasure and pain, is determined by past actions and formed out of the five great subtle elements, which become gross matter when one-half portion of one subtle element becomes united with one-eighth portion of each of the other four." Therefore: from ether gaseous matter is produced; from gaseous matter fire is produced; from fire water is produced; and from water earth is produced.

The five gross material expressions and the fifteen attributes earlier described, together with mind, the organ of intelligence, feeling, and ego make up the twenty-four underlying principles which make creation possible. In the *New Testament* these principles are referred to as Elders (*Revelation 4:4*): "And round about the throne were four and twenty seats; and upon the seats I saw four and twenty elders." God, then, *as* the twenty-four aspects mentioned appears as all that is. Again, the masters teach that there is no independent creation. There is nothing apart from *that* which is the cause and reality of all that can be perceived.

We are, in these pages, examining the teachings of the great seers of the ages who have shared with us their revelations. The masters recommend that one become acquainted with an overview of the cosmic process, also, that one be settled in patience in order to avoid stress which can result from trying too hard to understand too much all at once. Let us learn from the Old Testsment message once again. In *Ecclesiastes* (12:12, 13): "And further, by these, my son, be admonished: of making many books there is no end: and much study is a weariness of the flesh. Let us hear the conclusion of the whole matter: Fear God, and keep his commandments: for this is the whole duty of man." One might feel more comfortable with the word *respect* rather than the word "fear" as used in the above verse. Let us love and respect God and be true to natural laws, for this is the whole duty of each one of us.

A Realistic Approach to Study

The masters of perfection teach that, if we understand a thing, we should be able to explain it in sensible fashion, so that another person can agree with us because the explanation has been so clearly presented. We must also point out that a rational examination of the nature of Consciousness may satisfy the mind, and, as useful as this is, the next step for one on the path is to actually fully comprehend the Reality of God. When we know the truth about the life process from our inmost center and being, then we can be said to be possessed of true knowledge.

While continuing our studies, we do well when we also see to practical matters of living in harmony with events and persons in our present world. When we are possessed of correct Self-understanding, we are able to discern clearly and we are able to live in an appropriate manner in harmony with the flow of life. When the feeling nature is settled and when the mind is clear, when we are in health in every respect, we are then more open to clear perceptions. My guru would often talk to me of God and the great masters and, then, before ending the visit he might say: "Be sure you eat well. Be sure to get enough rest. Meditate on God and dedicate your life to God. Always be balanced and practical. You will then see how real God becomes to you and how steady you are on the path."

Our path is a creative tool. Our senses enable us to perceive the world without. Our body enables us to move through time and space in this dimension. The cause of unknowing is not mind, senses, or body. True, through unwise use of mind, senses, and body we can experience further confusion, but the problem is lack of discernment. The mind, senses, and body are but instruments through which we express and experience. When we truly know who and what we are, we can live free in a universe which is supportive and cooperative.

Chapter Five
The FOURTEEN SPHERES
of WORLD MANIFESTATION

As a result of deep introspection and intuitive analysis, the seers inform us that the manifest universe is graded into fourteen spheres of expression. For the purpose of our discussion let us consider a sphere as an area designated for specific activity and expression. The first seven spheres are areas of world manifestation. The remaining seven spheres are the corresponding vital centers in the body of man. The Spirit of God manifests as the world-process in a successive series of appearances, and the Life that is God awakens and ascends from identification with matter through a successive series of vital centers in man. The vital centers are known as *chakras*, and man limited by mental conditioning often considers the subtle spheres other than the physical plane as heavens. And, according to one's understanding and personal hopes, the descriptions of idealized heavens are various.

The manifestation of the spheres, from subtle to gross expression, is from the Godhead to the physical worlds. We are told that the description of these spheres is the result of personal experience as well as memory: personal experience because some souls have actually withdrawn from body identification, experienced the inner planes, and then returned to body identification to report their experience. If one person told of inner plane experience, we might be skeptical and presume the explanation was that of fantasy or hallucination, but, when people unknown to each other and separated by time and distance report similar experiences, we must at least be discerning enough to examine the details fairly.

In recent years there have been published reports telling of the inner experiences of many people who have been pronounced dead but who returned to life in the body to share unusual memories of what transpired during the time they are not conscious of the physical realm. Many people, either religious or not, tell of exiting the body and of moving through a tunnel of light at the end of which is a bright destination. Arriving at this destination they communicate with intelligent beings who are benevolent and supportive. Sometimes the communication seems to be with words, sometimes the communication is by mental telepathy, and often the information is shared by a process of mutual knowing. Many who have had such experiences tell us that this "place" is like a true home to them, as though they finally returned to the source from which they originally came. The usual report is that they are informed that they are "home"too soon and must return to the body to fulfill destiny. In almost every instance, persons who tell of the experience share the feeling they had when told they had to leave that special place, a feeling of reluctance and even of sadness. Frequently these people find their lives imbued with a greater sense of purpose of philosophical depth. We do not, of course, hear such stories of inner plane experience from those who remain there.

But all is not beauty and harmony for some souls who experience temporary transition. There are the purgatorial and hellish experiences also. The former experience is the occasion to be purged of confusion and internal conflict, and the latter is the occasion of pure misery. Both experiences are but for a duration because, when the emotional-mental problems are neutralized by experience and the passage of time, the soul soars free once again. Sometimes a soul in misery goes to sleep to rest and withdraw from upset and inner conflict. Then it either awakens in a new physical body or awakens in inner space and continues the drama of life according to the level of understanding and state of consciousness. The other alternative, for those who are temporarily detached from body identification, is that they go to sleep and awaken in the body just recently vacated.

The masters of perfection have long taught how to consciously leave the physical form at the moment of transition. Daily meditation is preparation for this. If one will daily "die" to this world, the final experience will be but a gentle occasion. By withdrawing attention and vital forces from the senses and then resting in the experience of *conscious Being*, a person overcomes death, as most people know death. The way to overcome death is to know life as it truly is. There is a meditation method by which we can learn to flow attention and awareness up through the spinal pathway, through the vital centers, and depart this world with full awareness and without any inner confusion. We shall discuss this process later in this presentation.

The Seven Spheres
of Universal Expression

Innate to the Godhead are the three electric attributes: positive, neutralzing, and negative. The positive attribute pulls creation back to the point of first beginning. The neutralizing attribute results in eventual balance between the poles. The negative attribute results in heaviness, inertia, and the outflowing of the creative current. As the current flows out from the center, it changes in frequency to manifest as all that is, from subtle to gross levels of appearance. When we use the word "gross" in this examination of the cosmic process, we refer to material substance in its fully combined form, as dense and more heavy and compact. God manifests in a graduated series of events and appearances as He sends Himself into expression as nature, the seeming unconscious aspect of Himself. Consciousness resides in a sleeping condition even in mineral form. Each atom which is a part of the known physical universe contains the power of God. This we know because of the demonstrations of scientists in the past few decades. The potential of the atom is the contained force of God's own creative energy. And though I am premature in sharing the truth to be revealed in these pages, I must share the special insight of the masters of perfection regarding our present time. I speak now of some publicly shared prophecies of world disorder and of mankind's mass suffering.

A large proportion of the current world population now suffers lack and seeming deprivation because many involved are still in human consciousness. That is, they are still involved with thinking and feeling that they are bodies only. They have not yet awakened to the realization of their spiritual nature, and they have not yet learned to use their creative imagination in order to visualize and believe in higher and better possibilities. This is not to say that God is in any way punishing such persons for past sins. God is not involved with personally punishing those who either consciously transgress natural law or those who are unaware of natural law. Every human experience is a reflection of a personal condition of consciousness. People who are awake flow with life. People who are not awake suffer the natural result of unknowing. This is how life works, and any discussion of right or wrong or good or bad is not relevant to the question. Some prophets of doom speak of worldwide catastrophe, almost with a sense of satisfaction, as though God would be happy to rid the planet of his own expression as man. These "prophets" see evil at every turn and do not know that God is present and that God is working through His own expressions. The intelligence of God is seeing to the orderly release of the divine potential and to the eventual fulfillment of all souls.

1. *The Sphere of God* — God is the first and only outward manifestation of Pure Consciousness as It moves in the direction of expression. In the Godhead are the three characteristics mentioned in the world scriptures: changeless being; intelligent awareness; and creative energy. These three characteristics are referred to as God the Father, God the Son or First Begotten of the Father, and as God the Holy Spirit. In Sanskrit we would say, in the same order, *Brahma, Vishnu,* and *Shiva.* A part of God remains forever stable, and a part flows out, expands, and makes manifestation possible. The outflowing results in:

2. *The Sphere of the Holy Spirit* — This is really the aspect of God that acts upon the field of maya and animates forms as well as causes the evolutionary activity. It moves in and through responsive souls as well as draws souls back to the source, causing spiritual awakening and the unveiling of the intuitive and intellectual faculties of the soul. One excellent definition of God's grace is, "The activity of the Holy Spirit, moving in and through a person, transforming and regenerating him." When we are under grace we are directed to live in harmony with all of nature. We move from event to event, from experience to experience, with perfect timing and in harmony with others always. We do not have to try to do this, for trying is evidence of ego, the sense of being

apart from the flow of life. The key is to relax the conscious effort and to surrender to the trend of evolutionary unfoldment. This is a major question: "How do we ascertain God's will for us?" We cannot always know ahead of time, but we can enter into an intimate relationship with God through prayer and silence and then we find that we are consciously aware of a supportive and benevolent presence which is taking charge of our personal affairs. One who lives by grace may say, "I do not know how I know, but I do know that all is well."

3. *The Sphere of Spiritual Reflection* — Here is where the soul's sense of separate existence begins. This is the highest sphere in which fully illumined souls function and it is the stage before the manifestation of maya. Maya, you will remember, is the realm of subtle material substance; the components are: creative current; light particles; time; and space. Souls at this level are known as Sons of God. They are not involved with the outflowing creative current and are, therefore, free from compulsive involvement with nature. Some souls never become identified with matter. Some do, while remaining conscious, and they are avatars (incarnations of God-Consciousness). Avatara means the descent of a God-realized soul into the flesh for the purpose of quickening the evolutionary process. Such souls remove the problems of the world. Then there are souls which become involved with matter and totally forget their real nature. These are the deluded people who populate the worlds. But there is no judgment here. All souls are rays of God, viewpoints of God playing various roles in the divine process. An unconscious soul is no less divine than a conscious soul. A few souls became involved with matter out of curiosity. Many became involved because it was God's intention to animate forms and carry on the play of lights and shadows. Let us see the world process as the masters of perfection see it. Why are the masters cheerful, relaxed, and optimistic? Why are they so patient and understanding in the face of confusion and even in a place of challenge because of error and unknowingness on the part of people? Because they know something the "world" does not know. They know that the world scene is but God's dream, a drama, a happening due to interchanging electrical influences. My guru, Paramahansa Yogananda, often referred to the world scene as a "cosmic motion picture show." He told us to see the heros and the

"evildoers" as God's instruments. Of course, no person is evil. There are only souls without conscious awareness, who are identified with the material universe and, because of inner confusion, perform in a manner which seems in conflict with God's good will. How do we handle such a personal challenge? We relax into God-awareness and we do our practical things, while, at the same time, we know that God is working out the process of fair dealing. It is not our role to judge another person or to try to execute God's will for another person. We may feel that we know what is right, but we do not always really know what is right as long as we are working from emotion. A rule to be followed is to ever be kind and fair. All people, including those whose motivations are seemingly negative, have their private times of personal soul-searching. Most people in human consciousness do the best they can from their current level of understanding. All of us are more wise than we seem to be, and we are better than we perform. Human nature almost always gets in the way of the divine impulse when we examine history (including our personal history) as our life-plan unfolds.

4. *The Sphere of Material Manifestation* — This is the door between the spiritual and material worlds. The term spiritual here refers to the subtle realms before the production of maya. From maya outward the realms are referred to as *material*: fine matter and then gross matter. The fabric of nature makes possible the various forms in the material realms. Remember, we have said that this basic fabric or substance is made up of creative energy, light particles, time, and space. It is through this sphere that souls pass when they move from the true heaven to material-world involvement. All souls "come from the Father"; they flow from the Godhead. All souls will return, through the sphere of maya, to a conscious awareness of their existence in God. It is with maya that a fully conscious being works when he causes unusual effects in the material universe. Unenlightened people refer to such effects as miracles, only because they do not know the principle by which these happenings are made possible. If one who meditates becomes aware of the sphere of maya and yearns to pass through it to the sphere of *spiritual reflection*, he may pass through this door (the connecting sphere) and transcend identification with matter. One need not fully comprehend the nature of maya before transcend-

ing it. After such transcendence one automatically comprehends the secrets of nature. To become overly involved with the material worlds, without attempting to see into the reason for them, is to become trapped in phenomena and relative happenings. Absolute truth cannot be known until one transcends the appearance-worlds and comprehends the cause behind them.

5. *The Sphere of Magnetism and Primary Electricities* — Sometimes referred to as the *causal* sphere because what occurs here is responsible for what is to follow. At this level we find the influences responsible for the manifestation of material appearances. The subtle electric influences blend and the result is:

6. *The Sphere of Electric Attributes and Manifestations* — This is the astral sphere. At this level there are universes with astral suns and planets. It is to this sphere that ordinary people retire between physical body experiences. These astral planets entertain life even as life expresses on the physical level. Here souls are still working out their salvation and here are to be found illumined teachers, representatives of God who work with seeking souls. Many at this level do not seek enlightenment, just as many on earth do not seek enlightenment. Many in this sphere will go to sleep eventually awaken in physical bodies as infants. Some will remain for centuries (according to earth-time calculations) on the astral level of awareness. This is the destiny of many souls. Astral-time is not the same as earth-time or solar time. Even earth-time is not the same for all planetary inhabitants because each has his own time-sense. For some time passes slowly; for others it rushes by. This has to do with the attention span of a person, as well as the level of body-mind-soul awareness. In the relative spheres (physical or astral) there are some souls who live outside of time; they are even aware of their changeless nature. When one great saint visited England some years ago, he was introduced to George Bernard Shaw. Mr. Shaw said, "You Indian holy men have no regard for time." The saint gently replied, "It is you who are slaves to time. I live in eternity." An enlightened person who lives outside of time still observes schedules and appropriate events and occasions, in order to be in harmony with the relative flow of time, events and, occasions.

7. *The Sphere of Gross Material Manifestation* — This is the physical universe. Matter is the energy of God formed as we per-

ceive it. But an examination of the physical universe shows it to be a play of electric interactions. The atom, as is now known, is a small universe in itself, and the components of the atom are in constant motion. We are told by scientists that a physical object actually has more space than solid particles. The average human body, without the spaces between solid particles, could be compressed to a mass that could be easily held in the palm of a person's hand and yet still weigh the same number of pounds as the body weighed before it was compressed. It has also been estimated that the potential energy available in the atoms on the tip of a person's finger could provide the electric power for the city of Manhattan for a short duration of time. The problem would be in how to release and fully utilize the available power. God-power is resident in the atoms which make up the fabric of the physical universe. This sleeping power is *kundalini*, the dormant potential. Kundalini also sleeps in the body as dormant-potential-force of the soul. Atoms have their own life, as the life that is God-given to the material manifestation. Cells have genetic memory and their own impulse to survive and flourish. The overshadowing mind of the soul also contains impressions and tendencies-to-fulfillment. The soul also has a personal destiny. Are we beginning to see how complex, on a body-mind level, we are as human beings? The soul is dominant as far as giving impulses to the mind and body, once one is aware at the soul level. The body reflects the mind and the mind reflects soul intention. It takes a while for this process to be even and correctly ordered because many awakening souls slip back and forth between soul awareness and body identification. We are not to reject the body we use; the body is our point of contact with the physical universe. We are to see to the body's needs, with rest, nutrition, and the input of soul intention and mind understanding.

The Remaining Seven Spheres of World Manifestation: The Vital Centers in the Body of Man

The masters of perfection teach that just as the soul is made in the image and likeness of God, so man's body is an image of the manifest universe. What is found inside, it is taught, will be found outside. As the Godhead regulates and nourishes the universe through levels of Self-expression, so the soul regulates and nourishes the body in an orderly series of stages. The seven corresponding spheres in nature appear as the vital centers in the body of man. Only in man do we find the highly developed brain and the subtle vital centers which make possible the soul's full conscious expression through a physical form. Man's body is referred to as the temple of God, and it is through and as man that God fulfills His highest conscious evolutionary purpose. God fulfills other purposes through various life forms, but the highest purpose is fulfilled through the human body.

When the soul is truly conscious, the body is nourished by descending soul force and the body reflects such soul awareness. The body is then glorified and made luminous. Descending soul force is distributed throughout the organism through the vital centers on the astral-vehicle level and through the nervous system on the physical level. When the organism is free from stress, then kundalini moves freely, flowing upward and causing a circulation of powerful currents: the creative energy which enlivens the body and encourages all systems to function freely. In a person who is almost totally sense-bound, kundalini is mostly dormant. When one experiences soul quickening, then kundalini begins to stir.

The seven vital centers correspond to and work with the major nerve masses in the spinal pathway as well as the endocrine glands. The vital centers are not the nerve masses nor are they the glands; the vital centers are the subtle astral counterparts which exert specific influences.

In meditation one can become aware of the vital centers as shining places and then advance through them, stage by stage, from lower to higher levels. Among the yogis these vital centers are known as chakras (wheels), and to students of the Christian Bible they are known as *churches*. In *Revelation* (1:12, 13, 16, 20) we read: "And being turned, I saw seven golden candlesticks, and in the midst of the seven candlesticks one like unto the son of man . . . . And he had in his right hand seven stars . . . . The seven stars are the angels of the seven churches; and the seven candlesticks which thou sawest are the seven churches." St. John, during meditation, perceived inwardly the vital centers with their subtle electric influences, the various frequencies of vital force or prana.

The masters of perfection have carefully examined, during meditation, the vital centers, and they know the energy influences as well and the corresponding subtle sounds emanating from them. Energy frequencies have corresponding colors and sounds. There are advanced meditation methods during which one can visualize the lights of specific vital centers and inwardly (or audibly) intone the appropriate mantra in order to activate the energies and encourage them to function freely. When meditation is a natural and spontaneous experience and kundalini ascends easily, one often perceives the lights and sounds automatically.

The Five Coverings of the Soul

The radiant soul, when becoming involved with material manifestation, becomes covered, according to the degree of involvement, with sheaths or coverings. These are, in order of involvement:

1. *The First Subtle Covering* — The free soul, dwelling at the level of spiritual reflection, has a sense of individuality but is free from identification with material expression. When it becomes identified with maya or fine matter, it takes on a sheath corresponding to the nature of this sphere and is then capable of enjoyment as a result of a feeling-relationship to the environment. The feeling here is sheer pleasure, sometimes referred to as bliss. This is the origin of the sense of separation or sense of ego. Because of this the soul tends to desire contact with external reference points in order to experience satisfaction. This can lead to further involvement with externals and to further dependency. One on the enlightenment quest is advised not to *need* external contact. To understand and to enjoy contact with the outer is all right as long as there is not a need. Need results in craving or desire. and this results in unreasonable actions. Renunciation is not rejection; renunciation means to be soul-satisfied while relating intelligently to the world about us. In deep meditation one can experience pure bliss, but this is not the final experience. The final experience is that of being. In the final stages of meditation, even the craving to experience the bliss of almost-pure meditation can be a barrier to full knowledge.

2. *The Intelligence Sheath* — The organ of intelligence enables

the partially deluded soul to examine the nature of consciousness and discern the truth about it. True knowledge is had when one uses the organ of intelligence correctly.

3. *The Mind Sheath* — This covering contains the subtle organs (counterparts) of the senses. The mind is fed through sense channels and data is accumulated. Memory enables one to relate present perceptions to past perceptions. The conscious level of mind receives and retains input. It records but it does not analyze. When inaccurate data is fed into the subconscious level of mind, if the data is not screened and analyzed, the input is recorded as factual. The subconscious level of mind will respond to negative and untrue material just as readily as it will to positive and accurate material. Also, memory is frequently related to pain, loss, or fear, and whenever memories come to the surface of the mind they cause one to experience again the original impact of pain and trauma. The greater area of the mind is the unconscious level, and most people do not have access to this level except on rare occasions. Little does the average person know about the strong and persistent influences flowing from the deep unconscious level of mind. We are assured, however, that the more we meditate and the more we live from the level of clear awareness, the stronger is the cleansing influence of higher energies upon the contents of the subconscious and unconscious levels of the mind sheath.

4. *The Life Force Sheath* — This is the astral vehicle containing the organs of action which make possible expression and relationships in the relative worlds. As we progress on the spiritual path we begin to feel strong surges of current at deeper levels, and this is evidence of astral body awareness. Initial energy surges may be body energies, but practice will enable us to discern the finer and more subtle energy movements. The practice of mantra, attention to inner sound and light, and Kriya Yoga pranayama will in time open the subtle channels so that astral perceptions are experienced.

5. *The Sheath of Gross Matter* — This is the physical body of man. The physical body of God is the gross material universe. Just as the universe emerged from the Godhead, so the human body is the result of the material provided by God plus the influence of the soul. The material for the body is already provided by nature, but the soul attracts to itself, after union of sperm and ovum, the

necessary components to form the physical body. The blue print of the body is already established at the astral level as well as imprinted in the sperm and ovum provided by the parents.

The final outflow of force from God results in the physical universe. The birth of universes is still happening. There are, somewhere in the universe, planets just being prepared for the emergence of life forms and there are planets which have already served their purpose of providing sustenance for organic life. It is so easy, at times, to overlook the obvious fact that we are not an isolated phenomenon. Over 100 million planets are similar to our own in the galaxy in which we dwell. There are countless other galaxies also. Even in our galaxy, the sun in our solar system is a small sun by comparison to the suns already known to exist. The universe is vast to the mind of man, yet it floats in the mind of God. One might flow the attention outward to examine the universe and the mystery of it and experience cosmic consciousness. One can also explore the inner universe and experience cosmic consciousness. Both directions, if followed to the end, result in the identical experience.

The universe itself will, in time, be redeemed or drawn back to the original condition as God. Billions of solar years will pass before this transpires. And it is no major event in God's eyes because, after a duration of rest, God will *exhale* and the process will begin anew. The flowing out is the cause of the manifestation of the worlds; the flowing back is the cause of the dissolution of the worlds. It is the drama of life and will continue forever. The foreverness of God is a matter to ponder. If Life began, where did it begin and who or what started the process? Let us be reasonable; something does not come out of nothing! If there is an effect, there must be a cause behind the effect. If there is an appearance, there must be an originating point. We can say there is a beginning, but what *causes* the beginning? When an event occurs there is, behind the event, that which pushed it into expression.

As God is without beginning and without end, so we are without beginning and without end. Here is a personal question for each of us, "What are we going to do with ourselves throughout eternity?" The masters of perfection constantly remind us: "If you are going to awaken sometime . . . why not now?"

The Opening of the Eye
of Intuition and Knowledge

A basic teaching of the masters of perfection is that the external world, while a play of currents, can never be exactly perceived by anyone. Since motion is built into the manifest realm (only the realm of Pure Being is motionless), by the time what we perceive is reported to the mind and examined by the intellect, that which was perceived is no longer as it was. This is not apparent to us because often the world appears to be solid and fixed, but at deeper levels even material forms are undergoing subtle change. We know that events are not static or frozen in time. By the time we analyze an event, trends are at work to result in a change in events.

Certainly people are not what they seem at first glance. We usually perceive only the outer dramatization of a person, not that which is the underlying cause of the outer role, and even the cause of outer dramatization is not the real person. The inner cause of the outer role may be subconscious and unconscious motivations and tendencies which modify outer behavior. Just as motion is built into the material world, so tendencies and motivations are in active expression through organisms. We therefore always perceive "what was" instead of "what is." This is also true as we perceive inner processes during meditation, until we experience a clearing of the mental waves and no longer experience modification or change in perception. Until we experience pure being we can infer what is perceived from the report received through the senses. Here is what an ancient text shares: "Just as objects seen in our dreams are found, when we are awake, to be insubstantial, so our waking perceptions are likewise unreal . . . a matter of inference only."

People who are without courage, when they learn of the insubstantial nature of the world, tend to become despondent or even to live in an unrealistic mentally created world of hallucinations. People who are possessed of the urge to know the ultimate truth are inspired to seek out that which is everlastingly true about the nature of consciousness. As a result of yearning to know the soul awakens from sense-limitation and is literally born into a higher level of understanding.

This higher level of understanding can be the result of soul awakening, without any phenomena attending it and without any dramatic inner perception during meditation. This understanding is a true knowing and we cannot always explain to others who have not had this experience just why or how we know. With this knowing, however, there is a serene inner sense that we are more cosmic conscious than ever before and that this initial knowing is surely the early stage of a greater knowing soon to follow. A frequent expression of Christian mystics is that the unfoldment experience is, "from glory to glory." Along with the inner "glory" experiences, there are often the outer severe challenges. This is not because God is setting up a contest for us to see if we will love Him more than the world; it is because with awakening on the soul level there is the personal challenge of relating new insights to mundane events. Spiritual laws or principles differ from those at the material level, even from those at the mental level. Material level awareness has to do mostly with survival of the body and we see how this is at the level of the animal kingdom. Animals do what they do to survive at the personal level and as a species. They often even live by eating those who cannot eat them or who would not eat them but cannot evade their survival needs. The mental level of understanding is often a matter of causing effect, making things happen, and sometimes surviving at the expense of others. One can live from a higher mental-law level and use the laws of mind fairly and without hurting other people. The higher law is the law of grace, where life unfolds in honest proportion to the benefit of all and everything. As we awaken, from level to level, we sometimes experience challenge while learning to remain centered and possessed of understanding and in the flow of life. This is the growing experience and is usually experienced in basic form as we make gradual transitions from infant life, childhood, the puberty phase, young adult opportunity, and through the stages of biological experience onward to the demise of the physical body. We never die but the body usually gives up, sooner or later. This is the way of this realm. Most souls participate with the graded trends, a few resist, to little avail . . . fewer still overcome while on the earth plane and manifest a glorified body which remains ever-renewed for as long as the soul has need of it. It is interesting to know of mortal-immortals and it is an uplift to know of worldservice, but even as heaven and earth shall pass away, so all bodies, even glorified ones, will fade from material view.

The purpose of spiritual discipline is to see to the full enlightenment of the soul, which is a viewpoint of God. Personal destiny can be left to the soul that knows its destiny and no judgment is necessary regarding relative levels of attainment. All attainment, until the final truth is known, is related to spheres of God-manifestation and there is no final Truth or Reality in any of them. All of the realms are caused by God and are God's energy in manifestation; therefore no extension of God contains the complete and total information. Only in God can all data be found.

All substance (the basic fabric of this world) is filled with God's intelligence. The *substance* of all worlds is creative energy, light particles, time, and space. From this the outer material worlds were born and of this they are made seemingly real. The intelligent-power which pervades the worlds is referred to (in metaphysical terms) as Christ Consciousness. To receive the Christ Spirit is to be empowered from on high, to be anointed of God. The intelligent power is the Christ and the Christ is God's manifesting influence. The Christ influence is now pervading every atom of all worlds and is also the residing and controlling intelligence of each and every soul. God, as intelligent influence, governs each person's life down to the most minute detail, if given the opening through which to move.

The Manifestation of the Christ
Spirit Now and Through Our World's History

It is surely true that all awakening souls will, sooner or later, have to confront the mystery of the Christ, of being anointed of God. When the intelligence of God moves fully into a person, all that is part of deluded consciousness is cleansed from that person. We can say that when we "are in Christ" we are truly redeemed. The masters of perfection teach that the intelligence of God is the Christ aspect of consciousness. This aspect pervades the Godhead and it pervades all of nature. Christ then is resident in the world as the evolutionary intelligence and resident in man as the grand potential. When we are led of Christ our self-willed desires and our unconstructive tendencies are neutralized and we do only God's will. The waiting-to-be manifested Christ nature is the hope of glory for everyone. The Christ nature seems to enter into us, but it actually emerges from us at the soul level and into mind and body.

Wherever the power and glory of God has expressed through any person and as any person, there is the manifestation of the Christ. The Christ aspect of the Godhead is the true avatara, that which comes into glorious expression through human agency. Again and again this process occurs, to awaken a sleeping world and to contribute to the liberation of souls. When virtue declines in the world, the activity of the Christ appears. Those in material consciousness do not understand the reality of the Christ; those looking for a savior outside of themselves concoct superstitious religious philosophies; awakening souls comprehend the truth.

We are never talking about a personality when we discuss the Christ activity. Jesus, to those of the Christian faith, is the embodiment of God, the Christ. This is true but only because the Christ activity is all that remains. The personality recedes in order that the glory of God might be fully expressive.

God anoints that most receptive vehicle available with His own Reality. True masters never debate the relative appearances of spiritual realization which appear from time to time on earth. True masters know that the outer appearance is but the shadow, the activity of God is the only operative influence. A Christ is the full manifestation of God's useful influence. Healing flows forth from the Christ. Lives are transformed. Planetary consciousness is infused with the Holy Spirit, that intelligently directed force of God which unveils the soul and all of nature so that sleeping consciousness is awakened.

Where is the Christ Spirit today? It is omnipresent, it is everywhere present. It is present in every soul and it is present in the atoms. It does not reside at some distant and inaccessible place, it is immediately accessible once we are open to its activity. God is available to anyone at any time and any place; God is in the air we breathe and in the food we eat. God expresses through people we meet and resides in the things we use as we go about our routine business. The creative current of God sustains us and is the true life and true light. "That was the true Light, which lighteth every man that cometh into the world." (John 1:9) And again, (John 3:3), "Verily, verily, I say unto thee, Except a man be born again, he cannot see the kingdom of God." Turning attention from sense-perceived things back to the source within, we are able to comprehend the subtle inner realms and experience a relationship with the creative current of God. The masters teach that there is an "attraction" from God which draws soul awareness back to full conscious awareness.

When mental and emotional impediments are removed, when purification is experienced, the reality of God flows into expression. In *The Gospel According to St. John* (1:12) we read, "But as many as received him, to them gave he power to become the sons of God, even to them that believe on his name." To believe on his name is to be attuned to and, immersed in, the consciousness of God. Christ Consciousness is the reflected consciousness of God in creation, pervading the Holy Spirit which is discerned and experienced as Amen or Aum (Om). This is why one is directed to contemplate, during meditation, the internal creative sound current and flow attention to its source. True *Bhakti Yoga* is experienced when we love God with all of our heart, mind, and soul yearning; then we surrender to God's love, the supreme attraction from the Godhead, and liberation is assured.

In a preceding segment of this text we discussed the *Fourteen Spheres of World Manifestation*, from the Godhead into material manifestation. The final seven spheres are reflected in the body of man as the seven vital places, thus the total of fourteen. The vital places are centers through which vital energy is distributed throughout the system and they relate to levels of partial soul awareness. As the soul awakens from material awareness there is a gradual detachment from gross aspects of nature, giving the appearance of gradual awakening to the truth through successive stages. The soul awakens from material identification and experiences: awareness of electric forces in nature; subtle mental influences; the nature of the world as a combination of *appearances* (i.e. creative current, light particles, time, and space); awareness of the soul nature; and finally fully God-realization or liberation of the spirit. As this process is undergone one is able to comprehend the inner side of creation and, therefore, know the truth.

A Possible Experience During Meditation

For some, soul awakening is an experience of being more clear and more discerning without any dramatic meditation perceptions. For others, there are inner perceptions which can be understood in the light of these teachings. When one meditates, with eyes closed and attention gently flowing to the *third eye center* or higher brain centers, one can often see a steady inner light. This light, when steady to our inner gaze, is known as the light of the spiritual eye. What happens is that dual electric currents in the nervous system are caused to flow upward, and these currents merge at the medulla and are then inwardly perceived as a single light. This light is the condensed manifestation of the energy-frequencies of God Consciousness which are described as:

1. *The outer golden light*, the frequency of the creative current: (Aum, Amen) the Word.

2. *The inner field of dark blue*, the frequency of the intelligence aspect of consciousness, the Christ light.

3. *The five pointed star-like silver white light*, the origin of the five frequencies of life force (prana) which extend into creation.

Seeing the light is the beginning. One is advised to surrender to the light and *consciously* experience the successive lights. Merging in gold light one experiences the Word, the creative energy in all vibratory manifestation. Merging in the blue light one experiences the intelligence of God, the Christ spirit. Merging in the white light one transcends all outer reflecting aspects of God and is stable in the experience of conscious being. Once one is drawn into the spiritual eye, all inner meditative processes are spontaneous and what is experienced will be due to the destiny of the soul.

I have known several persons who were able to see the inner light as a result of relaxation and steady concentration who, after a time, were still drawn into sense-involvement to the extent that the early attraction to God-realization was neutralized. Inner light perceptions should not result in pride due to supposed spiritual attainment nor cause one to become lazy regarding the practical need for daily self-observation and attention to mental and emotional purification.

Even soul powers (siddhis) which manifest must not cause one to forget the goal of total enlightenment. An enlightened person may or may not manifest soul abilities, and the presence of a few such abilities is not necessarily evidence of full enlightenment and soul purity.

The Possibility of Delusion
This Side of the Field of God

Tradition has it that even the gods are capable of losing their way unless they remain steady in understanding. In this world, for instance, we know of people who are possessed of great creative and intellectual powers who are still misdirected and who seek power and control rather than God's will. The masters of perfection teach that our surrendered ideal should ever be, "God, let your will be done always!" Any thought, feeling, perception, or activity that contributes to increased soul awareness and a closer working relationship with God is useful. Whatever does not contribute to increased soul awareness and a closer working relationship with God is not useful. This is the basic guideline on the enlightenment path.

The certain solution to facing the challenges of becoming entangled with the outer phenomena is to meditate regularly, fast from selfish cravings, and actively work for others and for the good of our world. When we are dedicated to a life of true service there is no possibility of our losing our way in life.

Text and Commentary on the Yoga Sutras

Chapter Six
The SOUL'S AWAKENING
and TURNING TO THE SOURCE

In this chapter we begin our examination of the *Yoga Sutras*. To enter into a careful study of the material we list, in consecutive order, the fifty-one verses of the first section. A commentary follows the final verse. These verses can be taken as themes for personal contemplation, the explanation found in the commentary will inspire deeper understanding.

1. Now the way of Self-realization is explained.

2. When mental modifications and conditionings no longer restrict soul awareness, then Self-realization is experienced.

3. Resting in Pure Consciousness, the soul is established in the Truth of its own being.

4. When not resting in Pure Consciousness, the soul identifies with the mind and its transformations and changes.

5. Modifications and changes of the mental field, according to the classification, can result in the experience of either pleasure or suffering.

6. Through the examination of the nature of consciousness one may be involved in a quest for knowledge. Or one may be involved with illusion, hallucinations, sleep, or memory.

7. Sources of valid knowledge are direct perception, inference, induction, deduction, or the testimony of a knowledgeable person.

8. By misinterpreting what we perceive, we suffer from illusion.

9. Hallucinations result when the mind projects a false reality, not based on an object, or truth.

10. Absence of waking consciousness is sleep.

11. Recalling experience through the aid of mental impressions is memory.

12. Mental modifications can be weakened and neutralized through practice and objective examination.

13. Firmly flowing attention to Supreme Consciousness is considered the highest spiritual practice.

14. Regular and correct practice of meditation results in psychological stability and steadiness on the spiritual path.

15. Upon mastering compulsions and useless urges for sense experience, one becomes established in detachment.

16. That highest renunciation comes as a result of Self-realization, which brings victory over the forces of nature.

17. Through reasoning and discernment one realizes the truth that the world is a play of Consciousness.

18. When the mental field is clear, then the Transcendental Awareness is experienced.

19. If, because of regular transcendental experiences, all mental

modifications are neutralized, one attains permanent Transcendental Awareness. If mental modification persists, even if one is highly advanced on the spiritual path, he will return to involvement with nature and the worlds.

20. The highest spiritual experience is attained as a result of self-confidence, self-discipline, strong enthusiasm and energy, constant vigilance, regular practice of meditation, and by self-analysis and Self-realization.

21. The highest attainment is soon experienced by one who is intent upon the goal and steady in practice.

22. To obtain superior and quick results, one should intensify his practice.

23. Surrendering the sense of separate self to God results in Self-realization.

24. God, though actively involved in and through the worlds, is untouched by anything that occurs in the worlds. That is, no trace of anything that occurs is made on God.

25. God transcends all of nature.

26. God is beyond the limits of time, space, cause, and effect. God is the teacher of even the ancient teachers.

27. The manifesting symbol of God is the Word (Amen, OM, Aum).

28. One should meditate on this Word, analyzing it, surrendering to it, and being conscious of its real nature.

29. By meditation on the Word, one experiences cosmic consciousness and becomes liberated from all obstacles in life, including mental and physical ills.

30. Disease, doubt, laziness, lack of genuine interest, clinging to

sense pleasures, faulty perception, poor concentration, and inability to maintain concentration during meditation are a few obstacles one faces because of the fluctuations in the mind.

31. Other distractions due to fluctuations in the mind are: grief, anxiety, physical restlessness, and irregular breathing.

32. The mind is purified as a result of one's cultivation of the virtues and the practice of being neutral in the face of that which is not useful to one's purposes.

34. Through the practice of certain breathing exercises leading to the regulation of vital forces and mental activities, one can definitely overcome mental and physical obstacles to concentration.

35. Mental and emotional stability are definitely experienced when subtle meditation perceptions produce a change in one's consciousness.

36. By meditation upon that light of Supreme Consciousness, one's consciousness is transformed and this beneficially influences mental states.

37. By incorporating the virtues and states of consciousness of a spiritual ideal, one becomes stable and develops self-confidence.

38. Knowledge acquired as a result of analyzing dreams and the state of dreamless sleep can contribute to the health of consciousness.

39. The mind becomes stable as one meditates upon a chosen object.

40. Through mastery of meditation and states of consciousness, one extends influence from the level of the atom to infinity.

41. When the mental modifications become weak and lose their influence, then the mental field becomes clear and becomes capable of receiving true knowledge and of supernatural powers.

42. In lower states of meditation there can still be confusion in the mind even while useful transformation is going on.

43. When, during meditation, the mental field is devoid of confusion, then the object of meditation shines in the field of the mind.

44. In deeper meditation experiences the process of transformation of mental states continues at more subtle levels.

45. Moving through subtle levels, one eventually examines the fabric of nature and then passes through it to final liberation of consciousness.

46. Meditation experiences up to and including the examination of the components of the relative worlds is still with an object of examination.

47. Upon moving through the veil of maya, the luminous light of Consciousness becomes self-revealed.

48. In this meditation experience one has direct perception of truth.

49. Intuitive knowledge obtained in meditation is different from that obtained from books or conversations.

50. Mental impressions caused by superconscious experiences resist and overcome mental impressions caused by sense experience, habits, and day to day living.

51. With the removal of lower tendencies from the mental field, the higher mental impressions which were the result of superconscious experiences also fade from the mind. The soul then experiences permanent identity as Supreme Consciousness.

COMMENTARY

Regardless of how long one has been involved with the material worlds, there will come a time, sooner or later, when a degree of awakening will be experienced. Seldom does the full experience of enlightenment occur all at once. There may be a flash of insight, during which "everything seems to be known," and then a shutting down of that awareness. The impact of a single illumination experience can transform a life forever. The more usual way is for one to begin to experience an inner yearning for greater understanding. This can lead to searching, study, and personal investigation into the meaning of life. It can lead, if one is highly resolved, to a personal program of intentional study and practice for the purpose of clearing the mind of all that restricts the inner light and innate understanding. Such an intentional program of study and practice will result in the harmonizing of all component aspects of one's human nature: mental, psychological, and physical. It can also result in the exploration of subtle aspects of mind and the contemplation of the true nature, which is Pure Consciousness.

Our true home, the origin of our awareness and being, is inner space. This inner space is explored through self-analysis and meditation. Meditation, followed to its ultimate conclusion, results in self-mastery and final liberation of consciousness. The masters of Vedic times referred to such an intentional process as *Yoga* and they defined it thus: *"When mental modifications and condition-*

ings no longer restrict soul awareness, then Self-realization is experienced. " This, then, is said to be the purpose of intentional spiritual disciplines.

One may be weak, mild, or intense in practice and results will be according to inclination and involvement. My guru said to me many times, that one on the spiritual path could *speed up spiritual evolution by condensing experience through concentration.* That is, by paying attention to the essentials and disregarding non-essentials, one could accomplish more in less time. We know that some get involved with spiritual practices because they are in pain, for some reason or another. Perhaps they suffer illness or limitation in relationships. We know that some people get involved because they want power and control over others or over nature itself. We also know that a few seek the highest goal of life because theirs is the pure and direct way. People, because of their subconscious conditionings and their state of consciousness, naturally fall into the pattern of study and practice which best suits their purpose.

Resting in Pure Consciousness the soul is established in the truth of its real nature. When not resting in Pure Consciousness, the soul identifies with the mental field and the transformations and changes which take place in the mental field. When involved with mental transformations one will, according to what is taking place in the mind, experience relative happiness or relative unhappiness. This is how it is with mental life. There is a way to freedom from unwanted experience, and this is the way of intentional spiritual practice. Even as we probe the recesses of the mind, we must be alert for the signs along the way and be attentive to that which is useful versus that which is not useful to our purpose. There is always the possibility of mistaking untruth for Truth, for mistaking illusion and fantasy for the real. Some are content with illusion and fantasy because it supports their present position in life, but one with strong resolve will recognize error whenever it surfaces and will move past it to the Truth. This is the teaching of the great masters who have given of their understanding so generously.

The sources of valid knowledge are many, once we know how to study and how to see clearly. The most direct source is *intuitional perception*, just knowing by knowing, but this is rare for new seekers on the path. Another source is our own ability to examine whatever evidence is at hand and draw correct conclusions. An immediate way, if we are fortunate in having such a relationship, is to trust the testimony of someone who knows. By taking on faith the testimony of a seer, we can then begin at a certain point and move on to our own final understanding. We really cannot honestly say that we do not have the shared testimony of enlightened people because we do have available the writings of such seers and we do have available the great world scriptures. In the latter instance we must, of course, be able to discern the inner meaning of what is shared in written form.

There is the ever-present possibility that we might not correctly interpret the information given us. This may be because the communication form is lacking in content, or it may be that we cannot see clearly. We may not interpret correctly what is there for us to understand. By failing to interpret clearly, we suffer from illusion. Sometimes it is a trick of the mind. We see a shadow and we project unreal value upon it; we may assume that a moving shadow is caused by a person or an animal in motion when, in relative reality, the cause of the shadow is but a plant or tree being moved by a mild breeze. Our reaction is, emotionally, as though an animate being were nearby. Our reaction has no connection with the source of the appearance, but it does have a relationship with what we *assume* we perceive. Illusion can go deeper into mental-emotional sources. We meet a person who is quite honorable in his intentions, but, because he reminds us of a similar person we once met who was not so honorable, we conclude that the present person must be just exactly like the previous person. We may be correct in our evaluation because intuition is active in us. We may be *incorrect* because the memory of past similar experiences invades the analytical portion of the mind and cancels out direct perception of *what is so*: the truth of the present situation. This is how it is with our conditioned mind. Our real nature is Pure Consciousness. We are as God is, in essence, but we have become involved with the material realms and this has given rise to all manner of confusion. At a deeper level, however, we are not confused. Confusion remains only at the level of mind-identification. The extreme, relative to non-communication with what is before us, is the experience of hallucination. This occurs when the mind manufactures its own reality, either because the world confronted is so impossible to deal with or because of chemical changes in the body. It is not unusual to observe fantasy and hallucinations exhibited by people who cannot handle their environment. It may be that one cannot say "no" to people with whom there is an emotional tie and who are very dominant, with or without malice. It may be that one cannot say "yes" to life because of fear. It may be that an insufficient diet (due to poor eating habits) has contributed to a chemical imbalance in the system. It may also be that hormone changes are a contributing influence. Now and then planetary influences invade one's energy field and tend to cause an imbalance of fluid, chemical, and electrical combinations.

Sleep is another modification of the mind. When the nerve force is temporarily exhausted, when we are tired of confronting our outer environment, when the system needs balancing, we sleep. Some experience dreamless, refreshing sleep easily. Others dream much of the time while they sleep. Dreams can offer the opportunity for the mind to rearrange sensory signals received during the day and mingle them with impressions already in the mind. Sometimes, when one is overstressed or emotionally upset, dreams are more chaotic as a result of the mind's attempt to sort out the confusion or to arrive at needed answers. There is also *enlightened sleep*, during which time the body is relaxed and the mind is relatively clear, while the person experiences a near-meditation condition. Some advanced persons report that they do not experience sleep as ordinary people do; they, instead, meditate before retiring and then experience conscious awareness while the body rests. Too much sleep can be a form of escape from handling ourselves in daily life and too little, for the average person, works a hardship on body and mind. Sometimes superconscious dreams can result in guidance during our hours of sleep. Knowledge from the soul level filters into the mind during superconscious dreams. Advanced meditators sometimes use sleep as a gateway into the subtle realms and experience astral perceptions; these are not subconsciously induced mental states but actual perceptions of the inner planes.

Mental Modifications, Their
Regulation and Control

When we have an experience, whether induced by sensory stimulation or whether created in the mind, impressions are put into the mental field. This is the seat of memory, for, by recalling the impression, we inwardly picture and to a degree replay the experience which caused the mental impression. These impressions, the masters teach, often interfere with creative living and certainly interfere with one's attempts to concentrate. Some people are almost entirely at the mercy of their mental impressions, their urges and tendencies. Intentional discipline is designed to give one control over the contents of the mind and to weaken and neutralize impressions, urges, and tendencies which one knows are not useful to higher goals and purposes.

Through calm self-analysis one can examine motives, urges, tendencies, and memories and learn to handle them as so much available data. A self-possessed person is in charge of his memories, feelings, and powers of imagination. When memories, feelings, and fantasy overwhelm the mind, one becomes helpless. Many people who are reasonably functional are still, to a degree, strongly influenced by feelings, tendencies, and memories of the past. Their creativity is restricted and they often experience accidents, failures, and even physical illness because of the influence of mental confusion. Cheerfulness, peace, confidence, love, and optimism about life contribute to health and actually cause the glands and organs to function normally. Depression, anxiety, fear, hate or distrust, and a negative outlook on life interfere with the body's normal urge in the direction of health and function.

It is a mistake to assume that regular meditation alone will result in a purified mind. The more rational approach is to practice self-analysis and also to engage in regular meditation as a truly creative experience. The highest spiritual practice, according to the seers, is to flow the attention to Supreme Consciousness. We do this totally while meditating and, during daily duties, in the background of the mind we can have thoughts of God. Meditation opens the mind to an inflow of superior energy from the transcendental field and thoughts of good keep one attuned so that the energy continues to flow steadily. This has a purifying effect on the mind and nervous system and weakens lower tendencies and urges.

We emphasize the importance of conscious meditation, during which we are aware of flowing with ever greater intensity to the source of life within us. Relaxed meditation for the purpose of removing tension from the system is therapeutic, of course, but the greater benefit results when we probe through layers of mind to the experience of Pure Consciousness. When compulsive tendencies have been checked and when mental impressions no longer control the mind, we are then psychologically stable and steady on the spiritual path. Detachment does not mean disinterest in life; it means relating with understanding.

By examining the nature of consciousness as set forth in the sacred writings and as taught by enlightenment teachers, we learn to see that there is, indeed, a unity underlying surface differences. This understanding also has a stabilizing influence on our lives. After intellectual insight into the nature of life, we then experience the higher and more revealing understanding of Pure Consciousness. This inner experience in the direction of Pure Consciousness is called *samadhi* in the Sanskrit texts. There are degrees of samadhi and these will be more carefully examined in later chapters. Being absorbed consciously in an object of meditation so completely that mental waves are put to rest, and entering into identification with the object, is samadhi.

The conscious transcendental experience must be entered into again and again until, after years of experience, all mental modifications with any possible influence to control the mind are weakened and erased. If they are not removed from the mind, one will again be impelled into unwanted relationships with the world in spite of previous success in meditation. By cultivating the virtues we can resist the influence of inner tendencies and experience a cleansing of the mind and emotional nature. The ideal is to be patient and persistent on the path: to be regular in practice and to be reminded that the inner way to understanding is a private and personal way which we cannot discuss with others. In fact, many teachers recommend that we never discuss our inner challenges or our meditation experiences with anyone but God and our guru or spiritual mentor. There is little value in explaining our inner processes to another who is not enlightened.

Self-Surrender and Meditation Experience

Even if we are proficient in meditation practice, if we are conscious that we are personality-involved, we will not be successful. Surrender of the sense of individual self automatically results in knowledge of the true Self. A useful procedure, during meditation, can be to release the belief of being separate from the Source. All that prevents one from experiencing Pure Consciousness is the sense of being separate. If we can renounce this sense of being separate, all that will remain to our experience is Being.

The scriptures reveal that God is beyond the limits of time, space, cause, and effect. God, it is taught, is the teacher of even the ancient teachers. The masters of perfection tell us that what they teach is revealed truth, that it emerged to the surface of many minds as a result of contemplation. We may have teachers and we may have a guru, but we are to understand that God is the source of all knowledge and that teachers and gurus are but instruments through which truth is revealed. It is further taught that though God is in the world, the world is not in God. We are here speaking of the intelligent principle of God. We know that the energy of God appears as the things of the world, but it is the intelligence of God that runs the universe. Nothing that happens in the relative spheres leaves any impression on the transcendental aspect of God because this aspect is above mind. Impressions can only be made on a material substance.

For centuries a most practical meditation method has been that of listening to the internal sound, the primal sound. This Word of God can be inwardly heard during very relaxed occasions of meditation. We know that this sound has a source, so we allow ourselves to become absorbed in the sound and then flow attention to the source, which is the realm of Pure Being. All of the obstacles to success in meditation are overcome when one contemplates the inner sound and experiences Pure Consciousness.

Specific gentle breathing exercises can be useful in calming the mind because through controlled breathing we can regulate the circulation of vital currents in the system. The current flows from the brain down into the nervous system and body. Therefore, starting at the body level, we can regulate the circulation of gross vital forces and, in turn, influence the subtle currents in the nervous system and brain. A useful program would be to settle into a meditation seat, regulate the breathing rhythm, pray and turn attention inward to God. In surrendering to the process, meditation then becomes natural and spontaneous. The intelligence of the soul will direct meditation once we have succeeded in reaching a certain level of consciousness.

One will experience changes in the body and changes in relationships due to the transformation of mental impressions. In the beginning, one has to pay attention to specific rules in order to avoid further confusion and to weaken traditional behavior patterns. As one becomes more successful in meditation and is successful in resting in the light of Pure Consciousness, guidance and direction will flow from within. As the lower tendencies are neutralized, the higher soul tendencies become more dominant in their influence. One no longer has to put forth effort to be good or virtuous because goodness and virtue are natural inclinations of the soul when restrictions are removed. Up until we experience this free flow of grace, we must persist with high resolve. Here is what the Buddha taught his disciples just before leaving them:

"And whosoever, either now or after I am gone, shall be a lamp unto themselves, and a refuge unto themselves, shall betake themselves to no external refuge, but, holding fast to the truth as their lamp . . . shall not look for refuge to anyone besides themselves; it is they who shall reach the topmost height. But, they must be anxious to learn!" His final words were: "Subject to decay are compound things. Strive with earnestness!"

We can go as far on the path as we are inclined to go if we will but extend ourselves correctly. I well recall how, when I was new on the path, I would sometimes become caught in the trap of mild despair because I felt that I was not progressing rapidly enough. I was embued with high aspiration, but there were times when the obvious inner challenges seemed unyielding. My guru would tell me, with gentle encouragement: "Roy, you have to want God so badly that you cannot wait another day for Him. But you have to have patience just in case God doesn't come that day." God does not keep His active influence from us; the light of God cannot enter into a confused and heavily patterned mind. We must, it is taught, do what we can to raise ourselves, to clear the mind, to do what we can do to afford the light of God entry. In the *New*

Testament (Matthew 7:7) we read: "Ask, and it shall be given you; seek, and ye shall find; knock, and it shall be opened unto you."

The Shivapuri Baba, who made his conscious transition at his forest retreat in the foothills of the Himalayan mountains in 1963, at the age of 137, in early life spent almost thirty years in seclusion to study and to contemplate the transcendental aspect of God. His central message was to live a life close to natural laws and to yearn for God always.

Enlightenment can be experienced by one in any walk of life as long as that life is constructive and in harmony with the evolutionary process for the world. Even with family and community responsibilities one can carefully schedule the expenditure of time and energy: so much time for work; so much time to family needs; so much time to community service; so much time for study; so much time for meditation; and always with the awareness of God as the underlying reality. Through careful attention to duty we work out karma, neutralize desires, and learn to replace negative drives with positive forces. Karma, the collection of mental impressions, is not of the soul because the soul is Pure Consciousness. Being identified with the mind, the soul experiences restriction because of the impressions until these restricting impressions are removed. This is the purpose of intentional spiritual discipline.

Finally, when negative or unwanted mental impressions are neutralized, only positive and constructive impressions remain to impel one along through life. Even these will be eventually weakened and neutralized so that there is no compulsion at all; there is only the moment to moment appropriate action and response as directed by higher consciousness.

Chapter Seven
KRIYA YOGA: The PATH
of DISCIPLINE AND PURIFICATION

Kriya Yoga is considered the practical way to purify the body, subtle coverings of the mind, and the mind itself. Kriya Yoga is more than just meditation procedure, it includes the entire range of philosophy and procedure which makes possible the enlightenment experience. This particular section of the text deals specifically with the way to experience perfect concentration for intended purposes.

1. **Intentional Disicpline of the Senses, Complete Study and Analysis of the Nature of Consciousness, and Surrender of Self-consciousness to God-Consciousness is the Practical Means to Attaining Perfect Concentration. Taken Together, This Constitutes the Path of Kriya Yoga.**

The term Kriya Yoga was first popularized in the West by Paramahansa Yogananda during his thirty-two year teaching mission to establish the foundation for later Yoga study by people in this part of the world. Many are of the mistaken opinion that Kriya Yoga refers only to meditation techniques. In the above verse the true definition of this procedure is given.

We have examined preliminary disciplines in the earlier segment of this work. These are considered to be the essential prerequisites to higher meditation practice and experience, for without a foundation there can be no assurance of psychological health. It is true, as we shall see later, that, as one advances on the enlightenment path, the light of the soul infiltrates the mind and works its purifying influence. There are things we can do, however, and we are well advised to attend to practical matters according to the instructions given by the masters. Without discipline, mind and feeling nature cannot be regulated and inner confusion as well as outer chaos will be the result. Intentional discipline of the senses is the very first step in the direction of success in meditation.

Complete study and analysis of the nature of consciousness will range from examining the constituent parts of the manifest universe to that which is behind the manifestation, yet which is the cause and nourishing influence of it. Mind, subtle elements, and the material worlds are all manifesting aspects of consciousness. Thorough study results in discernment, and then one fully comprehends the why and the how of world manifestation, one's place in the process, and the why and the how of the eventual dissolution of the worlds. Knowing this, there is nothing else to be known. Knowing this, one is a master of perfection.

Surrender to God is nothing more or less than letting go of the sense of separate existence, the condition known as self-consciousness, so that God can move freely as us to perform His appointed duties. We are not to do what we think is best and then give to God as the best we can humanly do. We are to release the sense of separate existence so totally that all that remains is God performing. If we are not yet able to do this we can, at least, see to it that we are involved in only useful and constructive work. If we do not know the highest way, we can live our lives so that we do not interfere with the process of world uplift and purification.

Attention to fine details results in the cleansing of the body, feeling nature, and mental condition. With such cleansing, soul light can shine into the mind and move through the feeling nature and physical form with transforming influence.

2. Kriya Yoga is Practiced for the Purpose of Weakening and Neutralizing the Subtle Restricting Influences of the Mind.

Our intentional program of spiritual discipline, then, is designed to enable us to concentrate effectively during meditation and, over a longer period of time, to weaken and neutralize all of the limiting influences in the mental field. We are all aware of obvious conditionings which must be cleared away, but we are not so immediately aware of the deepseated, subtle impressions in the mental field which make their influence felt. Careful attention to Kriya Yoga practice results eventually in purification of the mind and sheaths of the mind.

3. Restricting Influences Contribute to Pain and Suffering and are Due to Lack of True Understanding.

Several influences are mentioned as possible interferences with soul unfoldment. Ignorance or lack of understanding is the cause of all other problems. From this comes the "I" sense or ego-sense, which comes under the influence of inertia or heaviness. The results of this are various: attachment and clinging; aversion and repulsion; conflict between the inner will to live versus the urge to die or become unconscious. The combinations of influences on the lower mind are almost without end, thus further complications and confusions are the result.

4. Lack of Understanding (*Ignorance*) of the Spiritual Nature is the Cause of All Other Restricting Influences.

Being unconscious of that which is true about life gives rise to all of the following problems: egoism; attachment; aversion; death instinct. These obstacles may be dormant, weak, alternating, or fully operative. In their dormant state, tendencies are possible influences in relationship to the future when an occasion may arise for their emergence into active status. One may have repressed tendencies with the potential within them to cause pain and suffering at some future time. Weak influences cause little real problem, but they do contribute to emotional unrest, indecision, and lack of ability to concentrate perfectly. Alternating influences are those which surface and then recede, or which begin to influence us but then are neutralized through force of personal will or by intentionly cultivating the opposite tendencies and habits. For instance, one may feel inclined at times to moods and to purposeless behavior, but one can consciously decide to be cheerful and to be well-organized and goal-oriented. In time the negative tendencies will be overcome and cleansed from the system. When restricting influences are fully operative, we are caught up by them and our reason is overpowered. We examine a little more closely the nature of spiritual ignorance in the following verse.

5. **Assuming the Non-Eternal, the Impure, the Painful, the Deluded Mind, as the Eternal, the Pure, the Pleasurable and True is Ignorance.**

Here is the teaching of the masters of perfection regarding initial ignorance and the following effects. The first error is that a deluded person assumes the outer realms alone to be real (permanent) and forgets the existence of the inner realms which sent the outer realms into manifestation and continue to nourish them. Only that which is beyond duality is changeless. Even the heavens and the gods are subject to change. It must be remembered that it is one thing to have a degree of inner certainty about the reality of the transcendental field and the impermanence of the relative spheres, but it is quite another thing to possess true knowledge. One may be able to discuss the subject with brilliance and yet become weak and fearful at the prospect of actually departing the worlds.

Other errors are to regard things which are not pure and useful as being pure and useful and, in this way, rationalize one's experience and behavior while continuing on in a deluded condition. Another error is to falsely conclude that experience through the senses alone is the cause of highest pleasure. The major problem, always, is that the soul so strongly identifies with the mind and body that it takes itself to be a mind-body unit and it takes the external realms to be the most important and permanent.

6. **When the Soul Appears to Identify With the Mind, Then This is Egoism.**

The scriptures are very clear on this matter of egoism, even to the point of explaining that identification of the soul with mind is but an appearance, that is, it is not permanent. The soul does not become the mind, it only identifies with the mental field and temporarily forgets its true nature and origin. The soul, like God, is the power of consciousness. The mind is the instrument through which the soul perceives when relating to the relative worlds. When soul and mind seem as one, this is egoism.

7. Attachment is the Result of Being Attracted to an Object of Pleasure

We are naturally inclined to be attracted to a person, place, thing, or experience which offers us a degree of pleasure and satisfaction. This inclination has use to us for its survival value because much of what we do that relates to survival is accompanied by a sensation of pleasure and satisfaction. Shelter, warmth, food, security, sleep, supportive human relationships, and anything that contributes to getting along well in this world is pleasurable and satisfying, and we, therefore, gravitate to these things and experiences. But if we are immature, if we are deluded, we tend to become attached to things and relationships which offer a degree of pleasure and the satisfaction of seeming security, even when some things and relationships to which we cling are destructive to soul awareness and ultimate happiness. Often when we say that we love a person, we are really saying that the person has some qualities or does something for us that makes us feel good or secure. Such love-relationships are not based on true love at all but upon dependency.

We all know people who find a degree of security in the possession of material goods or who are almost forever looking outside of themselves for a source of sensory stimulation to cause them to feel more alive or to distract them from having to face the need for inner growth and transformation. Some meditators even turn their attention to the inner realms and to the study of philosophy, but their urgency and drive is really a quest for pleasure, power, or security and not for soul-realization. One can even become attached to visions, ecstasy, and expanded states of consciousness as a result of egoism, as a result of being driven by the pleasure seeking urge of the clouded mind.

8. Aversion is the Result of Being Repulsed by an Object of Pain.

As attachment through attraction to an object of pleasure is often called love, so aversion through repulsion to an object of pain is often referred to as hate. We love that which makes us happy and we hate that which makes us unhappy or hurts us in some way.

When we are confused we sometimes even hate ourselves. In this instance we are really experiencing aversion to the weaknesses of which we are aware and we hate that which we think ourselves to be. Some people, not understanding the true nature of God and God's role in the world, will even express dislike and anger toward God. Every truth teacher has met people who were so caught up in their own confusions and psychological defense patterns that they were afraid to even discusss truth principles for fear of having to face the possibility of change. These people, already wallowing in sense-related pleasure experiences, actually see the possibility of enlightenment as a threat to their unsatisfactory, yet somehow fulfilling life.

Those on the spiritual path should also take care not to allow aversion for "worldly" things to become a preoccupation. We are to aspire to the good and the pure while remaining free from the pull of sense attractions and from the influences which operate within us at deeper levels of mind. Both attachment and aversion should be neutralized as a result of higher understanding.

9. **The Instinct Toward Death Exists Along With the Inclination for Life, Even in the Wise. These Instincts and Inclinations Are Propelled by Their Own Powers.**

All beings have a strong urge to survive, to live, because this is the urge of life to express itself. In lower life forms we find this urge to live, to express, and to fulfill instinctual duties. Even simple organisms strive to live and attempt to avoid premature death. Ordinary human beings begin life on earth with a strong will to express and survive. This continues until life's purpose has been fulfilled, until desires are satisfied and thus neutralized, until one loses the will to live because of pain and disappointment, or until the relationship with the material worlds ends due to enlightenment.

There is the instinct, though not the conscious drive, to die in all living things, because it is the nature of things and forms to emerge, persist, and then to withdraw. Therefore, the instinct toward death and the inclination toward life are both directed by an urge, a power or drive in the direction of ultimate ends. Death is only the end of a form, not of the animating unit of consciousness which gives the appearance of life to a form. Death, the withdrawal of life from a form, does not mean the end of that form; it only means that the form will be changed into a different manifestation of energy. Energy is just as eternal as God is, but energy changes form while God does not.

While attraction and repulsion, love and hate, remain strong influences, one tends to be involved with his world. When these opposites no longer influence to any marked degree, one loses interest in the game of life. In ordinary people this disinterest results in their leaving the body. We see in people who are weak and tired, in whom the driving influences are no longer predominate, that the world is no longer as enchanting as it once was. In people who tend toward the direction of enlightenment, when attraction and repulsion no longer influence greatly, the inclination is to search out the meaning of life and to assist others who are so inclined.

Some say that we fear death because we have subconscious memories of previous death experiences and of experiences in between incarnations. This may be so, in some instances. In other instances we may fear death because we desire so much to fulfill our purposes without interference. Even without fear of death there may be a disinclination to die to this world because we have grown accustomed to this realm and we know our way around in it with reasonable certainty. If we are reasonably comfortable and happy, there will be no inclination to change environments. One may not fear death of the body but, at the same time, see no reason to leave the body. Advanced meditators have a premonition of soon departure from the body and they experience an inner psychological adjustment which results in their making a conscious transition with full cooperation of all of nature's influences and subtle forces.

10. The Influential Tendencies to Suffering Can Be Overcome by Being Resolved into Their Subtle Origin.

We can often be free from unwanted influences, originating in deeper levels of mind, by recognizing them for what they are and by being impervious to them. In this way they will be weakened and lose their influential power over us. Also, during meditation, when we experience deeper stages of samadhi the tendencies then settle in the subconscious level of mind and do not interfere with samadhi experience. But as long as they remain, even in dormant form, they still have the potentiality of again becoming active and becoming a disturbing influence. Through repeated samadhi experiences and through keen self-analysis and discernment, we eventually arrive at the clear realization of our true nature as Pure Consciousness. Knowing the truth, we are no longer ignorant of that which is so. Since ignorance, unawareness of the truth, is the field from which all problems arise, when it is banished so the obstacles to life are dissolved.

11. The Gross Modifications of Pain-Causing Tendencies Are to Be Overcome by Careful Self-Analysis and Deep Meditation.

It is easy for one to assume that the storehouse of the subconscious has been cleansed of dormant pain-causing tendencies when, in fact, these tendencies have only been suppressed. This is why meditation is recommended, long after one has experienced a considerable degree of enlightenment. As we meditate and experience deeper samadhi states, we are assured that the purifying light of the superconscious is steadily fed into the various aspects and chambers of the mind. The descending light and power eventually does its cleansing work, literally dissolving the seeds of possible future effects. It is taught by the masters that when one turns his attention toward God, the elevating influence of God's love lifts one partially free from bondage due to identification with mind and conditionings. The elevating influence neutralizes inertia and restlessness, sharpens one's power of discernment, and awakens intuition. The masters also teach that when we remain in the company of enlightened people and see to our attunement with their state of consciousness, this allows us to receive an infusion of spiritual energy which has a transforming effect upon us. We are advised that we also have to be responsible for self-honesty, living in harmony with natural laws, and for experiencing God as a reality during regular meditation practice.

12. The Storehouse of Subconscious Impressions and Tendencies is the Cause of Unplanned Experience in This and Future Lives.

Subconscious impressions and tendencies which propel us through life and which influence us from deeper levels are referred to as karmic patterns. They are causes which, unless neutralized, will result in outer effects or experiences. Some will assert that it is not fair that thoughts, desires, feelings, and reactions of the past, perhaps now forgotten, should have an influence in the moment or a possible influence in the future. What should be understood is that, even though impressions and tendencies have their origins in a moment now past, they still reside in the subconscious in this present moment. Because they reside within the deeper levels of the subconscious now, they can possibly be influential now, if the opportunity is present. Or they can remain dormant and be influential in the future when an opportunity arises.

13. As Long as the Roots of Probable Effects Reside in the Subconscious, They Will Tend to Mature and Come into Fruition According to Class, Span of Life, and in Relationship to Pleasure or Pain.

Unless some success in the direction of neutralizing subconscious impressions is realized, these impressions will tend to become active and influence one's life. This is the natural working out of causes leading to probable effects. Because the mind is conditioned by the storehouse of collected impressions, one's awareness is accordingly clouded. This results in a person gravitating unconsciously into life situations over which control seems hardly possible.

However, change is possible for one who is conscious enough to make decisions. One may be born into a social situation where poverty and seeming lack of opportunity prevails, but he may decide to rise above the situation. Most people who gravitate unconsciously into restricting environmental circumstances are not there as punishment for past wrongs committed but merely because they did not know any better than to flow with circumstances. On the other hand, one might be born into the most ideal human environment, with great opportunity for growth and education, and still fail to make use of the opportunity because of lack of interest or inability to resist negative influences in the mind. Length of life, is, in some instances, determined by impressions in the subconscious, either brought from past experiences or received during the present incarnation. One may have a weak constitution and fall prey to illness. One may be accident prone and die young through misfortune. One may be endowed with a strong constitution and the ability to move through the world with relative ease but lack the inclination to aspire to higher knowledge. Again, there may be subconscious tendencies from the very beginning of one's earth experience which incline one to seek out experiences which will result in pleasure or in pain.

14. Pleasure or Pain, Joy or Sorrow, Can be the Results of Maturing Subconscious Impressions According to Whether Their Cause is Virtue or Vice.

The impressions in the mind which were the result of positive thought, feeling, action, and response were caused by virtue and, when they mature, will reflect accordingly. Intelligent planning, a healthy self-image, psychological maturity, constructive actions to desired ends, and appropriate response to any given situation contributes to improved health and a more open and cooperative relationship with one's world. Failure to use the available faculty of intelligence, a negative self-image, weakness and meanness, destructive behavior, and immature or selfish response to life situations contribute to further confusion and a deterioration of mental and emotional health.

15. Enlightened People See the Possibility of Future Pain Even in the Midst of Pleasurable Experiences and Situations Because of the Existence of Latent Subconscious Impressions Yet to Be Influential and Because of the Tendencies and Actions of the Electric Characteristics in the Mind.

If one experiences a situation which is felt to be pleasurable and if this situation is the effect of a past cause, when the momentum of the cause is exhausted, then the pleasure-causing situation will dissolve. Unless one can flow from moment to moment, from event to event, there will be either an inclination to try to retain a pleasure-causing situation through attachment or an inclination to experience anxiety in anticipation of unwanted future change. Thus, there is the possibility of mild pain even during pleasurable experience. Then, too, even if all seems to be going well, there is the possibility of the unexpected coming to the surface to disturb one's present harmonious condition. Furthermore, due to the constant interplay of electric characteristics in the mind and body as well as in our environment, there is always the possibility of a restless mood canceling out our peace of mind, of inertia dulling our faculties of perception, and of inner conflict because of a surge of passion or strong feeling. As long as the mental field is not cleared and as long as the elevating characteristic of nature is not dominant, even during times of seeming happiness, the hint of unrest awaits just offstage.

16. Pain and Suffering Which Has Not Yet Resulted from Such Subconscious Inclinations Can Be Avoided.

If we are aware of thoughts, attitudes, actions, and habits which contribute to our suffering, we can, if we so decide, change these thoughts, attitudes, actions, and habits so that new causes replace old unwanted ones. But, what if we are not aware of patterns and inclinations within us which may contribute to future suffering?

There are two ways to approach the problem. First, we can be self-honest and explore the range of the subconscious mental field during occasions of conscious introspection or during times of reverie when the door to the subconscious is more open. We can become aware of our dreams, our mental conversations, and our not so secret hopes and dreams. We can examine our motives and analyze why we do the things we do and why we relate to life as we do. Having become aware of unconscious patterns which influence us adversely, we can change these patterns. Second, we can plumb the depths of the mind through conscious meditation practice and direct attention to the source of life, the Transcendental Field. This experience will result in a change of values and priorities and, in time, insure mental purity.

17. The Cause of Suffering is the Identification of the Seer With the Seen.

Again, we are reminded that the cause of suffering is due to the identification of the seer (the soul) with the seen, the (objective) world. Before losing Self-awareness as a result of identification with the material world, the soul is naturally luminous and free. During unconscious identification with matter, the soul becomes caught up in the movements and activities of nature and experiences variety. Upon awakening, the occasions of past suffering or pleasure are no longer real to the soul and not a trace of memory remains. Memory has only to do with material things in which impressions can be made and retained. The soul is non-material and therefore, upon final liberation, is free of the time-space realms.

18. The Objective Worlds, Consisting of Elements and Sense Organs and Influenced by Electric Attributes in Nature, are For the Purpose of Providing Consciousness With the Opportunity for Experience and Ultimate Liberation.

It is obvious that Consciousness is inclined, at times, to express through material forms. Many philosophers have pondered the age-old riddle of why the universe came into manifestation and what the purpose might be. Subtle elements combine to form gross elements and these further combine to appear as the material universe. Consciousness, expressing through nature, experiences life in the relative spheres. We cannot say that Consciousness wants to do this, we can only observe that it does so. We cannot say that Consciousness needs to do this because Consciousness is obviously superior to matter. The human mind may not be able to fathom this riddle of the play of light and shadows, but, we are told, the enlightened mind understands it without having to justify it or make anything out of it.

Throughout our examination of the life process we are reminded of the influences in nature of three electric attributes or characteristics. There is a trend toward brightness, clarity, and purity. There is a trend toward action and motion. There is a trend toward inertia, heaviness, darkness, and stability. Life forms tend to repeat survival behavior instinctively and this provides for the perpetuation of their species. The soul which enlivens forms, however, is destined to ultimate awakening because of the innate brightness which characterizes its nature. This is why, eventually, all souls awaken and withdraw from involvement in relative spheres. It is really a matter of God having become involved, God being involved, and God withdrawing from involvement; and the story is written as the journey of the soul.

19. According to Their Gross and Subtle Manifestations, the Cosmic Forces (Electric Attributes) Have Four Aspects. These are the Specialized, the Unspecialized, That Which is Only Indicated, and That Which Has No Characteristics Whatever.

In reverse order: that aspect of cosmic force which has no characteristics at all is cosmic force in the primal stage, before outward manifestation; that aspect which is indicated is the aspect which first emerges in the direction of manifestation; the unspecialized aspect is nature appearing in subtle electric combinations this side of physical manifestation; the specialized aspect is the full outer manifesting condition which we can perceive through the senses. The outer universe is made possible because of a subtle inner universe, which, in turn, is the result of fine causes. Gross, subtle, and fine aspects emerge from primal nature-energy.

20. The Seer is Pure Consciousness. Even Though it is Essentially Pure, When Relating to the Objective World It Cognizes Through the Mind, Senses, and Body.

Over and over the masters remind us of our essential and never changing nature as Pure Consciousness. As we ponder this truth, awakening can occur and we can know in an instant the reality of our own being. On such occasions the philosophical explanation given us by the masters makes the utmost sense. We see that which is so with brilliant clarity.

21. The Only Purpose for Nature and the Manifest Universe is For the Sake of God.

Nature is the unconscious principle of God. The conscious principle, the intelligence and motive force, animates nature and causes evolution, involution, and dissolution. This process of manifestation, unfoldment, and final rest continues forever.

22. Although This Universe No Longer Exists for One Who Has Transcended It, It Continues to Exist for All Who Yet Perceive It.

Nirvana, the "blowing out" of the sense of individuality and multiplicity, removes the appearance worlds from the range of the one who has experienced Pure Transcendental Being. We cannot be aware of that with which we have no connection. Others, however, who have a sense connection with the world will continue to perceive it and relate to it. Even while relating to our world, if we so purify the mind and consciousness that only harmony and fulfillment is real to us, we will know nothing of suffering and lack even though millions in the world continue to see it and experience it.

23. When the Forces of Pure Consciousness Mix With the Forces of Nature, This Becomes the Cause of Identity of the Supreme Soul With Matter.

There is an aspect of Consciousness which never becomes involved with matter. If this were not the case, then matter alone would be superior and life would forever be imprisoned in it. There are forces, influences, which infiltrate nature and in this manner God influences nature with directing intelligence. This directing influence is called the Holy Spirit by Christians and Shiva by yogis. The Holy Spirit moves in and through all of nature, transforming, regenerating, influencing, forever acting. The Holy Spirit also encourages the spiritual awakening of souls and assures their final liberation. As much as we are encouraged to seek out the truth, as much as we are encouraged to be attentive to needed disciplines and to practice meditation and samadhi, we are wise to be ever aware of the purifying influence of the Holy Spirit in our lives when we surrender consciously to God.

Even unconscious surrender to God can be useful for one new

on the path. That is, one may have little faith and even sometimes doubt the existence of God, yet this turning to God can bring forth a response from the soul level and be the start on the quest for enlightenment, knowledge, and freedom in God. Throughout the world scriptures we find mentioned the importance and usefulness of one's yearning for the truth, of one's experiencing a burning love and longing for God.

If one can conclude no other reason for the world, one might stand in amazement at witnessing the tremendous spectacle and conclude that all is the glory of God in never-ending expression.

24. Imperfect Cognition of the Nature of the Soul is the Cause of Its Becoming *Seemingly* Identified with Matter.

It is taught that correct Self (Soul)-understanding solves all problems, even this problem of world identification. When Sri Ramakrishna was ill and it was felt that his stay on earth was short, he was asked why he did not pray for healing of the body. He responded by pointing out, from a higher level of looking at things, that the existence of a body at all was, in itself, due to illness. Meaning that if there were no false identification with mind there could be no relationship with the body or the world. So, identification is relative, and suffering and/or pleasure is relative.

It is not the goal of all enlightenment masters to depart this world. For some the goal is to live within the framework of relative appearances and understand the process completely. With total comprehension there is no bondage and no pain.

Philosophical problems can forever plague the mind. Is the soul really clouded as a result of identification with matter and mind? Let us ask ourselves whether or not the sun in our solar system is clouded because clouds float over the earth. The answer is, of course, no. At a deeper level, behind the conditioned mind, we are as radiant as the sun and, unlike the sun, we will shine forever and forever. The problem we have is that of identification with matter and mind. We do not become matter or mind, we assume a point of view of identification. That is, a portion of our awareness does so, and then it is this portion of identified awareness of which we are aware this side of the field of subtle matter. The Sanskrit word for subtle matter is maya, that which veils the truth and that which is the substance of which things can be formed. Its component parts are: creative energy; light particles; time; and space. On the other side of maya is the clearly shining reality of Transcendental Being. Yet maya is not an illusion, it is the unconscious principle of nature. Being identified with it, however, we fail to see clearly and the objective realms seem illusory to us. Maya, as a result of its veiling influence, gives rise to the sense of illusion in the soul which is identified with matter.

25. By the Removal of the Sense of Identification (*of the Soul with Matter*), Ignorance (*Lack of True Knowledge*) is Banished and the Seer Experiences Absolute and Final Freedom.

We are here examining the possibility of directly experiencing freedom as a result of dissociation of what we are from that with which we have heretofore been identified. The contemplation of a phrase, during which we attempt to experience the truth (such as "I am Pure Consciousness"), can be useful but it is not the experience of freedom itself. There is a vast difference between knowing *about* something and actually *knowing* that something. Visualizing food will not take the place of eating the required food when the body is in need of nourishment. Having some insight into the nature of Ultimate Reality is not as liberating as *experiencing* Ultimate Reality. We must, of course, begin where we can and do the utmost of which we are capable at any given moment. Even right effort is some gain, and persistent striving will result in success.

The enlightenment path is not an easy way to the satisfaction of human whims. The masters of perfection have taught the basic steps to freedom. First, it is obvious that unenlightened man, no matter how perfect his present lot in life, is still subject to possible suffering and pain due to misunderstanding or the very influences of nature. Second, the causes of suffering and pain are now known; the basic cause is lack of awareness of the true nature. Third, there is a way to put an end to suffering and pain. Fourth, the way to end all suffering and pain is to awaken to the conscious realization of the Real Nature. If one can instantly awaken, this is the easiest and more direct path. If a procedure is needed, then

Kriya Yoga offers the plan of intentional involvement designed for the purification of body and mind.

26. The Means of Removing Lack of Knowledge is to Remain Firmly in the *Conscious Knowledge* of the Truth Regarding the Relationship Between Pure Consciousness and Matter.

Again, the actual experience of knowledge is not the same as thinking about it and almost-understanding of the Truth. Some have reported that insight came in a flash of recognition and that with this experience all doubts were settled and everything was known. The usual experience is that persons who have prepared themselves through discipline and meditation can more easily retain this understanding. They *remain firmly in the conscious knowledge of the truth regarding the relationship between Pure Consciousness and the manifest worlds.* A flash of insight is useful but it is not permanently result-producing. The stable knowing of the truth permanently burns out all remaining subconscious impressions that might have caused future unknowingness. Once ego-sense is dissolved, all of the other tendencies and confusions weaken and die because they have no soil in which to be nourished.

27. The Final Enlightenment is Experienced in Seven Progressive Stages.

One may move through the subtle experience slowly or quickly. As a result of samadhi experiences the soul actually experiences and comprehends the full range of manifesting nature and finally experiences total independence or liberation. The soul becomes free from compulsive involvement with the physical realm, the astral realm, the causal realm, and the inner fine realms or heavens. Degrees of freedom are experienced with each progressive stage, but the final freedom is that of complete transcendence. There are astral samadhi experiences, there are true cosmic conscious samadhi experiences, there are experiences during which one roams the heaven realms like a god, but these are still experiences in relationship with manifest nature. When unknowing is removed and when all attraction to any illusory manifestation is neutralized, pure awareness is experienced. During higher samadhi experiences there is no personal effort to gain the next level or to reach a goal; all that is required is to surrender to the inner activity and to renounce the desire to cling to any perception or experience. Being under grace, the advanced meditator moves through the progressive stages smoothly because the attracting influence of God unveils the subtle organs of perception of the soul, until the soul stands revealed in freedom and purity.

28. **Intentional Disciplines and Spiritual Exercises Result in Purification of the Mental Field and Gross Coverings. Enlightenment is Experienced and Further Experiences are Undergone Until Final Liberation is Assured.**

We are under no illusion regarding a cause and effect relationship between daily practices and the enlightenment experience itself. Enlightenment can be experienced spontaneously without prior expectation or preparation. What the text here suggests is that there are things which can be done to prepare for the enlightenment experience as well as to make possible its continuing influence as a result of our providing a suitable body and mental field through which it can be expressive. In the original work these disciplines and procedures are referred to as *accessories* rather than causes of spiritual effects. Up until now, in this section, we have been dealing with matters which will be acknowledged by many readers as abstract philosophical considerations. We now move on to extremely practical matters with which any reader will be able to involve himself.

29. **The Will to Restrain from That Which is Not Useful, the Will to Observe and Apply Truth Principles, Physical and Mental Exercises, the Regulation and Transformation of Vital Force, Intentional Direction of Vital Force, Concentration, True Meditation, and Samadhi are the Eight Steps in the Experience of Perfect Knowledge (*Yoga*).**

This is the famous eight-fold path of Raja Yoga (Royal Yoga). There are people who have known the truth without any such intentional discipline, indeed, without any knowledge that such a discipline even exists! There are others who report that they have spontaneously undergone each and every phase of this recommended procedure without having ever before heard of it. What we might find interesting here, however, is that such a careful step-by-step procedure has been clearly detailed and explained so that a seeker, whatever his present level of understanding or current need, might begin where he is inclined and go on from there to the intended conclusion of freedom in God.

30. The Five Restraints and Regulations Are: Harmlessness, Truthfulness, Non-Stealing, Right Use of Vital Forces, and Non-dependence Upon Things.

Harmlessness means to remove from mind and consciousness any intention or will to injure self, others, or the environment. One may lead a model life but inwardly resent others or dislike oneself. *Truthfulness* requires us to bear accurate witness in our communications with others, as well as to be self-honest. Of course, we would not appropriate anything belonging to another person, but *non-stealing* also means that we should not covet anything belonging to another. *Right use of vital force* calls for conscious direction of our available energies so that energy is used for intended purposes and is not wasted. To accumulate wealth for oneself, beyond one's own needs, and to deny others access to that which they could use with benefit is to be overly *dependent upon* and attached to things.

31. These Recommended Regulations are Considered to Be Universally Applicable as They Are Not Limited by Class, Country, or Time.

Regardless of the age in which one lives, regardless of the cultural life, these regulations are basic and applicable to all people everywhere; therefore they are universal. These regulations have been suggested to people throughout the ages by various enlightened teachers who had the welfare of humanity in mind. More than observing the letter of the law is required, one must enter completely into the spirit and practice of the principles.

32. **The Truth Principles to Be Observed are: Purity and Cleanliness, Contentment, Self-Discipline, Study of the Nature of Consciousness, and Surrendering Egoism to God.**

Purity is of body, of speech, of thought, and of action. *Contentment* is possible always, regardless of external conditions, as one rests in the understanding of the truth. *Self-discipline* refers to sense control, mind control, energy control, paying attention to duty, in fact, abiding by that which is useful and renouncing that which is not useful. *Study* of the nature of Consciousness and of the Reality of God is essential for ultimate understanding. *Surrender* of the sense of separate self is true surrender to God. What does God expect of one? We inwardly know the answer. In this manner we can conduct ourselves in harmony with nature.

33. **To Overcome and Neutralize Destructive Instinctual Forces and Tendencies, One Should Cultivate the Opposite Forces and Tendencies.**

We become aware of forces and tendencies within, and we know when they are not useful to our spiritual, mental, emotional, and physical health. What can we do with these forces and tendencies? We can check them by an act of will when they first make their presence felt. In this manner, by going against the current of destructive tendencies, they finally weaken and become neutralized. Unable to do this, we can intentionally think, feel, and act in such a way that constructive energies and tendencies predominate. Again, the unwanted tendencies will, in time, be dissolved. The ultimate end for the mind is to be purified by the light of the soul. In this case the only tendencies remaining will be positive and useful ones.

34. **Instinctual Forces and Tendencies May be Mild, Moderate, or Intense. These Tend to Result in Pain and Suffering; therefore They Should be Removed From the Mind and Body.**

Much energy is buried in the chambers of the mind due to confusion, repression, and misdirected attention. If destructive tendencies are not handled, if they are not neutralized, the result will be evidenced as personal problems, psychological unrest, and even physical illness.

35. When One is Established in Harmlessness, Then People and All Living Things are Free From Enmity in That Person's Presence.

It is taught that for one who is at peace with all the world, all the world becomes his friend. Such a person will never be hurt or injured by another person, by any living thing, or by any force or activity in nature. Having come to friendly terms with the universe, the enlightened person experiences nature as supportive and even benevolent.

36. When One is Firmly Established in Truthfulness, One Sees Immediate and Specific Results From Actions Performed.

When one is truthful, confusions are banished from the mind and emotional nature. As a result, one's intentions and actions bear immediate fruit. A double-minded person is unstable in all his ways, so the scriptures teach. When there is conflict between conscious and subconscious levels of mind there is no definite purpose in life. It is also taught that one who is established in truth can simply command a situation to be however intended and it will become so. When one is established in truthfulness, the forces of nature work through him.

37. When One is Established in Non-Stealing, True Prosperity is Experienced.

To prosper means to thrive, to flourish, to be successful. When we are in harmony with life, when we are in the stream of grace, it is our experience that life provides for us everything we need for comfort and for the fulfillment of personal destiny.

38. As a Result of Intelligently Directing All Available Energies (*Physical, Mental,* and *Spiritual*), One Experiences the Benefit of Transmuted Energy for Higher Purposes.

One on an intentional path, who lives with the ideal of experiencing the fulfillment of soul potential, is advised to make wise use of available energies. The first step is to refrain from wasting energy through non-productive activities. When we think or act without purpose, we waste mental or physical energy. When we allow ourselves to be emotionally upset or mentally confused, we waste energy. Anxiety, tension, and worry deplete our energy reserve. Frantic questing after sense experience is a waste of energy. Over-indulgence in any sense experience tires the system. Restlessness and excessive talking wastes energy. Because many people do not lead a planned and orderly life, they waste much of their energy. That is because what they do serves no useful or constructive purpose.

Unfortunately, many writers on this theme try to explain that the real subject here under discussion is that of avoiding sexual experience. That some people, who are making an advanced study of the nature of Consciousness, use the majority of their energy in the pursuit of knowledge is well known. Mental and spiritual preoccupation is bound to result in lessening of body urges. Enlightenment teachers do teach that sexual experience has its proper place in nature and that the function should not be abused. Physical energy can be transmuted into mental energy and mental energy can be transmuted into a finer energy. When the energies are strong in the body, health of body is natural. When mental energies are strong and harmonious, mental health is assured. The more one is established in soul awareness and the less he allows energy to be wasted, the more available energy he has to transmute for more subtle purposes. It will be observed that mere repression of natural urges will not result in enlightenment. Intelligent use of energies and the enlightenment experience contribute to a natural regulation of vital forces.

39. One Who is Established in Selfless Non-Attachment Acquires the Ability to Know the Processes of Birth and Death.

If we are materialistically oriented, we can hardly be possessed of an open attitude or enjoy keen powers of intellectual discernment. If we are not selfish, if we are not attached to things, we are then free to see in correct proportion the relationships we have with life. Being free from attachment and dependence, we function more and more from the level of soul awareness. As a result we gain insight into nature as only a free soul can.

40. As a Result of Purity and Cleanliness One is Inclined to Avoid Contact with Possible Sources of Contagion.

It is only common sense for one to avoid contact with people and conditions which contaminate the body and contribute to disease. But, as a result of purity, we also incline toward an environment which is free of mental confusion and emotional unrest. The undisciplined mind can be the target of negative suggestion, and a person who is basically endowed with pure motivation to action can sometimes be influenced to commit an immoral act. Sri Yukteswar taught new disciples the importance of spiritual fellowship. He taught that one's environmental influence is often stronger that one's will to resist. Physical cleanliness has to do with personal hygiene, selection of diet, and care of personal surroundings. A clean body, if well nourished and given proper exercise and rest, will be disease resistant. A pure mind, nourished with thoughts of God and the stronger energies of the soul, will be clear and well ordered.

41. As a Result of Mental Purity, One Experiences Serenity, Cheerfulness, Power of Concentration, Control Over the Senses, and Fitness for Direct Perception of God.

By attending to recommended disciplines and procedures, one can prepare the mind for success in life and for success in meditation. Success in meditation cannot be experienced if one is upset, depressed, lacking in sense control, and unskilled at concentration. A confused mind, a sick mind, cannot possibly receive the light of the soul.

42. As a Result of Contentment, One Experiences Supreme Peace and Happiness.

The supreme peace is the peace of Self-realization. The supreme happiness is the happiness of enlightenment, of knowledge of God.

43. As a Result of Purification and Self-Discipline, One Experiences Perfection of the Body, the Mind, and the Senses.

We see again the emphasis upon the total person. Kriya Yoga includes purification of the body, it includes purification of the mind, and it includes purification of the senses. The methods and procedures included in this teaching of the masters take in the whole of one's life. This procedure is not a part-time matter, it is a full-time process which has as its purpose the transformation of mind and body.

44. Through Study of the Nature of The World as Consciousness and Through Correct Use of Mantra, One Experiences Direct Insight into That Which is Examined.

One may examine the nature of Consciousness in a variety of ways. One may use keen intellectual powers to discern the truth about whatever is examined. One may experience identification with that which is being examined and thereby know about that aspect of life by being consciously at-one with it. One may use mantra correctly and in this manner enter into the core of the subject under analysis. The masters of perfection teach that the universe is made up of waves of energy. Variety in manifestation is possible because of different frequencies of a basic energy. If we know a mantra which will enable us to communicate directly with some aspect of the universe and if we use the mantra correctly, we will then experience pure communication with the intended idea or true knowledge inherent in whatever is being contemplated.

A basic mantra is OM, the primal sound. In the beginning, when the universe was originated in the ocean of Pure Consciousness, there was an urge, a movement. Increasing in force and complexity, the initial sound, the result of energy frequency, became varied so that subtle and then gross realms were produced. The sound, the *Word*, is the primal or basic vibration of the universe. One can, by chanting OM with surrendered devotion, gradually come into a relationship with this primal sound existing behind all surface sound variations. In this procedure one goes eventually beyond verbal chanting of OM and enters into the silence to actually hear the sound. Then the attention flows to the source of sound which is the pure field of Consciousness. During this process one will fully identify with, commune with, the ocean of primal sound and be one with all vibratory manifestation. Working from this level, examining various aspects of nature, one can know the truth about any aspect of nature because one is working from the level of knowledge. Knowledge is not superimposed upon the mind, knowledge emerges from the soul level to the mind level. Knowledge is self-revealed as it emerges through mental layers of the gross mind, which is the organ through which we perceive and know in the relative spheres.

Through the practice of mantra one can commune with subtle spheres which are presently existing behind layers of gross matter frequencies. Through such communion one can receive the beneficial influence of subtle energy influences which enter into the mental field and nervous system. In this manner the mind and nervous system are refined and the soul can then more easily express its innate knowledge and creativity.

45. Through Total Surrender to God One Experiences Samadhi.

When one is totally surrendered to God, all attention flows to God. Identification with the contents of the mind ceases and all that remains is the awareness of Pure Being. In early samadhi experiences there will be various cosmic perceptions according to the aspect and function of God with which one is communing. Samadhi is the most powerful cleansing and purifying experience possible to anyone. Perfection in samadhi experience results in fulfillment of the Kriya Yoga path.

46. The Ideal Meditation Posture is That Which is Steady and Comfortable.

Yoga students will know of many postures which are performed for specific purposes. Strain and discomfort is never involved in any of our practices. If there is discomfort, if there is strain, we then know that too much effort is involved. Especially for meditation practice, the body should be settled in a comfortable seated position so that full attention can be given to the inner process.

As meditation progresses, the body becomes increasingly relaxed, the vital forces become harmonized, and the mental field becomes clear. The nervous system is given almost total rest during deeper samadhi experiences. It is even taught in the tradition of Kriya Yoga that through these procedures the process of decay is arrested and the body does not show signs of aging.

47. Through Deep Relaxation One Experiences Purification of the Mind and Knowledge of God.

What happens as we meditate regularly and correctly is that gross energies are converted into finer energies and the quality of the mental field is likewise altered from gross to subtle levels. The character of the mind is changed as a result of the influence upon it of pure God awareness. The more regular our meditation practice and the deeper our samadhi experience, the more influential the fine spiritual energies become. This results in complete transformation from the inside outward.

48. When the Meditation Posture is Mastered, the Mind is No Longer Influenced by Tendencies of Nature.

Here is explained the ideal for success in meditation. When the body is so relaxed that we no longer have any sensation of it, all potentially disturbing influences are kept from interfering with concentration. True success in meditation also results in the removal of stress symptoms from deeper layers of the body. When there is no tension and when the nervous system is refined, the body is literally a pure vehicle through which the soul can express.

49. When the Meditation Posture is Mastered, Then the Circulation of Gross Vital Forces Ceases.

Even people who do not practice intentional regulation of the breathing cycle experience automatic pranayama during deeper meditation states. Prana is the energy flowing throughout the universe, from the Godhead into full involvement with gross matter. Prana frequencies perform specific functions in the body of man as well as in nature. Some meditators practice controlled breathing exercises before meditation in order to induce body relaxation and to harmonize the flows of subtle energies in the body. Others find that breathing is automatically regulated as they settle more deeply into meditation. There is a relationship between inhalation and exhalation and the circulation of nerve currents in the body. When these currents are balanced in force of flow, mental peace is more easily experienced.

In advanced meditation states, even though the body is completely still and no breathing action is discernable, there is yet a flow of sustaining prana from deeper levels of the mind. This flow of prana is cosmic energy which nourishes the mental field and finally the brain, nervous system, and physical body. Kriya Yoga pranayama is sometimes used by meditators because it relaxes the body, charges the system with prana, and encourages the awakening of dormant subtle forces in the body.

50. The Modifications of Pranayama are Either External, Internal, or Motionless. They are Long or Short and Modified by Space, Time, and Number.

If we will observe our natural breathing pattern, we will notice that there is a brief pause after exhalation, another brief pause after inhalation, and a duration of no movement at all, during which rhythm of inhalation and exhalation is restrained. References here to space, time, and number refer to specific breathing exercises practiced to give one mastery over the body and over prana. Masters of pranayama can feed the cells of the body with vital energy. Also, as a result of deep relaxation of the body and a slowing of the metabolic activities of the body, a greater degree of rest is experienced. The masters teach that breath regulation can result in health of the body, in mind control, and in longevity. The Shivapuri Baba once said, in a conversation, that it was possible through breath control and conservation and transmutation of energy to extend the body's life up to a thousand years or more.

51. Another Modification of Pranayama is That of Neutralizing Inhalation and Exhalation.

By bringing opposing currents into harmony we experience bodily relaxation, mental clarity, and eventual transcendence of the modifications of the mind. It is a common experience of those who practice Kriya Yoga pranayama that, as a result of extended practice, one can sit in meditation without any visible evidence of body motion. Breathing stops for a duration, but the nervous system is nourished from deeper levels of soul reality. Once waste gases are removed from the body through breathing and total rest is experienced, there is no longer any requirement for breathing, so the process ceases until the need arises once again. By consciously controlling the vital forces and by turning attention back to the source of vitality within, the advanced meditator restrains physical and mental influences from interfering with samadhi experiences. This restraint is not suppression, it is a stilling and quieting of body and mind forces and tendencies.

52. As a Result of Mastery of Pranayama, the Darkness Which Veils the Light of the Soul is Removed.

The light of the soul is screened through conditionings and impressions in the mental field. When one is successful in the practice and experience of pranayama, this collection of conditionings and impressions is removed. Subtle energy pervades the mental field and the illumined mind is then a reality. Mastery of vital forces is automatically experienced due to samadhi influence. Any spontaneous and useful alteration in the breathing rhythm during meditation and any spontaneous and useful energy-flow experience can be allowed, for this is the natural process of internal transformation. Specific and intentional exercises used for the purpose of regulating the breathing pattern or the circulation of vital forces should be learned from a qualified teacher during private instruction,

53. When the Mind is Purified, It is Then Made Suitable for Meditation on the Supreme Reality.

Not only does mental purity enable us to meditate effectively, it is also assurance that we will always be motivated in a positive direction and will never be tempted to use superconscious abilities for selfish purposes or destructive ends.

54. Interiorization During Meditation is Accomplished When Attention and Energy of the Senses is Withdrawn and Established in the Field of the Mind.

As attention flows inward during meditation it is withdrawn from externals. Also, mental energy which formerly flowed outward to the senses and their connections is withdrawn into the field of the mind, which is the origin of the senses. Gross energy, at the body level, is thus returned to the mental field and is there sublimated, transformed into finer forms of energy.

When external objects are no longer perceived, because of the energy having been returned from the sense organs to the mental field, inner sight opens. This inner vision can result in our being able to examine subtle aspects of the material world or the finer worlds contained within them. The organ of intelligence is purified and reflects perfectly the light of the soul. Because of this conscious introversion, without the support of sense organs or the mind itself, the soul can directly cognize the reality of God.

55. As a Result of Conscious Interiorization, One Experiences Supreme Mastery Over the Senses.

One may experience a degree of mastery over sense urges through discipline and will. If one uses the senses with intention and is not the compulsive slave of sense urges, then one can determine that he enjoys relative freedom. Supreme mastery is the result of mental purification through repeated samadhi experiences. As the nourishing influence of finer energy invades the mental field during and after meditation, the mind is cleansed, energy pervading the body is of a finer quality, and one's natural tendencies are wholesome and constructive. Insight realized through meditation enables one to see the objective world in proper perspective, in relationship to that which is behind it and which is the cause of it. This results in enlightenment and a natural and spontaneous relationship with life.

Chapter Eight
SIDDHIS: The POWERS
of PERFECTION

Mankind has always been attracted to the unusual, the super-natural, and the miraculous. This attraction can be attributed to curiosity, to a quest for ability that might end, once and for all, one's dependence upon externals. A more purified urge to knowl-edge of the powers of perfection would be the soul's natural in-clination to unfold and participate consciously with God's plan for the universe. The importance of a purified mind is ever stressed by the masters of perfection in this matter of siddhis. Siddhis are the powers of perfection. That one is a true master precludes the wrong or harmful exercise of ability. This is why all major teach-ing texts, while giving evidence of the soul abilities, explain that such abilities are not to be sought by one who is still on the enlightenment path because one who is still on the path to con-scious awareness should continue on that way until realization is experienced. When a master of perfection comes into a relation-ship with society, whatever powers are expressed are natural exten-sions of his soul destiny. When an unenlightened person comes into a relationship with society, even with partially unfolded soul ability, there will also be the obvious indications of ego, person-ality need, self-serving, and the manipulation of others even when such manipulation will be explained as being useful to the cause. The major challenge for one who is sincere on the path, who is curious about siddhis, is how to allow them to unfold and be expressed while still moving in conscious understanding to the ultimate freedom in God. Souls not yet decided on the course of full liberation of consciousness will often tend to settle for phenomena and miracle-experience. Partially awakened souls will be content to observe and talk about the miracles they have witnessed. Even disciples of enlightened gurus will often neglect their own needed disciplines. Such disciples will feel secure in their relationship instead of doing the inner work that is required to be as clear as their guru. It is not enough for one to say, "I am a disciple of a great guru" . . . or "Jesus is my example." One must exemplify the highest attributes of one's spiritual support and ideal. We cannot say that such hero-worship is not useful. Such idealism does, in the long run, contribute to soul unfoldment. However, in our present work we are emphasizing the now-possibility for each and every person who is inclined to true knowledge.

The several accounts preserved in printed form, in the various books and sacred scriptures, have a charming quality because of the simple and honest explanation of human versus soul challenge. We find Jesus, after his baptism experience, going into seclusion and there being tempted by the pull of the flesh and the suggestions of the ego-sense. His emergence as the full manifestation of the Christ Spirit is the story of initiation, of how the soul rises free from all mind-body tendencies. Jesus, moving about as God-as-man, openly displayed his siddha power. He healed the sick and performed minor miracles, such as making water into wine and making food expand to meet the present need. His greatest miracle was the transforming influence of true love and the quickening of soul awareness in those who came into contact with him. The greatest love, Jesus taught, was to love God and to love every person as one loved one's own self. True love of self is true Soul-recognition, and, if we have this, how can we not recognize other expressions of God as equals in the world process?

On the day to day scene we have our challenges, of course. On more subtle levels the challenges come more quickly and even more indirectly. Have we all not noticed that when a problem is seemingly solved, often, a similar problem, in more gentle disguise, comes to the surface? This is because deepseated tendencies are seldom neutralized quickly; the purification of deeper layers of mind is a gradual process as more-obvious and then less-obvious patterns of a similar nature are handled, or as gross and then subtle aspects of tendencies and desires are neutralized. Even advanced meditators are tempted to rest this side of liberation and accept, instead, lesser but still attractive experiences. One may be tempted to emulate the life pattern of another who seems almost as a god. One may be tempted from deeper levels of deluded mind to accept heavenly delights. The inner temptation may thus invite: "Come into the shining realms and be as gods and goddesses. Devote your attention to everlasting and radiant life in a body. Enjoy sense pleasures at a more refined level and experience exquisite, even ecstatic bliss and ever-new joy that mortals can never even imagine possible." Experience in subtle realms is the frequent destiny of awakening souls. A glorified body is sometimes manifested, for a duration. Blissful feeling is often experienced as perceptions become refined. One is counseled by the masters to experience what occurs but not to crave anything which is not lasting and not to cling to that which, while pleasurable, may cause one to cease from inquiring into ultimate truth. This is the teaching for souls aspiring to liberation of consciousness.

But not every person is destined to experience liberation of consciousness in this life-cycle. Many are destined, by God and by their own human needs, to work out their salvation in the relative worlds for a period of time. There is no reason why we cannot use whatever abilities we have to improve the world condition and to ease our passage through time and space. What is important here is purity of motive and the intelligence to work in harmony with the evolutionary pattern for our known world. "Not personal will but God's will" is the ideal. Since we are moving in the direction of an enlightened world, it is natural that awakening souls become aware of subtle laws of nature and that they respond to the challenge to utilize their knowledge for the highest good. We make a decision and we exercise wisdom-inspired will to set and reach goals. This is a siddhi, a soul ability. We use creative visualization to either attract desired circumstances or to cause useful effects. This is exercising soul ability. We examine a problem and we see through to the solution. This is soul ability also. So it is a matter of degree of involvement and, most important of all, purity of motive. A person can make unwise use of his creative powers of mind, but we do not condemn the use of creative ability by all people. Radio, television, and the printed word can be used to transmit negative information to the minds of the masses, but we do not condemn the existence of these communication forms. There is a positive side, a creative function, for every discovery in nature and to every power of perfection. For the average person, the unveiling of soul abilities will result in personal comfort, improved relationships, and unrestricted creative endeavor. When the majority on the planet exercise soul ability, then "heaven on earth" will be established. This will occur, according to the masters of perfection, a few thousand years from this present writing. Heaven and earth, so we are taught, will eventually pass away; therefore a glorified planetary condition is but temporary. Since, according to some calculations, planet Earth will continue to orbit the sun for some billions of years, several enlightenment ages will come and go before final dissolution. This is why the majority of people on the planet have a responsibility to unfold their latent abilities and to be consciously involved with the evolutionary trend. Now, let us examine the material which follows:

1. Concentration is the Directing of Attention to a Point (Object) of Focus.

For the meditator, concentration is necessary if success in practice is to be experienced. A person who has not himself experienced true concentration may contend that concentration is not possible for anyone. Yet, advanced meditators report that they do experience single-pointed focusing of attention. Preliminary training will result in eventual success in concentration. Also, if that which is concentrated upon is attractive to the soul or to the mind, then concentration occurs with little effort. As a result of mental, psychological, and physical disciplines; confusion, emotional unrest, and body movements no longer interfere with meditational concentration. Many people fail in their meditation attempts because they have not seen to preliminary disciplines by way of preparation. Some experience a degree of success because they are highly motivated or because they are attracted to the inner object of concentration, but they tend to have difficulty after the meditation experience because they do not see the importance of attending to mental, psychological, and physical health. If one is devoted to God and attracted by the love of God or lights and sounds perceived within, meditation occurs naturally and spontaneously. Also, if the meditation experience is pleasure-producing for the mind, the mind itself will be attracted to the experience of frequent meditation. That the mind experiences pleasure as a result of meditation is useful in the beginning because the superior pleasure of meditation is more enticing than sense-induced pleasures. Pleasure is not the goal of meditation; therefore even pleasure must be transcended if one is to experience pure awareness.

It is natural, in the early stages, for attention to wander a bit even during total concentration because, as long as attention is flowing to the object of concentration, there may be various aspects of that object to be examined. This is still considered to be concentration because the attention does not wander from the object, even though one is examining various facets of it. For instance, when concentrating upon the spiritual eye one might perceive changing patterns of light, yet concentration upon the spiritual eye is steady. When listening to internal sounds one might hear a variety of frequencies as one flows ever deeper in concentration. Even in listening to a mantra the quality and character of the internal sound may vary. Or when surrendering to the inner silence the quality of that silence may change as the attention becomes more introverted and flows from gross to subtle levels of awareness.

2. **A Steady Flow of Attention to the Object of Concentration is Meditation.**

Such steady contemplation is perfect meditation. If the attention is flowing to the object of concentration totally, there are no distractions. Since one is relaxed and in a quiet place during his meditation practice there are no messages being sent to the brain through sensory channels, therefore no interference from the outside environment. Since the metabolic processes are slowed down, the breathing is shallow, and emotional surges have been neutralized, there is very little that can interfere with concentration. All that remains to interfere with the meditation process is the restless nature of the as-yet undisciplined mind. If one is attentive to a regular schedule of meditation and if one is totally surrendered to God, in time the mental field will become purified and even subtle mental modifications will be put to rest.

3. When, During Contemplative Meditation, the Form (and, or Aspects) of the Object Concentrated Upon is Transcended and the Meaning (Reality) only Remains, This is Samadhi.

There are degrees of samadhi. This Sanskrit term refers to the fact that the waves of the mind are stilled, resulting either in absorption in that upon which one was contemplating or in the experience of non-mind awareness, while remaining fully conscious. In preliminary meditation experiences one may cease being aware of the object of concentration because the waves of the mind are stilled and the reality of the object shines in or pervades the mental field. In advanced samadhi experience, object and mind no longer exist for the meditator, as only the experience of clear Being prevails. This samadhi experience is not to be compared with trance due to one's consciousness having become trapped in deeper (unconscious or subconscious) layers of the mind. In the latter instance one may emerge from the experience with no greater awareness than was had prior to it. Or one may experience certain inner-mind perceptions and even unfold undeveloped psychic abilities. But this mind-trance has no transforming effect upon the mind or the personality. Samadhi, on the other hand, when experienced regularly, results in purification of the mental field, psychological adjustment, and the transformation of one's total life. However, even advanced meditators who are content with initial samadhi states can remain satisfied with light, bliss, or subtle perceptions and conclude that they have experienced perfection in meditation when this is not the case at all. One brother disciple of mine experienced deep ecstasy almost immediately upon learning to meditate. Some years later he experienced true initial samadhi. Almost twenty years later, after regular meditation and dramatic samadhi experiences, he experienced liberation of consciousness. Except in rare instances, initial samadhi experience is but the beginning of a longer process. Lahiri Mahasaya experienced the highest (pure) samadhi shortly after he was initiated by Babaji, but this was only after years of prior meditation practice as well as the fact that he was an illumined soul in a previous incarnation. He had but to wait for a few years to become settled in this world before being awakened to what he had consciously known before.

4. The Three (*Concentration, Meditation, Samadhi*) **Taken To-gether is Perfect Contemplation.**

When one is successful in gaining knowledge or true insight through experience of that which is being examined, then the process is known as perfect contemplation. A casual examination is not total understanding, so early stages of experience and per-ception are not the perfect or complete experience. Some will take months or even years to experience perfect contemplation. Others, who are either more naturally advanced (aware) or who have prac-ticed for a longer time, will be able to move through the stages of concentration, meditation, and samadhi very quickly. Yoganandaji and other masters of perfection could (and can) demonstrate almost instant samadhi experience. With advanced meditators, often just the thought of God turns the attention to instantaneous experience of samadhi. Understanding the process of concentra-tion, meditation, and realization helps one to understand much of what will later be explained in this text. What meditation masters tell us is that there is a precise training procedure which will enable any qualified person to experience success on the enlighten-ment path. It only seems, at times, that access to knowledge is for a special few with God-given soul endowments. We acknowledge that some are born into this world with a high degree of awareness and a natural aptitude for the enlightenment experience. But, in this study, we also acknowledge that any person who is sincere may begin where he is in understanding and work beyond his present capacity in a practical way. Steadiness, faith, and practical application of the principles will result in realization and perfec-tion. This is the great promise of the ages.

5. As a Result of Mastery of Perfect Contemplation, Enlighten-ment and Knowledge is Experienced.

Enlightenment refers to Soul-realization and to clear compre-hension of whatever is brought within range of contemplation. One might inquire into the nature of God and how God works in and through the worlds and see clearly that which is so about the nature of God and the world-process. One might inquire into the relationship of the soul to God and to the world and see clearly that which is so about the relationships. One might inquire into the nature of the mind and through direct intuitive insight fully comprehend the nature of the mind. One might even contemplate the inner nature and purpose of material objects and gain insight on all levels, from the obvious outer appearance to the finest aspect of that object. Perfect contemplation, it is taught, makes possible clear insight into the smallest unit of matter as well as to the far boundaries of the universe. Perfect contemplation makes possible understanding regarding that which is beyond (behind) the atom and the universe, including subtle dimensions, planes, and spheres. It is by revelation, spontaneous insight, and directed contemplation that all has been known by the masters of perfection. Do we desire to know the truth about anything? We have but to practice perfect contemplation and we shall know.

6. Perfect Contemplation Should Be Practiced in Stages.

"What is it" the ancient teachers asked, "which by knowing all can be known?" The answer comes: "That which makes possible all knowing is to know the Reality behind the appearance." One is to see the truth about that which is examined. According to personal destiny or present inclination, a person will examine that aspect of life which seems most useful to understand at the moment. Some are destined and inclined to contemplate the Supreme Reality behind and through all appearances. Patanjali wrote: "By the practice of yoga, the experience of yoga must be gained. Experience is the teacher of the highest experience in yoga. He who knows this secret remains in the state of Cosmic Consciousness forever." Yoga, regardless of whatever name we give to our spiritual disciplines, results in enlightenment. Early enlightenment experiences make possible higher enlightenment experiences. Without enlightenment, our seeming knowledge is but a collection of concepts and beliefs. All levels of consciousness can be explored by the right use of perfect contemplation.

Scientists explore the nature of the material universe, including that non-physical aspect behind forms which makes forms apparent. A scientist is not unlike the seer because both examine from the appearance to the reality behind the appearance. Seers tend to practice perfect contemplation in order to comprehend

Reality behind the veils of the mind, but a scientist, if he will follow his inclination to the end, will arrive also at that Reality behind the appearance.

As we proceed we shall become aware of matters both subtle and, to a beginner, fascinating and challenging. This can be a useful exercise for all of us, for in our examination of that which is advised we may find concepts shattered and clear understanding experienced.

7. The Three Disciplines Here Described are Internal Processes in Comparison with the Five Which Preceded.

Mastery of the above five disciplines will result in human fulfillment and the attainment of superior soul abilities. Some seekers who perfect the first five disciplines and who meditate superficially will be able to demonstrate remarkable abilities in this world, but they will not be enlightened because they have not explored the inner planes, the internal worlds. The internal worlds begin at the edge of the mental field and continue in the direction of Pure Consciousness. What those who are solely involved in outer concerns do not know is that the internal realms are even more vast and subtle than the outer ones. This is not to say that there is no purpose for outer realms, for there is purpose. What the masters of perfection have taught is that, for total knowledge, one should be aware of all planes, those outward from the mind and those inward to the Source. New seekers are sometimes confused because of the teaching emphasis of an obviously enlightened teacher. One will teach the importance of world service while the other will teach that to transcend this world is the highest ideal. We have to understand why they teach as they do and what each individual teaching destiny is for. God works through many enlightened expressions of Himself to do the work destined from the beginning. Some teachers stress the importance of devotion and service to one's fellow human beings. Others stress a balance between the inner and the outer, the way of standing at the edge between two worlds. A few teach that the purpose of spiritual discipline is to move from relative planes to the realization of the Pure Realm, the non-dual experience. Most teach all of these things to the particular souls who happen to need what is taught. A master of perfection will teach according to present need and according to his or her own destined role of service. If one will enter into a personal relationship with God, one will be shown the destiny he has for now, and there will no need to compare teaching methods or the seeming differences in emphasis. Differences have to do with the outer, understanding has to do with the inner. When the inner is experienced, the outer will be comprehended.

8. The Three Disciplines Here Described are *External* in Comparison With Higher Samadhi Experiences.

Here we are informed that even concentration, meditation, and initial samadhi realizations are *external* when compared with more subtle soul perceptions. Just as basic preparations preceding meditation are left behind as we move toward meditation experiences, so the techniques and procedures we use to meditate with benefit are left behind as we plunge into the realms of inner space where no sense-bound or mind-oriented soul can go. In the early samadhi stages the light of the soul infiltrates the mind with purifying influence, but there is often a combination of mind-influence and soul-influence. There is a mixture of influences, from below and from above. Then something happens and this mind-soul relationship is neutralized. What occurs is that the aspect of the soul which is aware of itself as a viewpoint of God becomes more influential in the process of complete soul unveiling. When we truly "stand naked before God," we are stripped of all coverings and there is no longer any possibility of pretense. There is only the experience of God acting as God wills to act. God knows what is best always. We, at a deeper level, at our Reality level, know what is best. The seeming interaction between God and the soul is but God influencing Himself in relationship to His own manifestation as matter. There is no compromise, there is only God working according to whatever is required to fulfill the predestined ideal. While still in soul consciousness we can but rest and surrender to whatever God does through us and around us. We watch the process, yet we are not unresponsive. We act as we feel inclined from within, but we are aware that we are not doers, we are participants on the stage of life. Even in higher samadhi experiences there is often an awareness of God and ourselves. It seems as though God indwells us and that God walks and talks with us moment by moment. Some scriptures inform us that for one to aspire beyond this level is a sin, it is wrong, it can only lead to self-punishment. We know that God does not punish Himself as us. What, then, is the problem? The problem with wanting to "become" God is that such aspiration is evidence of confusion. How can we aspire unto that which is really our very own nature? We are not God but God is us. Any suggestion of our trying to become God or of our yearning to be united with God is the result of our own error. Very few, even among advanced yogis and mystics of whatever religious affiliation, are conscious of the subtle stages of knowing. This is understandable because we are now attempting to explain that which cannot be known at the mind level. It can only be known at the level of personal experience, and this leaves mind-oriented persons at the outer door of understanding . . . until such persons take the next step and move from all frames of reference and concepts and begin to flow attention to that which is the most useful experience of all!

9. **As a Result of Samadhi Experiences, Higher (*Superior*) Influences of Consciousness Permeate the Mind. Destructive Tendencies are Neutralized as Constructive Tendencies Increase.**

As we continue to meditate correctly we experience occasions of clarity when mental impressions are neutralized or when we succeed in experiencing the spaces between the emergence of mental impressions. In early stages of meditation one may experience moments of being free of the interference of unwanted impressions and thought patterns, then attention is drawn again into involvement with mental processes. As a result of inner watchfulness and gentle intention one can succeed in controlling and suppressing the tendencies of mental impressions. During these occasions of non-interference the mental field is receptive to superconscious influences, the influence of the soul nature. When one surrenders to higher influences these influences then effectively neutralize lower tendencies, that is, the tendencies of conditioned mind to either be overcome with delusion or to be agitated by restlessness. During initial samadhi experiences one is conscious of being able to control the waves of the mind, direct attention at will, and be open to that influence which is outside the mental field. Through the regular experience of samadhi lower instinctual psychic influences are neutralized by higher enlightenment tendencies. This results in purification of the mental field and transformation of mind and lower nature.

In the preliminary states of meditation, when mental waves persist, one can interfere with the random flow of thoughts by directing attention to the object of meditation. If we do not struggle with thought activity but remain absorbed in our meditation ideal, the force of impressions from unconscious and subconscious levels will be weakened, and thought processes will become more subtle and finally cease entirely. If one is not successful in transcending awareness of thought activity, one can, in early stages of meditation, simply rest as the witness of thought processes without interfering. One may then observe the occasional moments of non-thinking. In this way one will learn, through direct experience, that it is possible to be aware even when thoughts are absent. One can then turn one's attention to the intended object of contemplation. Some of the non-useful instinctual influences upon the mind are the tendency to allow attention to wander, being sluggish and preoccupied with matters of no importance, and being easily distracted from the purpose of meditation.

10. The Flow of Superconscious Influences Becomes Peaceful, Calm, and Serene.

As the instinctual influences within the mind become neutralized by the superior influences of superconsciousness, the flow of superconscious influence becomes serene. That is, there is little or no contest going on between opposing tendencies. As we realize at this stage that the battle to control the mind is not ours, in the ego sense, superior superconscious influences can continue their cleansing work. Superconscious influences are not struggling with the mental field itself, they are resisting and neutralizing impressions rooted in lower levels of the mind. All who have meditated for any length of time have experienced a shift from personal effort to surrender, thus allowing the higher influences of the soul to naturally bring about useful change in mental patterns.

11. **Samadhi is Experienced When Mental Modifications are Settled, Distractions No Longer Interfere, and When Attention is Absorbed in the Object of Meditation.**

Sensory input disturbs the calm nature of the mind by causing thoughts to surface. Feelings can also cause ripples of activity in the mind. Tracings of memory can result in the recollection of past experiences and this, too, can interfere with the process of concentration during meditation. When all mental modifications are settled and the attention no longer wanders from object to object, samadhi (superconsciousness) is experienced by the meditator.

12. **When Concentration is Steady, Then the Mental Impression of the Past is Similar to the One Which is Present.**

We are still dealing with imperfect samadhi experience, during which superconscious influences are present in the mind, but final transformation has not yet been experienced. Therefore, even during this samadhi there will be subtle mental impressions as the result of inner perceptions, but each succeeding impression is similar to the one which preceded because attention is flowing without interference to the object of meditation. If there were no subtle changes in perception and impressions, it would mean either that the meditator had become unconsciously absorbed in the meditation object (light, sound, et cetera) or had consciously transcended identification with relative objects of perception. In the former instance it would mean that inertia had overcome the meditator, and in the latter instance it would mean that lower samadhi states had been transcended and the soul's experience would be that of conscious Being.

13. **By What Has Been Explained in the Preceding Four Verses the Property, Character, and State Regarding Elements, Body, and Senses are Explained.**

To summarize the preceding four verses: impressions perceived by the mind are resisted and held in check; the flow of superior influences over inferior ones becomes steady; that which was resisted is no longer a challenge; concentration is steady and one-pointed.

Elements make up things and forms in the material realm. There is one basic *thing* or substance out of which all things and forms emerge due to a mixing and blending of subtle elements. The property of a thing is its basic make-up. The character is its form. States may be altered through the passage of time due to internal and external causes. Lumber (wood) has a property which reveals it as wood. Wood can be fashioned into furniture. The property (wood) remains but the form changes. The state of wood changes due to decay or due to external influences such as weathering, burning, infestation by parasites, or by whatever external influence.

Our perception of our world is due to the interaction of properties of what we perceive and the subtle sense receptors in the mind. Things have color, texture, odors, and other properties which make possible our perception of them. An unenlightened person sees things as things, according to sense communicated data. An enlightened person accepts, as a matter of convenience, the role of a thing but knows that behind that appearance is the basic fabric of which all things are made possible. As a practical matter man may alter the properties of a thing by a scientific process. The masters of perfection can, if they are inclined, work from the inside-out and cause a change in the material universe through an act of will, working not with the thing itself but with the primal substance of which all things are produced. Matter can be altered in appearance, as wood is changed into furniture and wool into cloth. Chemical change is possible by knowing the scientific process which will cause such a change. A change in state is possible. For instance, water can be changed to steam through the application of heat or it can be made solid by freezing. A chemical change results in an altering of the properties of the original thing, while an altering of form does not result in a change of properties. One great master would, at times, convert water into oil to use to burn wood. When asked how it was possible he said, "I *look* for the oil in the water." That is, he looked at only the basic properties of the kind of oil he wanted and let the properties in water which did not relate to oil be released into the air. Remember, even though a material scientist may say that the ingredients of the new form do not exist in the things from which the new form emerges, behind appearances there is only one substance, and from this, any form with any needed properties can be called forth by a true master.

14. The Substratum or Primal Substance is That in Which the Properties (*Latent, Active, or Unmanifest*) are Innate.

That which is innate to anything is that which is inborn and has been a part of the thing from the very beginning. For instance, *Being, awareness*, and *power* are innate to the soul as they are innate to God. But in this verse we are still examining the primal substance which makes possible all that appears in the relative spheres. Even if a property of the material universe is not known at present, that property still exists in latent form, active form (either noticed or not noticed), or in unmanifest form. One description of substance is: "That which has inherent quality and action and that which is the material cause of its effect." Some properties in nature are latent and will emerge at some moment in the future or at least the potentiality for their emergence is there. Some properties are not active and fully manifesting, making the visible world real or apparent. Other properties are unmanifest either because they have not emerged to the latent stage or they have expressed and are now in the past with no further reason for being expressed. The basic substance which exists remains regardless of whether or not all properties of this substance are in evidence. Forms change, events seem to come, remain, and go, but substance is ever what it is. The force within substance makes possible its movement and change and this force is directed by the intelligence of God. When a master of perfection is inwardly led to mildly interfere with the surface arrangements of a material thing by working from the level of initial-cause, then what the world refers to as a miracle happens. The intelligence of the soul is identical with the intelligence of God, and where there is direct knowing about the usefulness of an intention, a master can exert influence as a representative of God. No personal will or ego is involved when a master participates in evolutionary matters through the exercise of siddhi power.

The change in form and properties of a thing is made possible by a subtle change being made in the electrical characteristics or qualities inherent in matter. What takes place is a rearrangement of properties due to a change in internal relationships between electric characteristics. We might relate intentional change to what can occur in one's mental field. Nothing can emerge in mind without its already being innate to that mind. We are aware of currently active thoughts, moods, and attitudes, and we are conscious that thoughts, moods, and attitudes can be changed either by a conscious act of will or by allowing superconscious influences to enter into lower mind levels. We also know that there exists in the mental field certain tendencies which are now dormant but which can, in the future, become active. The neutralizing of unwanted dormant tendencies is the real purpose of our spiritual practices.

15. A Variety of Underlying Influences and Occurrences Are the Causes of External Changes in Basic Substance.

The material universe, seen and unseen, known and unknown, is made up of basic particles. Making up any form we see is the arrangement of electrons, protons, and neutrons restrained by a blueprint or pattern for that arrangement. Seers, in meditation, see through matter to the smallest units and behind those units they perceive Consciousness-as-Light. This is why masters often refer to the universal activity as a play of lights and shadows. Matter can be changed in form, in chemistry, and in states, and the total energy and total basic substance will remain the same. There is no creation and no destruction, there is only an exchange of energy and matter from one form to another. The outer appearances change constantly, for this is built into the life process. But available substance does not increase nor does it decrease; behind appearances is that which never changes.

When nature is in perfect harmony energy flows, forms emerge, and then withdraw from visibility; transformation is constantly taking place. Even when a form persists for a duration, at a deeper level there is constant motion taking place which enables a form to persist. When life-motion ceases or withdraws from a form or when the pattern holding energy in form is released, the form disintegrates. Things emerge (they are "born"), they persist or live, life withdraws, and the form dies. This is inherent in the natural process going on about us. In the *Bhagavad-Gita* Krishna instructs his disciple Arjuna not to grieve when forms come and go because forms are temporary. We are advised, also, not to overly rejoice when things (forms, events, relationships) come into manifestation because they, too, are subject to transformation, change, death, and decay. The masters of perfection have taught that one should live in a responsible manner in the world while understanding the process of nature and living without attachment or aversion. In this way one comes to experience changelessness from the soul level of awareness.

16. Through Perfect Contemplation on the Three Kinds of Transformation, Knowledge of the Past and Future is Acquired.

As there can be no effect without a prior cause, if we become aware of the causes behind current effects and experiences in our life we have greater understanding. We are also in a position to change inner causes so that outer effects will be altered. What is happening to us and about us now may be the effect of causes set in motion in the distant or immediate past. Past causes emerge as current events, current causes result in future events, and the stream of causation flows through time until a person either interferes with the stream or rises free from its influence. A probable future exists and can be known by knowing present causes. But the future can be altered by making a change in present cause-patterns. For instance, if we agree that we are as we are because of past causes and that there is nothing that can be done about past or present, we will tend to continue in a pattern similar to the one we now experience. Removal from the subconscious and conscious levels of mind of causes of outer events will result in a change of life experience. Often what is required is deep and honest self-analysis in order for us to become aware of the contents of the subconscious level of mind. Desires, tendencies, and patterns of response to life situations often dictate our daily experiences. By changing desires, neutralizing tendencies, and becoming consciously and appropriately responsive, we can redeem the past, change the present, and influence the future. What is not generally known is that mental impressions often precede the physical body, as the soul takes the mental field from sphere to sphere and from body-experience to body-experience. The history of incarnations is recorded in deeper levels of the mind. Not only our personal history, but, due to our attunement with universal mind, at a very deep level are recorded the histories of all life forms and the motions of the universe itself. By examining physical changes, changes in character, and changes in psychological states and states of consciousness, it is possible for one to become aware of personal past, personal present, and personal future . . . as well as the past, present, and future of the world.

It takes perfect contemplation and extreme self-honesty, when dealing with personal matters, for one to see clearly into causes of present effects. It is human nature to deny that the problem is within us. We often want to place the cause elsewhere, with others or with conditions which are beyond our ken and control. It may be that our present experiences are not due to past causes but to our present attitude about life, our own self-image, and what we feel worthy of experiencing. Even if one is not the cause of a problem, for instance, one may be accepting it.

17. Through Perfect Contemplation on Sounds One Comprehends the Meanings of Sounds Uttered by Any Living Being.

By examining the ideas, feelings, and emotions which prompt verbal sound, one can comprehend the meaning of that sound. People who work with animals learn to fairly accurately communicate with animals by understanding the feelings, needs, and emotions which prompt the animals' "speech." Anyone who has had occasion to mingle for a time with persons who speak a different language can, with practice, comprehend the intention and meaning of their speech even if the words are not understood.

By examining the ideas, feelings, emotions, and intentions of a person we can easily understand what that person is attempting to communicate even if that person fails to explain himself clearly. The idea behind speech contains the true meaning of the person who speaks. We also observe that communication is possible and understanding can be clear without the use of sounds or words. The general attitude and behavior of a person or living form can communicate intention. Sounds uttered by humans and animals, even if not clearly defined as words, convey the idea, feeling, emotion (need), and intention. We acknowledge the scream of terror, the whimper of loneliness, the sigh of contentment. Humans can "talk" with animals through sound, tone, and attitude, as many will attest from experience.

18. Through Perfect Contemplation of Subtle Subconscious Impressions Comprehension of Past Incarnations (*One's Own or Another's*) is Experienced.

Subtle impressions or memory due to experience are stored in the deeper layers of mind. With each new physical emergence or birth, a new body form is manifested so the body cannot be the storehouse of past incarnation memories. The body may, however, record tracings of pain or pleasure experienced during this present incarnation. Subtle mental impressions certainly influence the physical form. In this verse we are informed that by examining the impressions in one's subconscious one is able to revive memory of previous time-space experience, in this physical world as well as subtle spheres between physical body experience. Because of personal interest some seers have examined the contents of their own subconscious levels of mind and have recalled previous experiences in minute detail. On the other hand, there are enlightened people who are not at all interested in looking back through time. Yet again, some report that knowledge of previous experience has surfaced spontaneously during occasions of quiet.

I, at present, know little about previous experience. I do know that I came from realms of light into this present body and that, in a recent incarnation, I was on the yogic path. This has also been confirmed to me by my guru. The occasion of this verbal confirmation took place during an evening's quiet walk in 1950 at Yoganandaji's desert retreat in Southern California. He told me that we had been together before and that I had come this time to be with him and assist in his mission. Paramahansaji also knew his previous earth experiences, as well as his experiences between physical bodies. He also knew his future. He knew his destined mission from 1893 to 1952 (his physical birth and time of transition), he knew when and how he would leave his body, and he knew that his body would remain intact after his conscious exit from it. He knew the sphere to which he would retire for a while after his conscious exit and that he would return in a new physical body in the future and reside in the Himalayas with Mahavatar Babaji. While not an uncommon event in the lives of the saints, Yoganandaji's physical form did remain intact after he left it. He told a few close disciples, before he left, that his body had been purified in the fires of Kriya Yoga and that it would not decay. This "phenomenal" occurrence was merely part of his teaching mission to the world and does not represent a personal goal to be achieved. It seems that deep meditation, the circulation of creative energies, and the harmonizing of innate subtle properties of the body resulted in a permanent condition of non-decay of his physical garment.

Paramahansa Yogananda lived only for God and to do God's will. He often said that he was but God's servant. He wrote in a poem that his eyes were made to see beauty everywhere, his lips were made to sing God's name, his hands were made to serve God as people, his heart was made to love God alone. In this idealism did my guru represent the highest aspirations and the clearest realization of a true devotee of God.

While we are about our examination of the siddhis, the powers of perfection, let us be ever mindful of the true use of soul abilities. We cannot hide from the fact that soul abilities will unfold. They will unfold because, as we become more aware, more conscious, we are certain to become more creative and more able. To deny this urge in the direction of total knowing is to attempt to suppress the natural and predestined trend of evolution, the trend in the direction of unconsciousness to full awareness. If we affirm that we do not want to know or that we should not know, we are reacting from fear and deep delusion. After all, darkness does not want to know the light. There is nothing wrong, the masters of perfection teach us, about scientific inquiry into how and why things work. There is everything *right* about our using soul ability to inquire more deeply into the nature and workings of the mind in order to understand more completely and to move through all mental impressions to that final experience of Reality.

When confronted by soul ability the mind can run in several directions. We can become emotionally involved and run after the phenomena itself. We can let ego become involved and then use new abilities for selfish purposes. The most useful way to go, for one who is dedicated to freedom of spirit, is to consciously utilize increased powers of perception to further liberation of consciousness. We then inwardly inquire about the true nature of God and of God's role in the universe. We inquire about who we are and what God wants of us. We learn to relax and flow with the movement of life. If God, as us, feels inclined to demonstrate the powers of perfection, we rest as a witness and we allow God to do what God will do. There will never be a moment of personal challenge in the matter.

19. Through Perfect Contemplation of Another's Mind, Knowledge of That Person's Mind is Obtained.

The indirect process of knowing the contents and motivations of another person's mind is to observe behavior. We can tell by how a person acts and reacts what the mental patterns of that person are. This indirect approach, however, does not tell us the whole story because there are deeper tendencies and causes which are not always revealed through surface evidence, as well as deeper tendencies and causes which may be masked by a person's public behavior. The person being examined may be skillful at putting up a facade, an outer pretense, which will result in a superficial examination being incorrect in relationship to deeper levels of that person's mind. The direct process of knowing the contents and tendencies of another person's mind is to practice perfect contemplation on that person's mind. Through attunement and direct perception, a seer can see into another's mental processes as well as he sees into his own. An enlightened person does not pry into the secret recesses of another person's mind unless there is a valid reason for doing so. Valid reasons might be that a relationship of some sort is about to be established and that one will want to know that which he is really relating to, or a person may come to a teacher for assistance and the teacher then has the privilege of examining the deeper levels of the student's mind in order to give the greatest help. The practice of perfect contemplation of another's mental processes is not a matter of telepathy, it is a matter of actually identifying with the mental field of that person so completely that full comprehension of the mental field is known. It must be understood that many sincere people do not even know their own deeper motivations. As honest as they might be with themselves, there may be areas of mind currently hidden from them. Such persons may mean to do well, but deeper tendencies and impressions interfere with good intentions.

Since every human mind is a particularization of Universal Mind, it is even possible for a master to gain insight into the mental processes of people who dwell at a distance, on the planet or in subtle realms. Yoganandaji would contemplate the mind of an original author of a scripture, even though the author had lived on this planet hundreds or thousands of years before. In this way, he told us, he could enter into the level of understanding the author had when he first wrote the text and, in this way, accurately interpret his meaning in modern language to meet current needs. At times, to practice perfect contemplation of another person's mind, all that is required is for one to be still and turn one's attention to that person. At other times it is useful to have a specimen of handwriting, a photograph, or some object previously owned by the person in order to establish subtle contact. Yoganandaji told us that he inwardly examined his disciples on a regular basis by turning his attention to them in meditation. Wherever the disciple was, Yoganandaji could attune his mind with that disciple's mind and know exactly that disciple's mental, emotional, and spiritual condition at the time. He taught us that we could assist him in his efforts to help us by remaining in tune with him, by thinking of him, by meditating upon God, and by being open to God's grace in our lives.

20. **Perfect Contemplation Which Reveals the Knowledge of Another's Mind Does Not Reveal the Deeper Contents and Supporting Influences.**

The verse preceding this one specifically refers to the seer's ability to know another's mental condition, while this current verse tells us that merely knowing another's mental condition does not give us access to deeper contents and supporting influences. For this, more complete practice of perfect contemplation upon the mind is necessary. It is possible, through deep identification with the mind of another person, to actually know the causes of present conditionings and tendencies. Whether or not these causes related to a previous life-cycle or this present one. One can know who has been influential in another's life, as well as the major situations and experiences which have contributed to the present mental condition. For instance, with superficial examination we may see certain behavior patterns and know specific psychological traits but not the persons and events that played a role in forming these patterns and traits. With deeper analysis we can clearly see a strong father influence or a strong mother influence, or the influence of peers and authority figures impressed upon the subconscious level of another's mind. We may see how a person's reaction to something observed, heard, or experienced has left its almost indelible mark. All of us have observed something which has resulted either in desire for it or a sense of aversion. We have heard statements or comments, with or without any basis in fact, which we yet retain and accept subconsciously as completely true. We have had experiences which have left us with the yearning for more experience of a similar kind or have resulted in our putting up our defenses so that we will never have a similar experience again. The causes of patterns in the mind do not have to be understood in order for one to become free from dependence upon them, but often insight as to why we think and feel the way we do affords a reasonable explanation for our letting go of undesirable and unwanted patterns.

21. By Practicing Perfect Contemplation on Body Form, on Suspension of the Receptive Power, Contact Between the Eye (of the Observer) and Reflected Light From the Body is Broken and the Body Become Invisible to Others.

Our perception of things in this world depends upon the existence of a thing in form, light sufficient to allow light reflection from that form to our eyes, and the optic nerves themselves. If a form is not present we obviously cannot see it. If it is too dark, we cannot see the form. If reflected light from an object is not received through the eyes and transmitted to the brain, we cannot see a form. Here is suggested the idea that if, through inner control, one can interfere with the light reflecting from one's own body so that the light cannot travel to the eye of another, one will, in effect, be invisible to others. This does not refer to dematerialization of the physical form but to merely being no longer present to the sight of others. We would "be here" but would not be observed. If an observer suddenly experienced an interference of reflected light from our body, all other conditions for sight being normal, it would seem to him that we had vanished into thin air. If the observer were then to see us again it would appear as though we had emerged from subtle space or another dimension. In fact, however, there would be no vanishing and reappearing in the sense of our leaving this dimension and then returning to it. The phenomenon would merely be due to the stoppage and then the natural flowing of reflected light from our physical form. We sometimes experience partial disappearance when we attend to our private business and remain aloof from interpersonal communications with others. In such instances, even though we are physically present we are, to them, not present because their attention is not upon us.

22. From This the Disappearance of Sound, Taste, Touch, Smell, and Hearing is Explained.

Having understood that we cannot see that of which we are not aware, we can also understand that if we are not aware of the source of sound we cannot hear a sound. Also, we cannot taste, touch, or smell that of which we are not presently aware. Our world has reality to us only because we perceive it. If we could not perceive our world, it would not exist for us although it would exist for all others who continued to perceive it. Even if no living forms were in the universe, if a universe were in manifestation, the universe would exist because its existence is not caused by the perceptions of beings. The manifest universe, even without life forms in the early stages, still remains as an energy manifestation due to God's impulse and will.

Many times we say that we experience suffering and pain because of our imperfect relationship with our body and/or our world. We sometimes say that we experience pleasure and happiness as a result of such relationships. In either situation the cause of pain or pleasure does not lie in the world but in our relationship to it. If we were not aware of the world, others, or our own body, we could not possibly experience pain or pleasure due to relationships. If one succeeded, during meditation, in withdrawing attention from the physical environment, nothing in the physical environment could then intrude upon the mind. But a meditator might still experience pain or pleasure in relationship to feelings, thoughts, and the influence of memory which often prompt the emergence of feelings and thought patterns to the level of conscious acknowledgement. Upon withdrawing attention from the mental field, one then has no contact with any pain or pleasure causing influences from without. This happens in deep samadhi experience. However, upon returning attention to a mental field yet unpurified, to a body with illness, and to a personal environment as yet not harmonious, one may again experience pain and pleasure in relationships. It is not always practical or wise to withdraw attention from environment, body, and mind in order to be free from influence. What is often required of us is that we learn to relate with understanding and be free while involved with appearances, events, and changes. This is the way to live liberated in this and all worlds.

We have all experienced moments of concentration, during an interesting conversation, while reading a book, or during times of idle contemplation, when we did not even know what was going on around us. We were oblivious to happenings because of our own preoccupation with an idea or something of interest. We do not consider this to be strange at all because it is natural to everyone at one time or another. A wise person sees the usefulness in clearing environment, body and mind of all pain causing influences. This person also sees the usefulness, at times, of purposely withdrawing attention from such an environment for the purpose of becoming inwardly settled in order to again return to the environment with understanding and increased ability to function. We testify that we feel pain and discomfort when something is not right with the body. Yet, pain and discomfort is not experienced by us when we are mentally distracted or when we experience deep sleep. The cause of pain is there, perhaps, but the report of discomfort is not reaching the mind, so the mind does not respond. We often experience pain in relationships because we insists upon maintaining relationships which are no longer useful to ourselves or others. Or we insist upon becoming involved where we have no legitimate business. Sometimes such pain is due to our inability to relate intelligently and appropriately. In the latter instance there may be nothing wrong with the connections between things or people, only that communication required for healthy relationships is lacking. Bodily discomfort is closer to us and we can learn to free the body of illness and malfunction so that we can live without pain. Mental and emotional discomfort is even closer to us, but we can also see to health of mind and emotional nature so that we can be free of restrictions, thus allowing our attention and energies to flow to constructive purposes.

23. Through Perfect Contemplation on Subconscious Impressions, Knowledge of the Time of Death and Indications of Unusual Happenings is Acquired.

There are different types of subconscious impressions or karmic patterns. Subconscious impressions often determine our conscious experience in this world as well as in worlds yet to be known. First is the total collection of impressions stored in the subconscious as a result of the soul's mental experience from the beginning of material involvement. Second is that portion of mental impressions released from deeper levels which now must be handled and which seek expression. This determines the course of one's present incarnation. Third are the impressions now being received on a day to day basis, some of which are immediately handled and some of which sink to deeper levels of the subconscious to become part of the first portion, adding to the accumulation of impressions to be handled in the near or distant future. Let us say that a young lad were to be given the task of standing beside a container of water and was instructed to remove water soaked leaves from the bottom of the container, as well as leaves floating free at varying depths, and also to remove immediately, if possible, the newly fallen leaves floating on the surface. If the container were a large one, and many leaves had already fallen and many leaves were still falling, the lad would find himself busy indeed. He would have to remove free floating leaves from the surface of the water as well as at deeper levels. While he did this some leaves, newly fallen, would settle to the bottom to mix with the ones already there. Unless the water was protected from newly falling leaves and, barring some extraordinary process being used, the task would be a time-consuming one. This is what happens to the average person who is attempting to clear the mind of mental impressions. While working with surfacing impressions and handling currently in-bound impressions, new impressions are bound to slip through into the deeper levels and there mingle with the material in the unconscious. And without some disciplined method of approach, the average person seldom succeeds even in handling tendencies, urges, and desires of which he is now aware.

The motive force of some subconscious impressions result in their speedy fulfillment while some, by character, are more slow in their outward movement. We have tendencies which are quickly exhausted or neutralized and we have tendencies which will not become exhausted or neutralized for a longer time, either because the inherent motive force is not strong or because external conditions are not suitable and appropriate for their expression. In the latter instance one may generally enjoy peace of mind and harmony in relationships because of a well-ordered life and because the environment is ideal for this. There may be little or no anxiety, little or no emotional unrest, and little or no temptation which cannot be resisted. Allow the environmental condition to be drastically altered to a situation which gives opportunity for the tendencies to emerge, and one is often surprised to be overcome with fear, a tendency to anger, and the whole range of negative emotions, finding it almost impossible to resist even the mildest temptation. The seeds, then, of possible effects were resident in the mind all along, but the opportunity for expression was not present.

To know when in the future one will die to this world is an ability natural to many seers. However, many people who live a normal life often know shortly before their time when death of the body will be experienced. They are then able to make whatever needed arrangements and whatever required inner adjustments so as to meet the experience without resistance. Again, one may have a correct precognition of the time and method of leaving this plane, due to subconscious patterns now working out, but may decide to neutralize this trend by clearing the subconscious of the urges and tendencies which contribute to the present course. Everyone leaves this world sooner or later. What the masters of perfection teach is that it might be useful to think in terms of using this present body for as long as possible in order to experience enlightenment, instead of having to form another one, if this is our destiny, in order to complete the enlightenment process. Why should one be forced from the game of life just because of insistent subconscious tendencies? On the other hand, fully conscious persons also often know the hour of their earth departure because they know of their future soul destiny.

This verse also informs us that by observing internal signs, evidence of impressions now in force, one can become aware of future happenings. Causes, unless neutralized, produce effects. Effects, now maturing, frequently give surface indications of growth and fruition. With the eye of discernment we can learn to read subtle signs and thereby anticipate future events and experiences.

24. Through Perfect Contemplation on Friendliness, Compassion, and Other Noble Qualities, One Experiences Mental, Moral, and Spiritual Strength.

By fully understanding the meaning of friendliness, one respects all living beings as expressions of Divine Power and enjoys open and clear relationships. By recognizing the pain and discomfort of others, we share with them their needs for understanding and we feel compelled to offer them help in the direction of health and freedom. By acknowledging all of the noble qualities and by being gracious, appropriate, kind and fair, we contribute to the happiness of all people and assist in the spiritual quickening of world consciousness. While relating to the relative worlds we understand that, because we work through a body and mind, our lives are intertwined with all other beings who share this world with us. It is natural then for us to be concerned for the welfare of the world and to be considerate of others. An enlightened person is not a selfish person and does not think in terms of personal liberation exempt from relationships. Just as we have all been given a helping hand along life's pathway, so it is our moral and spiritual duty to share as best we can with others who are yet seeking.

We should, according to the great teachers, be friendly, compassionate, and helpful because it is our duty and because it is the soul's inclination. Also, there is a deeper purpose. If we are not developing the virtues, it means we are restricting our own unfoldment. One is unlikely to awaken spiritually while persisting in negative emotional surges and holding on to harmful thoughts about others. There is always the possibility, of course, that a mean-hearted person could have a conversion experience, resulting in a complete and instantaneous change of outlook. The usual ideal is for one to consciously cultivate the virtuous life in order to cancel out negative tendencies and to encourage the further awakening and expression of ideal characteristics.

25. Through Perfect Contemplation on Various Aspects of Power, One Attains to Comparable Strength.

Few people fully comprehend the range of power available to them. All power has its origin in the source of our own being. When we contemplate weakness we manifest weakness, when we contemplate strength we manifest strength. There may be a limit to bodily strength, but there is no limit to Soul power. Soul power, flowing through mind and body, can accomplish that which mere physical or mind-related willpower cannot accomplish. A wise person knows that God is the only power there is and that God will flow through one, or through any needed agency, to accomplish useful purposes. We know of unusual feats of physical strength and endurance performed by athletes who are well trained and who have that "all things are possible" attitude. We know of remarkable abilities of people who work mostly from the mental plane of visualization and will, in cooperation with universal mind. Both body and individualized mind efforts have natural limits, but the influence of Soul power has no limits at all.

26. Through Perfect Contemplation on the Light of Consciousness, One Acquires Knowledge of Things Which are Veiled, Subtle, and Remote.

Most people are restricted in their powers of perception according to the organs of perception they are accustomed to using. In general, we can only perceive through our outer sense organs the various aspects of the physical universe. We, of course, have internal mind perception during dreams and during occasions of relaxed reverie. By contemplating the Light of Consciousness, that Light behind all outer appearances, we learn to perceive directly from the level of Soul awareness. Also, we become accustomed to working through the internal organs of perception, of which the outer organs are but extensions. Being able to use internal organs of perception, we can then explore subtle spaces and realms not accessible to casual sense contact. Through the use of inner organs of perception, we can examine fine matter, subtle aspects of nature, and even events distant from where the body is located. There is no need for astral travel in order to see into the inner realms or to see at a distance on the physical plane. The subtle realms are here where we are, veiled by gross matter because we cannot see through the veil. Also, using the inner organs of perception, we can see, reflected within us, scenes taking place at a distance on the physical plane. Advanced souls can even see what is going on anywhere in the physical universe merely by assuming the viewpoint of being there. In the cosmic sense it is only due to body-mind identification that we are restricted to one location in space. At the Soul level, since we are viewpoints of God, we are everywhere present just as God is, and we can assume any position in space we elect to assume. Imagining we are at a specific location is not the same as actually being aware at that location. In the latter instance we have full cognition of what is taking place at the location being examined. In the world's religious literature, there are accounts of seers being aware at more than one location in space in the same time reference. That is, while talking with someone at one location they are also aware of what is taking place at another location. An instance follows:

Sri Satya Sai Baba was once speaking before an audience of several thousand devotees in Madras. At the same time a close disciple of his was in the hospital some distance away, recovering from a serious illness. After his talk, Sai Baba told one of his representatives to go to the hospital and give the patient some medicine which he (Baba) materialized with a rapid motion of his hand. He explained that while he had been talking, the disciple had almost died and had to be brought back through Sai Baba's inner-plane intervention. The representative went to the hospital as instructed and found that the disciple had indeed undergone a near-death crisis during the time Sai Baba was giving his lecture.

Paramahansa Yogananda was also known to have this ability to be fully functional at one location while being aware of the activities of disciples who lived miles from him. He was also aware of the needs of disciples who were still working out their salvation on the inner planes and sometimes told us of his experiences in assisting them.

27. **Through Perfect Contemplation on the Central Sun of This Solar System, One Experiences Knowledge of Regions and Planets and of Evolution, Maintenance, and Involution of the Universe.**

Through inner organ perception, while contemplating the central sun of our solar system, there arises understanding of the sun's relationship with the planets and the relationship of our sun, with its planets, to other suns in the galaxy. Our sun is not really very large in comparison with other suns in our galaxy. On the physical level the radiation of a sun nourishes its environment so that solar energy sustains nature. No life would be possible without the sun's radiation and influence. It is through the process of internal contemplation that knowledge of the sun and planets and their relationships and external influences on nature was revealed. We know that living things are influenced by the radiant energy of the sun as well as the emanational energy of the planets. The combinations of energy influences also affect living things. Man is influenced directly by the moon, which orbits the planet and reflects the light of the sun. There is gravitational influence also which influences the fluids on the planet and in bodies. When the moon reflects the sun's light, man's emotional life is more unstable and mental activity less regulated. When the moon is dark, man's emotional nature becomes more settled and thoughts quiet in the mind. It is for this reason that some teachers suggest that deep meditation can more easily be practiced during the dark phase of the moon. Also, during winter months nature turns inward and man's nature is inclined more to inner matters. During occasions of transition from night to day and from day to night, at dawn and dusk, there is a short duration of energy balance in nature which makes it easier for a person to meditate and quiet the system.

It is also known that a central sun, around which our sun and solar system orbits, influences the aspect of the mind known as the organ of discrimination, resulting in increased awareness when the nearest point is reached and in dullness when the most distant point is reached. This contributes to the various ages of enlightenment, less enlightenment, darkness, more enlightenment, and full enlightenment. Elsewhere in this text we will deal more fully with world cycles and the rise and fall of civilizations, in relationship to celestial influences.

There is order in the universe and interaction between all bodies in the universe, from the most distant galaxy to the nearest organism. There is an intelligence which directs the entire process. By awakening to the level of true Cosmic Consciousness one can know the full story of how the universe functions. One can know how the process began, how and why it functions, and how and why it will eventually dissolve. All of this can be seen through the inner organs of perception.

28. **Through Perfect Contemplation on the Moon (and Star Systems), One Experiences Knowledge of Their Workings and Relationships.**

This is a continuation of the preceding subject. Seers also teach of meditation experiences in relationship to the sun and the moon. Yogis teach of the sun current and the moon current in the body, both physical and astral. The sun current is positive and the moon current is negative. When the sun current moves strongly in the system, one is more dynamic and forceful. When the moon current is most influential, one is more retiring and imaginative. The sun current encourages knowledge. The moon current encourages fantasy because of diminished awareness and the soul's identification with the subconscious levels of mind.

A fully illumined soul is not unwillingly influenced by currents in nature, but such a one often works in harmony with existing natural influences. Not a few masters have timed their earth transition to coincide with favorable planetary influences. Others who made no public statement to this effect were later found, as a result of examining the master's horoscope, to have departed precisely on schedule when planetary influences were most helpful.

29. **Perfect Contemplation on the Pole Star Results in the Understanding of the Motions and Movements of Planetary Bodies.**

This refers to the contemplation of bodies in space, in relationship to the pole star, the central star. Once basic understanding is acquired, understanding of other similar relationships is possible. It is well known that many masters of perfection were versed in esoteric astrology and could determine precise effects of planetary influences upon the evolutionary process as well as upon individual life forms. Sri Yukteswar was a wise astrologer who discovered mistakes in the Hindu almanac and clearly explained the reasons for world changes. He was also able to assist some disciples who were under heavy adverse planetary influences to somewhat neutralize planetary emanations by an adjustment of mental attitude, deeper meditation, and the practical application of gems and metals worn for the purpose. Sri Yukteswar taught that the planetary emanations are not intentionally harmful or beneficial in themselves but that the energy influences afford a natural opportunity for the expression of subconscious tendencies.

30. **Through Perfect Contemplation on the Central Chakra, One Experiences Knowledge of the Nervous System and of the Physical Body.**

Reference is here given to the method of contemplating the center of vital force which corresponds to the solar plexus at the body level. The centers through which vital force flows are nonphysical, but they do relate to nerve centers in the body. Through contemplation of the centers through which vital force flows, one understands their function and the interaction of vital forces between subtle sheaths and physical body. While it is not essential for one to fully understand how a machine such as an automobile works in order to operate it, it is not always essential for one to fully understand how the body works in order to express through it. But there are some who are inclined to examine the inner workings of bodies and thereby contribute their discoveries to the welfare of mankind. Seers examine the nature and workings of bodies in order to contribute to the health of others. Advanced knowledge results in increased soul ability, as we shall see in the following verses.

31. Through Perfect Contemplation on the Throat Center, One Experiences Freedom From Hunger and Thirst.

One can neutralize the urge to eat and to take liquids by concentrating on the throat center. It is well known that some masters of perfection enjoy radiant health and abundant vitality in spite of the fact that they partake of little or no food for considerable periods of time. This is possible because of the increase in the force of flow of creative energies which have been aroused from their former dormant state, the increase in the flow of soul force which vitalizes the system, and, in some instances, the ability of the master to absorb solar radiation directly into the system without having to take it in through the medium of food. Food contains trapped solar radiation which is released into the body during digestion. If one can absorb solar radiation directly, then food is no longer such a necessity. The throat center regulates the ether, the fine matters, in the body. Subtle energy flowing from the fine matter level can flow into grosser expression and nourish the physical form. This is the teaching of some seers who have demonstrated the ability to enjoy perfect health without eating food, as well as the experience of a few mystics who have manifested freedom from material food needs as a result of ecstatic contemplation, even without knowing the method. Advanced masters live through a glorified body as a result of the infusion of the light of Consciousness. The practice of certain breathing exercises, which gives conscious control over vital forces, is also often used by seers. Through such a process one can convert free energy into a form usable by the body, one can increase the flow of internal creative energies, and one can take in subtle units of life force. Sometimes *mantra* is used to open the door to the inner planes and draw upon subtle energies existing therein.

32. Through Perfect Contemplation on the Center of Gravity Within, One Experiences Steadiness and Stability of Consciousness.

In the average person the psychic centers are not in a state of harmony; therefore some imbalance is experienced. This usually relates to emotional unrest and mental instability. By being self-contained or centered, by being peaceful and established in soul awareness, all of the currents in the system are encouraged to flow in harmony and interact perfectly. Steadiness and balance can be experienced through the practice of being self-contained, by retaining awareness and by not allowing attention to become diffused. Controlled breathing can often be useful as this will harmonize the vital currents as well as the circulation of current in the nervous system. The most potent centering procedure is to inwardly acknowledge the truth of being: "Pure and Changeless Consciousness am I."

33. Through Perfect Contemplation on the Light in the Center of the Head, Liberated and Perfect Souls Experience Direct Perception.

In preceding verses we examined the possibilities inherent in examining lower vital centers and centers of consciousness for specific purposes. Here we are advised that when one contemplates in the highest center, one rises above all lower identifications and experiences pure awareness. This is the experience of the siddhas, the perfected beings, the masters of perfection. Resting at this level of awareness, one experiences direct perception and knowledge, one experiences Ultimate Truth. That which seems true and useful at relative levels is necessary for world function, but at this higher level all dualities and differences are transcended. In early stages of meditation one may see an inner light while contemplating this higher center. In the intermediate stage one becomes absorbed in the light and experiences this clear light reflected in the mental field. In advanced meditation one experiences one's nature as the light of Consciousness Itself.

Some translators explain this verse as meaning that one established at this center gains the ability to commune with perfected beings through direct soul-to-soul means. We may be in the same room with an enlightened person and not know it. There may be bright beings all around us in subtle form and we may not be aware of them. However, once we have become established in the realization of our soul nature, we will recognize the masters of perfection on both outer and inner planes. As we advance in the awakening process, before complete awakening we may be telepathically and intuitively in communication with the perfect masters, even if there is not yet visual perception of them or concrete proof of their existence.

34. Through Perfect Contemplation on the Source of All Knowledge, (*Then*) Knowledge of Everything Positively is Revealed.

From whence does knowledge come? Knowledge comes from the source of all, from the field of Pure Awareness. Just as by attuning oneself to the mind of another one has access to all data in that mental field, so by becoming aware of the field of all knowledge, all is known. This spontaneous enlightenment can be experienced without going through the stages previously mentioned. There are some masters of perfection, who have had little or no relative experience with stages of unfoldment or experiences corresponding to these stages, who can easily explain the most subtle matters because they work from the level of all knowledge.

Because of the personal experience of different masters there are different teaching traditions. One tends to teach what one has experienced and what one has found to be useful. Some masters will teach the basics and then go on to a step by step program during which the student has the opportunity to become proficient in the practice of techniques and methods leading to higher stages. Some masters will teach the importance of living in harmony with the environment; others, the importance of doing one's duty and the importance of yearning for God and practicing meditation on the transcendental aspect of Consciousness. They take the most direct route to God-realization and the liberation of consciousness. It is not that one way is better, safer, or faster than another necessarily. It will depend upon the teaching mission of the master and the personal needs of disciples with whom he works.

35. Through Perfect Contemplation of the (*True*) Heart, One Experiences Knowledge of Universal Mind.

Reference is here given to the true heart, the central heart, not the heart of the body which pumps blood through the circulatory system. The word heart here refers to that source of involution, maintenance, and evolution of subtle vital currents. Where is this heart? This heart is at that point between inner realm Pure Awareness and outer realm manifesting aspect of Consciousness. On the personal level it is the soul; on the cosmic level it is God. If we are poised and centered, we can be established in that place within us from which our very life issues forth. This is the heart. When the sages teach us to "seek out the truth in the heart," they are literally suggesting that we go to the core of the matter. Just as God is the Self-effulgent Light which makes possible all other light and material manifestation, so when we rest in the awareness of our true nature, in the heart or vital core, we know that we, too, are Self-effulgent Light as God is. This is a more stable realization than partial realizations relating to the contemplation of relative happenings and manifestations. Relative events are subject to change, clear soul-awareness is not subject to change. Pure Awareness is not related to chakras or to anything which is an expression of the time-space worlds.

36. Through Perfect Contemplation on Soul Reality as Being Distinct From the Organ Which Makes Possible the Experience of Relative Perceptions, One Awakens to the Knowledge of the True Self.

The true Self, the soul, is self-complete and self-fulfilled. The basic organ or instrument of the soul is a sheath containing mind, ego-consciousness, and root-organs of perception. Through this sheath the soul can work in relationship with the material spheres and can experience pleasure and pain. Even if one succeeds in putting away the internal causes of pain and suffering and experiences unending pleasure, one should ask: "Who and what is experiencing?" The experience of experiencing is not the changeless state. The experience of experiencing is possible because of subtle organs of pleasure in the mental field, the ego-sense which causes the impression of "I am experiencing," and the organ of discernment by which one determines.

Having the *experience* of being is not the same as *Being*. Having the sense that we now possess knowledge is not the same as being knowledge itself. The soul is Being, is knowledge, is what God is as an extension of God. In the exact sense, nothing worthwhile is acquired by the soul because the soul already is that which for so long it mistakenly sought. However, one of the ways to liberation is to examine the difference between being and nonbeing and the difference between being the truth versus knowing about the truth. One may falsely conclude that as a result of true soul-awareness there is but emptiness. This is because the mind cannot picture how the soul can be self-complete without reinforcement from external sources. We experience sensory perception and we inwardly feel a pleasurable response. The response comes from within, not from without. The outer may have contributed to the inner response, but the response is from within. Therefore, the seat of satisfaction is within, at the center of Being.

37. (*One of the*) Results of Perfect Contemplation on the Soul Nature May be the Appearance of Extrasensory Abilities.

As the inner organs, corresponding to the outer organs, of perception are awakened and used consciously, one may exhibit signs of extrasensory perception. We may see subtle aspects of our world which ordinary people cannot see. We may be able to easily determine the thoughts and intentions of others or to read evidential signs of forthcoming events which are already predetermined because of existing causes. We may find that we have a knack for intuitively understanding the scriptures or that whatever we apply ourselves to, we succeed with relative ease.

38. These Extrasensory Abilities (*if Allowed to Flow Mostly Outward*) Are Obstacles to Samadhi. If Used Properly They Become Supernatural Powers Which Combat and Neutralize Lower Tendencies.

Here we find the major reason why many masters advise students on the enlightenment path to steer clear of preoccupation with the siddhis, the powers of perfection. If one is not oriented in the direction of soul awareness and final liberation, there will be a tendency to allow the out-flowing attention to cause ego-involvement with merely selfish interests or interests relating to material world consciousness. Many people with partially awakened extrasensory abilities pass themselves off as prophets, healers, and spiritual teachers when, in fact, they are merely working out of confused human consciousness. Not only do they mislead sincere seekers but they interfere with their own soul unfoldment. The siddhis should be used to further explore the nature of the mind and the nature of Consciousness. One who is established in the pattern of natural and honest living can, of course, allow the use of soul ability to result in a more fulfilling life. But always there must be that sense of balance and the understanding that, under no circumstances, must involvement with the outer interfere with examination of the inner.

There are certain siddhis which can be taught to aware students, but a master will never teach them to students who are not qualified as a result of inner purity. A guide to the exercise of soul abilities is: if what is done or experienced leads to greater God-realization and in an improved world condition, it can be considered useful. If what is done or experienced leads to further involvement and confusion and reinforces negative and destructive tendencies, then it is not useful. The text clearly teaches that if siddhis are unwisely used, they are then obstacles to samadhi and higher realization. If used properly they will enable one to overcome all obstacles and will actually be useful in the attainment of samadhi states.

39. As a Result of the Causes of Bondage Being Relaxed and By a Penetrative Flow of Consciousness, One's Consciousness Can Enter into Other Bodies.

Some causes of bondage (to a body) are fear of leaving the body, strong identification with the body, and the restrictions due to subconscious impressions and subtle mental modifications. One who is not clear in understanding regarding the difference between the true self or soul and the body can hardly have the awareness, the inclination, or the ability to leave a body, much less enter into another one. Traditional texts assert that it is possible for one who is highly advanced and who knows the method to actually depart one body and to consciously enter another. Usually, however, it is not a matter of a person actually leaving a body in order to enter another one, it is that the person is able to direct his attention to the mental field of another and fully invade that mental field to the extent of being able to assume that point of view and operate that body. We have discussed concentration, meditation, and samadhi, the cycle of perfect contemplation. If one follows this procedure of perfect contemplation with the intention of merging with the mental field of another, we can see how one can literally identify with another's body.

If a disciple is receptive to the guru's intention, then the guru's consciousness can enter into the mental field of the disciple. The guru does not, in this case, displace the disciple's awareness of sense of personal control but enters the disciple in order to share his God-realization. Even if one were to seem to fully enter into another body, it would be but an appearance of that because we have not fully entered into the body we now use. We have only almost-fully identified with it in order to work through it.

One with this ability to direct attention for intended purposes can also leave the body at will when the time comes for final departure. We are told that some spiritually advanced souls actually will themselves to be born into a body in a certain part of the world where they know they will have the best opportunity to continue their mission.

40. As a Result of Mastery Over Internal Processes, One is Able to Walk on Water, Walk Without Touching the Ground, and Levitate.

Various frequencies of vital force circulate throughout the body. Soul force is changed in frequency to perform specialized functions in the body. When one is able to neutralize the down-flowing aspect of vital force, one can then, it is taught, literally levitate. Great masters are not in the habit of saying things which they do not mean or claiming things which are not possible. Even if we have not seen a demonstration of physical levitation, we can take it on faith alone as a possibility if an enlightened person tells us it is possible. The body has mass and is, therefore, influenced by the gravitational pull of the planet. What the masters say is that if we can neutralize the pull of gravity we can experience bodily levitation. Yoganandaji has said that he had a levitation experience while meditating, during which time he saw the nature of the universe as light. Yogis report that as a result of advanced pranayama (breathing exercises which give control over internal vital forces) the body will, in due course of time, hop, hover for brief moments, and finally hover above the ground. If one can hover above the ground at will, one can certainly walk on (above) water.

There are reports of some of the early Christian saints who

were observed levitating during occasions of mystical rapture. Their supreme and total devotion to God undoubtedly regulated the vital forces in such a manner so as to allow this phenomenon. Some siddhas, the scriptures inform us, do not leave any footprints, even in soft soil, when they walk. And, of course, we have the account given us in the New Testament about Jesus walking on the water. The suggestion given in this narration is that it was possible because of faith. Pure faith transcends believing and enters into the realm of knowing. And with knowing one can do whatever is possible in all the worlds.

More direct than the practice of pranayama and more controlled than occasional experiences during rapture is the exercise of "gentle inclination" to levitate during occasions of nearly-pure transcendental awareness. If the transcendental experience were total there would be no awareness of body, therefore no intent to levitate. In our modern age we have little practical use for levitation since our need to walk above water and pass without injury over extremely rough ground is seldom. What the experience of levitation can do for one is to prove to the mind, by way of experiential feed-back, that soul awareness is superior to all material restrictions.

The sensation of rising above one's body while in a meditative state is not the same as actual levitation. Such an experience is due to our having temporarily broken free from usual connections with the nervous system or gross and subtle sheaths. What we are discussing now is a body happening which can be experienced and observed. More recent research, as a result of concentration in this direction, reveals that levitation can occur when the meditator is fairly well established in the transcendental experience, with a mild body awareness remaining. At this point, for the purpose of experimentation, the person very gently "wills" the body to rise, and it does. The most valuable result of such research is that one can prove to oneself and to others who may be interested that what the masters have taught to be so for many centuries is actually true. Once one has proof and breaks conditioned agreements with the mind, one can then move on to further exploration and greater soul freedom. This is a practical reason for investigating siddhis.

The possible value then is not in performing. The real gain is that we experience more freedom in a world where many feel too bound and restricted. Our own freedom is important to us. The evidence of our own freedom that we share with others can give them hope. We already know, through personal experience, that we can modify our environment, our personal world, as a result of purposely altering our own state of consciousness and taking control of the mental field, our mind. We can also beneficially influence our world by becoming more clear, more aware, and more soul-oriented. Levitation has another implication: we can rise above the concerns and mental-gravitational pulls of the world around us when we rise above all restricting influences. We can then move freely through our world and we can see all that unfolds as a play of lights and shadows. We still perform whatever duties are ours, but we do so with clear understanding.

41. As the Result of Mastering the Inner Fire Influence, One Can Then Control and Regulate Internal and External Heat (*Fire Influence*).

Earth, water, fire, air, and ether are material influences at work in the body. It is well known that persons skilled in consciously directing the fire influence can increase body heat at will, lower body temperature, increase the power of food digestion, and even flood the body with light from within, thus causing a visible radiance in and around the body. Mastery of the fire influence enables a person in a very cold environment to generate internal heat to warm the body and, if in a very warm environment, cool the body from within. Yogis in the Himalayas have occasionally been observed in below freezing weather and being perfectly comfortable, wearing nothing more than a light garment.

42. Through Perfect Contemplation on the Primal Sound, One Experiences Divine Hearing Perception.

Om is the primal sound behind all external sounds. It is the pure sound out of which all sound variations emerge and into which they return. As one meditates upon the primal sound it may first seem that the sound is heard within the ear. With deeper practice it will be heard in the crown chakra in the head and then will be heard throughout the nervous system and inner spaces of the body. At times, in the beginning stages, according to the sound frequencies which emerge from within, one will hear various sounds. Eventually one will clearly hear the pure sound and, surrendering to this, the attention will be led easily to the transcendental experience. This form of meditation is one of the more direct methods taught by the masters.

Even if one uses a special mantra in early stages of meditation, if one is surrendered to the inner nature, the special mantra will be transcended when the pure sound is heard. Inner sounds are often heard during meditation after one has first practiced certain breathing exercises, Hatha Yoga poses, mudras, and when mild stirring of kundalini results in increased force of flow of the creative energies in the body. Inner sounds are often heard by one as a result of deep relaxation and interiorization of attention. As a result of regular absorption in internal sound, one becomes calm and peaceful and the often discordant sounds of the average environment, while at times tolerated, are not attractive to the meditator. Frequently, along with awareness of internal sound, one will experience corresponding light perception in the third eye or crown chakra.

43. Through Perfect Contemplation on the Relationship Between the Body and Ether, One Experiences Lightness of the Body and has the Power to Move Through Space.

We have already discussed levitation of the body in an earlier verse. Here, again, mention is made of that possibility by contemplating on the relationship between the body and ether or subtle matter. Interesting stories have come down through the ages telling of spiritually advanced persons who could literally fly through the air without any visible means of transport, and of persons who could move from point to point in space without actually transporting the body over a distance. There are stories told of highly advanced masters who can dematerialize the physical body and rematerialize elsewhere by an act of will; and of masters who can literally walk through walls because of inner knowledge that a seemingly solid object really has more space than particles. One then simply moves through the spaces available. The inner gain

one experiences as a result of such contemplation is soul freedom and release from any material restriction. Also, by understanding the subtle side of the body, one can by an act of will
change the body and heal illness and regenerate the body.

**44. Through Perfect Contemplation on the External Modifications
of the Mind, These Modifications are Understood, and This
Results in the Destruction of Ignorance Which Veils the Reality
of the Soul.**

By careful examination of the conditionings and impressions
of the mind, one sees clearly their nature and influence and is
able to discriminate between the mind, with modifications, and
the true soul nature. This results in awakening, the vanishing of
not-knowing, and perfect understanding. Through meditation and
intentional discernment one can realize: "I am pure Being, I am
not the mind with its modifications." Some people are so firmly
identified with the mental field that they feel they are the mind.
Others are aware that they are not mind, but they are trapped in
the mind through involvement with its tendencies and conditionings. Freedom is experienced when one clearly experiences the
true Self as being separate from mind. Then the light of Pure
Consciousness shines without restriction.

**45. Through Perfect Contemplation on Gross Matter, Its Essen-
tial Forms, Its Subtle Essence and Particles and Their Purposes,
One Experiences Victory Over Matter and Energy.**

Any reader desiring information so far available regarding the
physical structure of the universe can easily obtain books which
share these findings. A seer explores matter at the finest level,
the level of subtle-element combinations which result in gross ele-
ment-manifestations. The elements designated by early sacred
books are said to be ether, air, fire, water, and somewhat solid
matter termed earth. It is taught that there are subtle aspects which
mix and result in gross appearances or compounds. The teaching is
that one-half of one subtle element mixed with with a one-eighth
part of the remaining four subtle elements results in the gross
manifestation of the element influence of the greater proportion.

For instance, one-half subtle ether element mixing with one-eighth part each of subtle air, fire, water and earth elements results in the manifestation of gross ether. The process continues and results in gross manifestation of air (gaseous substance), fire, water, and earth.

Scientists of this century have explored to a degree the inner world of matter and many useful results have benefited mankind. We are in the era of such discovery, when man learns to understand and wisely use the forces hidden in matter. The electric interactions taking place in element compounds result in specific forms, tendencies, and purposes. The physical universe is an extension of creative energy and is animated by the vitality of Consciousness. There are some masters of perfection who openly demonstrate mastery over the elements by materializing and dematerializing objects by an act of will. One such master, when asked how he was able to do such things, said: "I have self-confidence!" Such instantaneous response of matter to perfected will proves that matter is the effect of inner causes. We are here speaking of materialization of objects directly from available energy in space around us. In the fall of 1972 I was given a gold ring inset with rubies which was materialized by Satya Sai Baba. I have seen him materialize rings, prayer beads, food, and other small articles just as easily. Of course one who can produce a thing can also cause it to vanish by releasing essential subtle elements from their combinations.

It is also possible, by those who know the process, to transport objects from the astral realm to the physical realm and back to the astral realm again. When the veil between dimensions is seen through, such transfer is easy.

46. **As a Result of Mastery Over the Elements, One Experiences Supernatural Powers, Perfection of Body and Mind, and the Understanding of the Indestructibility of the Qualities of Matter, Energy, and the Elements.**

One who understands the nature of the world as Consciousness has overcome the world. He is then a perfected being and nothing ever again restricts without his consent. Many masters of perfection who possess total understanding still agree to play a role of sometimes seeming restriction because they are working with people of lesser understanding and helping them along life's pathway. Outwardly conforming, for the most part, to the pattern of society and to the usual way of doing things, such masters inwardly see it all as a drama and remain settled in understanding.

A master of perfection, being unrestricted, can demonstrate, if if so led from within, a variety of siddhis or soul powers. Eight specific siddhis are referred to in classic texts dealing with this verse. They are: the ability to identify with the smallest particle of matter; the ability to be light as a result of being free from gravitational influence; the ability to identify with heaviness or come under the influence of gravity; the ability to expand awareness to fill all space and experience Cosmic Consciousness; the ability to fulfill wishes and desires of self or others through mere assent or agreement; command over the environment; the ability to influence evolution, maintenance, and dissolution of events and things; the ability to change the course of destiny by neutralizing existing tendencies and introducing new ones. These are the siddhis most commonly referred to when discussion on the subject arises. Beginning students often ask why, if the masters have these abilities, they do not intercede more obviously in the affairs of mankind? The usual answer is that even a master does not have the right to overly interfere with the natural trend of human events. They will share their consciousness, they will instruct and motivate, they will occasionally weaken the trends of karma so that the full impact is not externalized, but their work is to call forth the sleeping divine nature of all and to assist in the direction of world purification.

While not all masters of perfection demonstrate perfection of the body, it is within their capability to do so. One with perfect understanding can easily control the elements of the physical form through which he works. Some masters allow subconscious tendencies, inherited with the body, to run their course because they know their mission on earth is but for a brief duration of time. A few masters, knowing that their work will require many years, even centuries, retain a youthful and healthy body indefinitely. There are several authentic accounts of masters who retained the body in excellent health for one hundred, two hundred, even three hundred years. There are stories of a few who retain the body for thousands of years. Some accomplish this through Kriya Yoga pranayama which keeps the body energies balanced and the system purified. Some are also skilled in the use of herbs, metals, and rejuvenation processes. No truly enlightened master is under any bondage to the belief that he will maintain the physical form forever, he simply elects to retain the form for the duration of his earthly mission. Even while retaining the body such masters freely move, in awareness, through inner spaces. While pranayama, rest, nutrition, cleansing procedures, and other methods are extremely useful in contributing to health and function of the body, in relationship to extremely long life in the body, the most important thing is superior soul realization.

A fully liberated master is not compulsively tied to any sphere or to any outer condition. This is what it means to be liberated, to be free from dependence upon anything. Such a master comprehends that matter is energy formed and that energy is not created nor is it destroyed, it only changes form. Energy does not increase and it does not decrease. Even when it is in a state of rest it still exists.

47. Perfection of the Body Consists of Beauty, Complexion, Grace, Strength, and Adamantine Hardness.

Continuing along the lines of the preceding verse we are told of the characteristics evident in the body which is perfected. Chinese alchemists referred to the immortal body as a diamond body to indicate its indestructible nature. All of the characteristics natural to purity and unrestricted expression of innate soul tendencies can manifest through the perfected physical form. While the form and features of a master may not meet the requirements set by fashion experts, regardless of the body style and features, there will be always in an enlightened person the reflected characteristics of true beauty, natural grace, radiance, and appropriateness.

48. One Experiences Mastery Over the Senses Through Perfect Contemplation of Their Power of Cognition, Inherent Characteristics, Pervasiveness, and Influence.

It is easier to obtain mastery over something which is understood. Perfect contemplation and thorough examination of how we perceive through the sense channels gives us this understanding. Information about external events flows through sense organs and the nervous system and is received and interpreted by the mind. The mind contains subtle counterparts of the sense organs, for, if it did not, sensory information could not be received and interpreted. But not only do we actually see, hear, taste, smell, and feel in the mind, there is an aspect of mind which analyzes and makes higher evaluations. The mind is not limited in function to data stored as a result of experience or preconditioning. There is the intelligence aspect of the mind, the discriminating organ, through which the soul is able to examine and evaluate. One who is intelligent does not make judgments solely based on previous experience and of previous examination of a similar problem. Soul awareness is present during an intellectual exercise which is obvious to us when we become conscious of the fact that we are making unique and independent judgments and drawing special and appropriate conclusions which fit the occasion.

Shankara wrote, in one of his treatises, that the soul's initial point of contact with the mind is with the organ of intelligence or the faculty of discernment. This is why it is taught that super-conscious perception, transcending conscious and subconscious, originates with the soul and not with conditioned mind. The examination of situations and problems through the intellect is called the wisdom path. This path is not for all seekers, in the beginning, because it calls for objectivity and incisive examination, putting aside all emotion and relying not upon previous experience.

How do we see the world about us? By what means is it possible to receive information through the organs of the senses? These are questions one can examine, and the answers are forthcoming. The inherent characteristics of the organs of relative perception can be understood. No perception of relative matters is possible without the existence, as the medium of communication, of elements such as fire (light, for seeing), ether for sound, radiation from the object examined for smell, resistance to touch for feeling of the object, and characteristics given off to allow taste. But still, all interpretations of what is available in the world outside is the result of corresponding responses with the subtle counterparts of the organs of the senses which are established in the mind. Our cognition of the world around us is only possible because of the prior existence of the ear behind the ear, the eye behind the eye, organs of perception behind the corresponding nerves, and so on and on; all of which exist in the mental field.

The rudimentary constituents of the organs of the senses are all pervasive because the same characteristics are found throughout the universe, from subtle to gross levels of expression. The elements and electric attributes inherent in nature are omnipresent and are a part of all that is in manifestation, from the highest heaven to the most inertia-dominated world. The only difference between the spheres is that the more subtle the sphere, the more close to the Source, the more the elevating influence predominates. The tendency toward enlightenment (completion) is ever in contest with the tendencies in the direction of activity and gravity. When heaviness dominates, the mind is dull and sluggish. When the movement-to-action is dominant, the mind is restless. When the elevating tendency overcomes the former two tendencies, then the mind is inclined in the direction of light and knowledge because the Soul influence predominates and God's grace begins to influence the mind.

49. As a Result of Understanding the Senses, One Has Direct Insight From the Mind Level, Can Perceive Without External Sense Organs, and Experiences Total Ability to Stand Free from Nature.

Upon clearly understanding the relationships between subtle sense organs and external sense organs, a master, through intuition, can examine the external world. That is, one can know by knowing, as the soul's intuition works through the mind. The internal worlds can also be investigated through the use of intuition and the subtle organs of sense rooted in the mental field. This has to be possible because one cannot examine non-physical objects with physical sense organs. Inner plane perception is only possible through subtle sense organs and intuition. The result of clear understanding is that one is no longer trapped through identification with nature, and stands free from nature, as well as having dominion over it.

50. Through Perfect Contemplation on the Process of Discrimination, as Well as the True Nature of God Beyond Nature, One Experiences Omnipotence and Omniscience.

Being identified with the organ of discernment, the faculty of intelligence of the mind, one experiences true soul awareness while yet identified with the intelligence aspect of the mind. Because of true soul awareness one is aware of the nature of the soul as omnipotent and omniscient. It is only because of identification with the mental field and its modifications that the soul experiences restriction and limitation. When this identification is transcended, the soul experiences the Truth of its being and the Truth of its abilities. At this stage of realization there are subtle impressions remaining at deeper levels of the mind which will have to be cleared or neutralized.

51. Renouncing Identification With the Experience of Omnipotence and Omniscience, One Completely Transcends the Relative Planes and Experiences Final Liberation of Consciousness.

As long as there is realization of anything or any state, there is still a mild degree of "I am experiencing this or that." Upon releasing attachment to the higher perceptions and powers, one experiences pure Being. This results in the latent impressions in the mind being neutralized or the mind itself being transcended.

52. There Should be No Attachment to Spiritual Attainment Because This Could Possibly Lead to Further Bondage.

Pride in one's spiritual attainment is a pitfall on the path. Pride reveals ego-sense and false understanding. The soul is merely awakening to what it has always been; therefore there can be no sense of pride in any seeming attainment experience. Temptations abound on every side for the person who is moving through the final stages of soul freedom and mental purification. Not that God tempts us but that opportunities in nature attract us, or the lower tendencies of the mind influence us. All of the great masters have taught the importance of total surrender to God, from the beginning to the end of the enlightenment path. As we surrender to

God there must be no outer evidence that we are being humble on purpose, for this, too, would be proof of role-playing. One can even err by being inwardly smug about the fact that he is a renunciate and the servant of all. One way to avoid preoccupation with ego-sense is to surrender all to God and to engage in truly selfless world service. Even in rendering service to others, if we feel they do not appreciate us or if we feel they need us, we are missing the point of the opportunity. One who truly serves inwardly knows that he needs nothing because life supplies all his needs. He does not need recognition because he, as an independent entity, does not exist. People do not need him because people need only God. When we serve truly it is God serving as us.

53. Through Perfect Contemplation on the Moments of Time and Their Succession, One Experiences True Knowledge Through the Power of Discrimination.

True knowledge here refers to the experience of Pure Being and not to the knowledge of something. The Transcendental Experience is devoid of any characteristics. The experience of Being is clearly understood as just that, in contrast to not-being. Seers of ancient times considered a moment to be that interval between which an atom moved from one point in space to another. We see, then, how incredibly brief a moment is. As moments flow, so does time seem to flow. Yet, we are told, time is not really as it is perceived to be. Moments follow one another even when an analytical mind is not present to examine the process. Trees age, events leave their impression on the planet, bodies come and go. Two moments cannot exist together. The present moment is not the previous moment nor is it the moment to come.

The basic substance of which the worlds are made possible is a combination of creative energy, space, light particles, and time. These are essential to the manifestation and continuing of the relative universe. Without motion, without a succession of moments, creation would be changeless. Yet we know that change is built into the fabric of nature. Through perfect contemplation on moments and their succession, one gains insight into the nature of what we call time. One pierces the veil of illusion and experiences eternity.

54. Through Perfect Contemplation of Moments and Successions of Moments, One Obtains Discernment of Similar Things and Events Which Cannot be Measured or Recognized by Any Outer Signs.

We can determine to a great degree general facts about a thing being examined by knowing about its class or species, its origin, and its particular properties and characteristics. Things which seem to be exact copies of similar things really are not, as there are subtle differences at some level of their make-up. Events which seem identical are really different, even though alike. If one will use keen powers of discernment, one will be able to tell the differences between things and events examined. How did that which we examine originate? What are its characteristics? What order or class does it occupy in relationship to other things or events? We have never seen a thing or an event which is exactly like the one we are now examining. If we see a rose today and tomorrow see a similar rose, the similar rose will be a new rose and a new experience if we are examining our world closely. One of the greatest errors a person can make in ordinary life is to wish for an experience exactly like the one that was previously experienced and enjoyed. One may enjoy a similar experience but never the same experience. We can never do anything again, we can only do a similar thing. We can never experience anything again, we can only experience in similar fashion. Clinging to memories of the past, indulging in wishful thinking about the unclear future, and attempting to maintain present situations in order to avoid change are a waste of time. We may recall the past without regret, we may plan the future with mild anticipation, but only the moment can be experienced fully.

55. Absolute Knowledge is That Which Includes the Universe and Every Aspect of It.

It is obvious that one could not function with total attention through a body while simultaneously being aware of the entire universe and all aspects of it. But, when attention is withdrawn from objects and is allowed to roam free, one then experiences unbounded awareness or true Cosmic Consciousness. Also, one can examine any aspect of the universe from this overview and have knowledge of that which is being examined. One can also withdraw attention from the relative worlds and experience Pure Being.

56. When the Organ of Discernment is Purified and as Devoid of Characteristics as is The Soul, Then Final Liberation is Experienced.

We have explained how the soul uses the organ of discernment in the mental field in order to examine relative matters. When the organ of discernment in the mental field is completely purified so that intelligence is always keen and discernment is always clear, then the soul using that mental field is liberated even while moving through time and space and relating to events and situations. The soul's awareness and ability, this side of liberation, is screened through the field of the mind, which is conditioned. When all restricting impressions are removed from the mental field, when the mind is illumined, then liberation is experienced. That there are degrees of soul freedom is well known to the masters. When one is Self-realized and does not falter from this knowledge of the nature of the True Self, even with karmic patterns yet to work out, this is salvation: the condition of being spiritually free even while involved with the world. The next stage, experienced as the result of greater purification and higher understanding, is the level of mastership, the level of Cosmic Consciousness. A master of perfection is one who has gone beyond Cosmic Consciousness to the realization of the Pure Realm beyond appearance and form and who clearly understands the world-process as a play of Consciousness.

Chapter Nine
ENLIGHTENMENT and
FINAL LIBERATION

The final thirty-eight verses of the *Yoga Sutras* begin this chapter. A commentary follows, which explains the theme.

1. Siddhis can be the result of the force of previous attainment, the intelligent use of chemicals, the power of mantra, austerities, and samadhi.

2. The transformation of mind, senses, and body is the result of the natural flow of creative forces.

3. The natural flow of creative forces is possible when obstacles to the flow are removed.

4. Individual minds can be produced by the power of Cosmic Consciousness.

5. The original mind is the director of all other expressions and alterations of conditioned mind.

6. Of all classifications of the mental condition, that one resulting from samadhi leaves no impression of such influence.

7. Mental impressions of dedicated meditators do not result in

constructive or destructive outer effects. Mental impressions of other people are of three kinds.

8. From the storehouse of subconscious impressions, forces and tendencies are manifested according to available opportunities for such expression.

9. Because impressions and memory are directly connected, there is a direct relationship between mental causes and outer effects, even if seemingly separated by class, space and time.

10. Because of the urge to life and expression which is innate to consciousness, there is no beginning and there is no end to the flow of causes and their respective consequences.

11. All tendencies and karmic patterns are made possible because of cause, effect, the mind itself, and the support of objects of perception. When these no longer exist for the soul, then tendencies and karmic patterns no longer exist for one.

12. Past, present, and future exist in their own real nature. Tendencies and impressions in the mind are changed when their driving forces are transformed.

13. The tendencies and cause of effects, whether manifested or remaining in subtle form, are made up of fine cosmic forces.

14. That there is unity throughout the universe is evidenced by the unity of the transformation process.

15. Even though an object is the same, what is perceived will depend upon the nature of the mind in relationship to the object.

16. An object cannot be said to be dependent upon the perception of one mind. For what would happen to the object in the absence of that mind?

17. Objects are known or unknown to a person depending upon whether or not they affect the person's mind.

18. Due to the changeless nature of the omnipresent soul, all mental modifications are known to it always.

19. Since the mind is an object which is perceived, it cannot be self-luminous and self-conscious.

20. Full identification with God and with mind, at the same time, is not possible.

21. If all minds could simultaneously perceive the contents of every other mind, this would result in confusion of memory.

22. The Supreme Soul is omnipresent, omniscient, omnipotent, and changeless, but, due to the reflections of mental modifications in Itself, It identifies with Its own material organ of perception.

23. Mind, influenced by Supreme Consciousness, is omniscient.

24. The mind, equipped with varied and innumerable forces, exists for the sake of the soul.

25. When, through discrimination, one experiences complete separation from the mind, one is free.

26. Having overcome identification with body, senses and mind, the soul becomes serene and calm and attention then flows in the direction of absolute freedom.

27. Even when inclined in the direction of the contemplation of Reality, there are intervals when the mind experiences an invasion of thoughts because of old habits, tendencies, and impressions which retain some influence.

28. One must renounce beliefs, fantasies, and untruths as these are obstacles to the experience of truth.

29. Having given up any selfish craving, even for liberation of consciousness, one experiences complete awakening and true freedom.

30. With the dawning of true knowledge all obstacles and restricting influences are banished.

31. With the dissolving of all mental restrictions individual mind is transformed into Cosmic Mind.

32. When, with the dawning of knowledge, the cosmic forces (gunas) have served their purposes, they cease to be influential.

33. No longer restricted to time, no longer perceiving the changes from moment to moment, the soul experiences timelessness and true knowledge which is beyond time and change.

34. Absolute freedom (independence) is experienced when the influences of the gunas become dormant or when, as a result of Self-realization, all forces in nature are transcended.

35. This is absolute liberation of consciousness.

36. Liberation is that experience where only Pure Consciousness remains.

37. If liberated while embodied, one sees the universe existing in God and one sees God in and as the universe.

38. Absolute Being is the nature of the Transcendental Reality. Mixed with electric attributes (gunas), Supreme Consciousness manifests as nature.

COMMENTARY

In the opening verse of the fourth section of the *Yoga Sutras*, the author shares unusual information: "Siddhis can be the result of the force of previous attainment, the intelligent use of chemicals, the power of mantra, austerity, and samadhi." In a world where personal freedoms are acknowledged, all people are born equal under civil law. But it is obvious that not all people are born with equal capacities and abilities! The masters of perfection teach that the average soul undergoes a series of earth-sphere experiences. When the urge of the soul is to identify through the mind and senses, attention flows outward and the soul becomes involved with the material realms. When the mind is clouded by the accumulation of impressions, soul awareness is screened and inertia and restlessness predominate as one moves through time and space as though in a dream. We have discussed, earlier, the intentional disciplines, the austerities which burn away the restricting patterns in the mind. Patanjali also informs us that other factors can contribute to the awakening of soul ability.

Some people are born almost completely unconscious. They are functional, but they live from the level of understanding that they are material bodies, almost always at the mercy of environmental forces. Others are born with a greater degree of intelligence and they are able to make the most of their present opportunity. A few come into this world with the natural capacity for experience and adventure and they make remarkable contributions to the world community. Now and then, with increasing frequency in this New Era, souls come into the world with an inclination to higher knowledge, the aptitude to learn quickly, and a refined nervous system which allows the consummation of life's purpose through the human form. These latter souls either come with knowledge, from realms of light, or they have been purified through previous involvement with study and spiritual disciplines.

The momentum originating in a previous sphere often carries over to the next. If cultivated, this momentum grows in force and progress continues. If not cultivated, the force of momentum can run its course and weaken; the soul then begins to sink into a less than conscious condition. Many bright souls spend but a few years on earth before awakening to God-knowledge. Some such souls have a little karma yet to work out before final liberation is experienced. Others, with a different mission, are here to assist the enlightenment trend of the world. When we see a person who is naturally endowed with keen intelligence and unusual abilities, we know that person to be one who was born with knowledge. We are also reminded, however, that supernormal powers are not evidence of liberation of consciousness.

It is common, because of mutual destiny, for enlightenment masters to incarnate during a time-cycle when their advanced disciples also incarnate. In this way the disciples can continue their instruction and become a part of the guru's teaching mission. While knowing that Supreme Consciousness is the true guide and teacher of all, gurus still play their traditional roles in the relative spheres. They know that as long as souls identify with the relative spheres they will be involved with relationships, and the guru-disciple relationship is considered to be the most important one of all.

Certain siddhas know how to wisely use herbs to contribute to health of the body. Sometimes, specific herbs are mixed with metals and other ingredients for the purpose of cleansing the system, stimulating function of the glands, and for the purpose of balancing the electrical characteristics of the body. Mind-altering drugs are not recommended by enlightenment masters because they often result in illusory perceptions and tend to weaken the mind's power to concentrate. The idea behind ingestion of a pure diet and taking certain herbs and prepared specifics is to do what can be done to contribute to health and long life so that one can have full use of the body while spiritual practices are continued. It is said that certain masters, through meditation, pranayama and the use of herb-mental combinations, extend their lifespans to hundreds of years.

Mantra is the time-proved method most suitable to all for the purpose of cleansing the mental field of impurities, refining the nervous system, and entering into more subtle levels of consciousness. The greater our awareness, the more refined the mind, nervous system and body, and the easier it is for natural soul abilities to be expressed.

The Purifying Influence of Samadhi Experience

Through the regular practice of samadhi, the soul realizes its true nature. As one awakens in the direction of Self-realization, to whatever degree experienced, there is a corresponding ability to function in the relative worlds. The transformation of mind, senses, and body is the result of the natural flow of soul force. This transformation is more than mild improvement of a condition, it is a change in quality from gross to subtle and from subtle to fine. The masters teach that man does not become divine, but, as a result of mental purification, the innate Divine Nature is allowed to express. When we rest in the conscious awareness of our nature as Pure Consciousness there is, in time, a descent of force and power which infiltrates the brain, nervous system, and body. This descent of superconscious force not only transforms the life of the person in whom it is active but it flows through that person into planetary consciousness. Fine energies, with the influence to transform, move from subtle spheres into the realm of this world. In this way the power of God moves to regenerate the planet.

The flow of creative force is possible when obstacles to the flow are removed. Nature is naturally inclined to express and nourish when given the opportunity. We allow this by attending to our studies, our practices, and our meditations. We create a condition which makes possible the in-flow of energy from the Source. Man is not blessed by God when he is good. Man experiences goodness when he is good because he is in harmony with nature. Man is not punished by God because he is bad. Man suffers when he is out of harmony with nature because nature cannot support that which has been deprived of its willing influence.

By the force of Cosmic Consciousness all seeming individual minds have been produced. We know there is but one Mind, the Mind of God. When viewpoints of Supreme Consciousness push out through the screen of Mind, seeming individual minds are produced. God, as Oversoul, is playing all roles and assuming all viewpoints through billions of seeming individualizations of the one Mind. At the level of One Mind, all is known about the relative spheres because all activity is contained within the range of Mind. But, seemingly individualized, relative mental units are, as far as they consciously know, endowed with personal reality. From the viewpoint of possessing a unique mind, my mind contains only impressions of my own experiences. I may be able to attune to another mind and know some of the contents, but I can never totally recall the experiences had by another. If there were no seeming separation between relative minds, there would be planetary confusion. Impressions, memories, motivations, goals, and purposes would be shared among all planetary residents and all universe-residents.

Of all classifications of mental states and impressions, the states and impressions resulting from samadhi influence do not contribute to destructive behavior. Samadhi influence is only constructive and contributes finally to full illumination of the mental field. Samadhi influence results in cleansing of the mental field, not in further conditioning of it. Influences upon the mind from subtle realms during meditation leave no tracing of memory which can cause effects in the relative world. The karmic patterns or collection of subconscious patterns of most people are of three kinds: one, resulting in positive behavior and constructive pleasure-causing effects; two, resulting in negative behavior and destructive pain-causing effects; three, a mixture of both. One who regularly practices samadhi creates no karmic impresssions and no longer ties himself to the future or adds to the weight of present psychological problems. He has only then to weaken and neutralize destructive tendencies and allow the working out of constructive ones. When he is no longer driven by any subconscious compulsions, if he retains a body at all, he lives by grace as an illumined person.

How Mental Patterns Manifest

From the storehouse of subconscious impressions, forces and tendencies are manifested according to available opportunities for expression. Unless a person has a psychological problem, he is usually appropriate to his present environmental circumstances. If things go well the average person will be reasonably calm and even-minded. If tendencies toward anger, frustration, hate, revenge, fear, cowardice, and whatever else may be semi-dormant in the subconscious are given the opportunity to be aroused and stirred into expression by environmental pressure, they will tend to manifest. A thief will not steal unless he has the opportunity. A liar cannot lie unless the opportunity is there. One may go for years assuming he has no serious psychological challenges with which to deal until the time of challenge and opportunity is met. Then, one who has long felt that he had made progress on the path of self-mastery is often shaken to his depths to find that the seeds of misery were but dormant, awaiting the moment for expression. On the other hand, given the environmental opportunity, seeds of positive response and constructive reaction to life situations can also be encouraged to sprout and manifest, if conditions are arranged for this to occur. It is understood by the enlightenment masters that it is useful to intentionally neutralize destructive patterns by replacing them with constructive ones. What is not always clearly taught in popular systems is that even constructive patterns, if they compel, interfere with spontaneous response. One who works to "build good karma" for a future reward is still working with mental conditionings and remains a victim of compulsive urges and drives. But this can be a start in a useful direction. One who is problem-oriented can, through intelligent effort, overcome the effects of past destructive causes and bring himself into a much better human condition. It is still a conditioned-condition, however. The next state is soul awareness and God-influence.

The electric influences, the gunas, also play a role in our lives. We have all experienced, seemingly with no cause and effect relationship being apparent, that we have changes in moods. At one time we are bright and optimistic, at another time we are restless and without apparent purpose, and then there are those occasions of depression and dullness. What is happening? Sometimes it has to do with the influence of the gunas. When the elevating influence is predominant, we are bright and clear, imbued with a sense of noble purpose. When the restless influence is predominant we are confused and easily distracted, or we are power driven or sense urged. When inertia prevails we are down in the emotional basement. Again we are advised to overcome inertia by implementing intelligent and purposeful action in the setting and reaching of goals. We are then advised to come up a little higher and practice the virtues so that action is truly constructive and in harmony with the highest ideal. We are finally advised to rise free of all three influences and live from spiritual understanding. Being intelligently active is more useful than being dull and overcome with the wish for death. Being idealistically and intelligently active is better than just being active according to traditional standards. Highest of all is to be in the stream of grace where only God's influence rules.

Regular practice of samadhi will result in a weakening of subconscious tendencies and a more conscious and even-minded relationship with life. Sometimes we must exercise our will to check the urge to mistaken action. We can often divert the force of a compulsive drive and thus transform the energy to a more useful purpose. When we are surrendered to God, God's force moves into our mind and changes everything.

There is, on the subconscious level, a direct relationship between mental causes and effects even if not obvious at the surface level. From the surface level we can be confused when things happen which we do not expect. We say, "I can't recall desiring or expecting this situation! How can there be a mental cause of my problem?" If what we are now experiencing is indeed the effect of a mental cause, we can be sure that somewhere in our life experience we accepted a mental impression which corresponds with the outer effect. We may not have *desired* the present outcome, so desire would not always be the cause. We may have *accepted* the possibility of the outcome, and the cause and effect mental result is the same. Whatever we *expect*, whatever we *believe ourselves worthy of*, can also be a cause and effect relationship. Karma, cause and effect in the mental sphere, is not punishment unless we so label the consequences. It is just that mental impressions cause us to meet corresponding situations.

To take extreme examples, let us look at the following possibilities. A man is told when he is young, by an authority figure he respects, "Life is tough. There is no way you can win. In the long run, life will grind you down!" The man works his way through college, applies himself with diligence, becomes successful and reasonably secure, only to make a "mistake" and fail in the end. He may not have failed because he deserved to fail or wanted to fail, he may have experienced the cause and effect relationship of the mental impression "life will grind you down!" And, sure enough, what his mind accepted, he experienced. Or a young woman is informed by "knowledgeable" people, "You're so pretty that all men will want you for is your body and as a decoration to impress their friends!" She knows better, her sense of self-worth makes her feel good about herself, but what happens? She finds that her life is the fulfillment of someone else's prejudiced prophecy. It is still cause and effect at a mental level.

It works the other way also. If someone in whom we have great trust says to us, "I believe in you. You will do wonderful things and you will have a wonderful life!"; this is just as likely to come true because we have accepted their pronouncement and it has given us a wholesome outlook on life and the marvelous gift of expectancy.

Our hopes, our dreams, our desires, our self-generated beliefs about life tend to externalize. A selfish person will constantly have to be on his guard against the selfish desires and intentions of others who are similarly selfish. A generous and fair person will meet generous and fair people the life long through. We tend to become what we think about because the mind will absorb whatever is presented to it. This is the law of cause and effect. Emerson said it: "A man becomes what he thinks about all day long." The subconscious level of mind does not analyze, it only reflects that to which it is exposed. Intelligence analyzes and discerns, but the subconscious level of mind is reactive, not discerning.

Much of what happens to us is not tied to a cause and effect relationship with roots in the past. Much of what happens to us is because we are attuned to group-thinking. We say, "I am only human and human beings think the way I do and their attitudes are like mine, so we, as human beings, experience similar situations." When we are in a mind identified state, whatever can happen to another human being can happen to us because we accept this as our lot in life. We can win and we can lose, we can experience pleasure and we can experience pain, we can be born and we can die, time and time again. Remember the rule: we become like the people with whom we associate. We take on the attitudes and life reactions of those with whom we choose to relate. Whatever is impressed upon the mind, the mind will express into outer manifestation. This is one reason why the masters suggest that we be attentive to the environment to which we subject ourselves. We cannot always completely determine our associations, but we can always be alert enough to monitor what is presented to us.

If present subconscious causes are not weakened and neutralized, they will eventually have to be faced because they will remain dormant in the mind and will tend to remain so until an occasion is presented for restimulating them. Even on the cosmic scale, at the level of Mind, causes and effects have no discernible beginning and there will never be an end to them. The initial cause was the motion of Life to express. Even when the worlds are dissolved, Cosmic Mind impressions will be in a dormant condition and will contribute to the next outward flow and the next universe to follow this one. This leads to the question: "What happens to souls who, billions of years from now, when the worlds are dissolved have not experienced conscious knowledge?" The answer: "Some will awaken and realize their participation was part of the plan, and others will remain identified with dormant mental impressions in subtle nature and will go forth once more to participate according to personal destiny." Since even the outer destiny is God's experience, this is quite all right with God.

It is natural to relate to our present world. But problems come when we are not in control of our mind and when deeper urges influence us unwisely. One way to put order and balance in our lives is to meditate deeply and correctly and experience samadhi states. We can only have a relationship with the relative world when we are aware of it, when influences from our environment make impressions on the mind. During occasions of partial or complete soul awareness we transcend, for that period, the mind and all possible mental influences. We can then return to mind identification with new perspective and strengthened by soul understanding. There will always be a past, a present, and a future for us when we are relating to outer matters. Causes will always tend to result in effects. However, tendencies and influential mental patterns are gradually weakened when their urge to express is transformed. Fine energies, working through subconscious patterns, move in the direction of expression. These energies can be intelligently directed and in this way they are transformed in a useful manner.

As a result of careful examination of our world we can see an underlying process at work. Life is a continuum, a series of connected relative parts. From one point of view "everything is one thing," and yet, from a relative point of view, because of the mixtures of electric influences and combinations of subtle elements, there is seeming difference. Water and poison may come in liquid form, but one will contribute to health and the other will not. While Supreme Consciousness manifests equally in both sinner and saint, the former is overcome by inertia and mental confusion while the latter is clear and knowledgeable. All environments are made up of essentially the same basic elements in combination, but some environments are uplifting and others are depressing. Order, cleanliness, and good taste in an environment contributes to soul satisfaction and peace of mind. Disorder, filth, and little sense of appropriateness contributes to activate the baser tendencies in a person. Natural food contributes to health and mental peace. Stale food or devitalized food contributes to mental sloth and physical disease. Love of beauty and an appreciation of order and harmony will not cause enlightenment but can contribute to a brighter mental condition which can be the beginning of the enlightenment quest. There comes a time when we are no longer influenced by environmental influences, but until this moment comes one is wise to arrange his environment to his highest advantage.

A Deeper Look at Mind and the World

The world does not exist because of our perception of it. If this were true (if the world existed because of our perception of it), when we went to sleep or left the world the world would cease to exist. Nor is the world the result of collective perceptions. For if no one were on this planet the planet would remain. There are galaxies of which we have no awareness, yet their influence on the whole is still evident. But, for us, only that which makes an impression on our mind is real to us. If we do not receive mental impressions of subtle spheres, they are not real to us even though they exist. While experiencing subtle spheres, if we do not receive mental impressions of the physical realm, the physical realm will not be real to us, although it will be real to persons who experience it.

The true soul nature is omnipresent, as God is omnipresent. Therefore, when established in Cosmic Consciousness while yet identifying with the mental field, all mental modifications cease to be known by the soul. We use the mind and we can examine it, so the mind is not self-luminous. The illumined mind is the result of soul light shining in the mental field. If the soul is fully God-conscious, that is, aware of the Reality of God beyond the relative spheres, it cannot at the same time know the mind or the mind's contents. It works the other way also; if one is even partially identified with the mental field, the totality of Supreme Consciousness cannot at the same moment be experienced. As long as we are working through the mind, there will be incomplete experience of Pure Consciousness.

How Supreme Consciousness Becomes Involved with Mind

Supreme Consciousness, influenced by electric characteristics, manifests as the Godhead or the Oversoul. When the light of God shines in the medium of Universal Mind, a portion of that reflected light retains images causes by impressions in Mind. This is how Supreme Consciousness becomes involved with the universal mental field. When Supreme Consciousness has influential dominancy, It is omniscient or all-knowing regarding the contents of Universal Mind. The stuff of material creation is unconscious, as it is the material medium. But Supreme Consciousness shining in it gives rise to the appearance of consciousness. Universal Mind, with its various aspects, exists for the expression of Pure Consciousness just as the particularized mental field exists for the expression of the soul. We must work through a mental medium when relating to the material worlds. Even the gods cannot relate to subtle or gross realms without the material medium of a mental field. On the other hand, restrained by a conditioned mind, we cannot be aware of the realms of the gods.

Being Free from Mental Influences and Restrictions

When, as a result of higher samadhi experiences and the use of discernment, we clearly see ourselves in relationship to the mind we use, we experience soul freedom. Before this we may have an intimation of what freedom is, but it will not be an experience of freedom. Having overcome identification with the mind and its contents, one then experiences unrestricted flowing of attention to the Source. From this point onward all personal effort to attain liberation is renounced and the process occurs spontaneously. In the early stages one experiences freedom from mental restriction only to again be pulled into involvement with the mental field, either through force of habit or due to restlessness and inertia which still retains influence over the soul's attention. It is for this reason that the masters teach that experiencing the final realization is not easy for everyone. It is often true that one can be almost clear, almost liberated, and yet be held back because of mental influence.

We are told in the *Yoga Sutras* (Verse 28) that one must, at this stage of experience, renounce beliefs, fantasies, and untruths because these are obstacles to the experience of final realization. One may ask, "Is it possible for a highly advanced person, standing almost at the threshold of liberation, to become prey to mental influences?" Yes, until final liberation there is always the possibility of becoming caught up in the surges of nature. Beliefs should be replaced by experience, fantasies should be replaced by accurate perception, untruth should be erased by the knowledge of that which is so about the nature of Consciousness. It is common knowledge among mystics that even highly aware souls, through whom God often does mighty works, can be partially deluded and given to the habit of defending cherished beliefs. Some also mistake celestial experiences for the final liberation experience because of the freedom enjoyed. Some, too, while possessed of almost-pure understanding, retain just a shade of lack of knowledge.

However, with the dawning of true knowledge, all obstacles and restricting influences are banished, as light replaces darkness. Darkness does not become light, darkness vanishes. Untruth cannot become truth, untruth vanishes. Higher samadhi experiences cleanse the mind completely and dissolve all mental restrictions. When this occurs, if the mental sheath is retained by the soul, the mind is transformed into Cosmic Mind. Then, working through the mind, the soul possesses inner and outer knowledge and is capable of knowing anything that is required to be known in the relative spheres. There are instances of saints having no formal education, who were able to interpret the scriptures with accuracy and insight so clear and pure that even learned philosophers could only stand in silent amazement. From whence does such knowledge come? It comes from the Source of all knowledge and filters into the conscious level of mind. There are things we all know that we cannot explain how we know because we have never been taught them in this incarnation. Some things we innately know were not learned in previous incarnations either. We contain all the truth there is in the deepest core of our being, and when it is allowed to surface we then experience revelation or direct understanding. The home of the *veda*, the home of "revealed truth," is Supreme Consciousness. We are, at the soul level, Supreme Consciousness. We, therefore, already inwardly know the truth.

The soul is often under the influence of the gunas even when mental modifications are no longer influential. This can explain why some bright souls experience a fluctuation in awareness. Once we know that all effects of past mental causes have been weakened and even neutralized, there can still be the influence of the electric characteristics inherent in the mental field. We can suddenly feel altruistic, we can suddenly feel restless, we can suddenly be influenced in the direction of inertia. These influences are usually the last to be neutralized. These influences, having "served their purposes" by assisting us in getting through relative experiences, are finally overcome. This is when one truly "overcomes the world" as Jesus testified in his own experience. Then, no longer restricted by time, one experiences timelessness and the true knowledge which is beyond time and change. We may have inquired as to why some of the service-oriented masters seem to be so patient with the slowness of world change. Now we know. The masters live in time-lessness and they participate as they are inwardly led. They are as patient as God is patient. We can only be truly patient to the de-gree that we have no expectations of a personal nature. When we see the process of life-unfoldment from the overview, we realize that events transpire on time, every time.

While we are relating to the mind and body, absolute liberation is experienced when the influences of nature no longer interfere with clear awareness or God-led intentions. There is also the possi-bility that the soul can simply depart the mental sheath and leave behind all of its characteristics. If we are not the mind, why can we not leave it when the moment is appropriate? Why do we have to "work everything out" in order to earn our liberation? The latter idea is only for those who not know the truth. I am con-vinced that a larger percentage of almost everything we have been taught about spiritual freedom is the result of unclear teaching. Much of what has been taught is useful to certain people along the way, if the teaching meets them at their level of need. We have been given guidelines for social comfort and these are useful for people who need instructions along these lines at the appropriate time. We have even been told how to believe and what to believe in order to be saved, and this is also useful for those who have the need at the moment. There are lower ways, there are middle ways, and there are higher ways . . . and each way is useful for those at each stage of understanding.

Relative to higher ways one is reminded of the incident which is recorded to have taken place in the ashram of Ramana Maharishi in the south of India. The sage was asked if one should carefully analyze the contents of the subconscious level of mind as a part of the enlightenment process. He responded, "When you throw out the garbage, do you examine the contents of the container? No! One simply throws it out!" We do not have to "pay" for past mis-takes and we do not have to understand why we made mistakes in the past. Along the "middle-way" it can be useful to under-stand the mental processes. Such understanding can result in re-lease and greater soul freedom. While about the "lower way," pre-occupation with subconscious tendencies will only result in a deeper and more confusing involvement with memory and emotion.

Many meditators are concerned about the importance placed on rising above mental influence or of clearing the mind. This is because they still retain feelings that they are mind and not Pure Consciousness. It is natural not to want to do away with what one feels to be one's own self. If I feel myself to be a body I will quite naturally not want to die, unless I am tired or weary of relationships. If I feel myself to be a mind I will quite naturally resist all intrusions which may challenge my mental condition. This is human nature and we can understand the urge to survive on the part of one who is identified with body and mind. We have no judgment on the matter. We understand. To understand is not the same as to put-up-with. Understanding springs from love and insight, from self-recognition, and true comprehension.

Absolute liberation of consciousness is the result of the soul's freedom from all external dependence, and this includes dependence upon mental states. Absolute liberation occurs only when Pure Consciousness is experienced. This is the Transcendental Experience, without form or name. One identified with mind cannot comprehend this state, but such a soul "almost" knows it. When that soul's destiny with relative-plane experience is ended, complete liberation is assured.

Not all souls experience liberation of consciousness as a result of carefully planned meditation schedules. Some are liberated due to God's grace, when they surrender fully to Him. God then pulls the veils from the soul and redeems Himself. Yearning and love, when honest and pure, can result in such a liberating process.

One can surrender to God while performing whatever useful duty and, in time, experience freedom in God. One can know, "Here am I, Lord, I do the best I can and whatever I do, I offer to you alone." Useful duty is whatever work is at hand and whatever duty is at hand. When we work with full attention and give our best, we are then conscious. When we serve our family and our friends with total attention to their *real* needs, we are then conscious. Being conscious and aware is essential to the awakening process.

One can also enter into a personal relationship with God and experience liberation of consciousness by going consciously with the flow of personal destiny. What does God expect of me? What do others expect of me? What should I do next? These are questions we often ask. The first question should be examined. The rest can await the final answer, and the final answer will emerge in due time. The straight message is that we can enter into the kingdom whenever we are receptive to it. The kingdom of heaven is available whenever we are ready to accept it.

Acceptance is the easy key to the knowledge of God and to all that God is. Do we not feel worthy? Are we not ready for truth? Shall we wait for some other moment before we even look at what is?

The nature of changeless Reality is absolute Being. Changing reality is referred to as nature and is Being mixed with electric attributes. One who is established in the vision of perfection sees the truth about the nature of God and the world. Is it possible to know the final truth even while working through a mind and physical body? The masters of perfection teach that it is possible to know the final truth and, by knowing, be truly free.

Epilogue

Epilogue
The EMERGENCE of the NEW ERA
and CYCLES of WORLD DESTINY EXPLAINED

The history of man on planet Earth can be traced with a fair degree of accuracy, by closely examining the cycles through which the world has passed in relationship to planetary influences. Though some masters of perfection have hinted at highly intelligent human life on other planets (in solar systems far removed from ours), we will confine our study to planet Earth.

Moons revolve around their planets, and planets, with their moons, revolve around the sun. The sun of our solar system takes a distant star as its central point of influence and orbits it in about 24,000 years. This movement of the sun through space results in the backward movement of the equinoctial points around the zodiac. The sun and the orbiting planets, our solar system, moves through the galaxy and participates in the interchange of universal energies. The masters of perfection teach that the sun also orbits a *central sun: the seat of power for this solar system.* This is the point in space from which Universal Magnetism (that fine aspect of God which plays the role of world transformation) acts upon all life, using heavenly bodies as distribution points through which energies are channeled. This true *Center* of vital force, in this given portion of space, regulates the mental forces on the inner planes. When the sun, in its orbit, comes to the place nearest this *Center*, the mental condition of man on the planet is so refined that the soul can readily comprehend the nature of God. When the sun, in its orbit, moves to the point most distant from this *Center*, the mental condition of man on planet Earth is dull and only outer objects can be perceived. In the former instance, we have what has been termed a Golden Age, or a true age of enlightenment. In the latter instance, we experience a Dark Age because the majority of people on the planet cannot comprehend the inner side of nature. Between these extremes we have varying degrees of mass enlightenment or mass delusion, depending upon the distance of the solar system from this *Central Point*. Because the orbiting of the sun (and our solar system) around this *Center* takes about 24,000 years, the peak of the Golden Age and the valley of the Dark Age are approximately 12,000 years apart.

Influences on Internal Changes

Each of these major 12,000 year periods brings a complete change in the inner nature of human beings, which reflects in the outer world. The world itself undergoes change as a result of various stresses due to planetary-energy interactions. The complete 24,000 year cycle is called an *Electric Time-Cycle*. Starting from the lowest point, the bottom of the Dark Age, the unfoldment of the mental condition is gradual and is divided into four noticeable stages. The time of 1,200 years, during which the sun passes through 1/20 of its grand orbit, is called the Dark Age. In relationship to mass consciousness, the mental ability of the average person during this period is but one-fourth unfolded and man cannot grasp anything but the most obvious external matters. Most people who are at this level of understanding can only perceive what is revealed to them through their sense organs. The intuition, the faculty of the soul, is not yet operant.

The second period of 2,400 years of the ascending cycle, when the sun moves through 2/20ths of its orbit, is called the Electrical Age because, during this period of time, human intellect begins to comprehend the fine forces in nature: the electricities and their attributes which are the creating principles of the external world. This is the time-cycle in which we now live, rather than being in a Dark Age, as some would have us believe.

The third period of 3,600 years, during which the sun passes through 3/20ths of its orbit, is called the Mental Age because the human intellect is then able to grasp the *source* of electrical forces upon which creation depends for its existence.

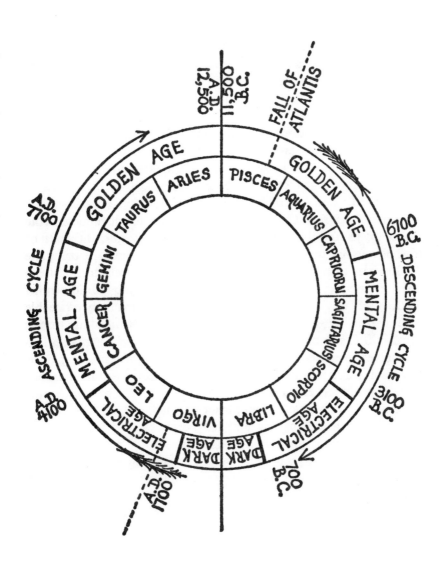

The remaining fourth period, during which the sun passes through 4/20ths of its orbit, is called the Golden Age or the Age of Enlightenment because, during this period, the human intellect can grasp the nature of God; that from which the material worlds have emerged. This period is 4,800 years in duration.

Reaching the peak, the descent begins, in reverse order, as the sun moves away from the *Central Point of Power*. So we see that the Golden Age period is the longest of all, totaling almost 10,000 years (4,800 ascending and 4,800 descending years, plus the durations of mutation between cycles before and afterwards). Manu, the ancient sage, wrote, "Four thousands of years, they say, is the Golden Age of the world." He referred to the very peak, since there are many centuries before and after the highest point experienced.

From 11,501 B.C., when the sun began to move away from the point in its orbit then nearest the *Grand Center*, the intellectual powers of man on the planet began to diminish. During the 4,800 years of the descending Golden Age, the intellect as a whole lost the power to grasp spiritual truth. During the following 3,600 years of the descending Mental Age, the majority of people on the planet lost the ability to grasp the subtle realms. During the 2,400 descending years of the Electrical Cycle, the masses lost the power to understand the nature and use of electricity. During the final 1,200 years of the descent, man dropped into the Dark Age. This process explains, simply and directly, the reasons for the rise and fall of civilizations on planet Earth.

Civilizations, then, rise and fall because of the electrical influences by which all of nature is ruled. People incarnate during Time Cycles when their personal soul needs and karmic patterns indicate an opportunity for experience and unfoldment. The period around A.D. 500 was the darkest part of the last Dark Age. From that point, the sun began to move again toward the *Grand Center* and the intellectual capacities of man began to be unveiled, resulting in the gradual awakening of people on the planet. According to historical records, the 17th century was the time, in the West, when man began to "discover" once again the existence of electricity, magnetic substances, and subtle influences. Since then, because the awakening process has been accelerating, science has progressed with amazing speed. This is part of the cosmic plan for, as seers of times past predicted, due to their knowledge of time-cycles, this present era would be the occasion of space exploration and interplanetary travel.

As we understand the workings of God through nature we see that there is, indeed, a Creative Intelligence which is responsible for the destiny of man and his worlds. Many historians have incorrectly blamed man for past major world catastrophies because they did not understand that the true cause of major outer effects is not man but subtle influences behind nature. The greater one's soul awareness the less he is influenced by forces in nature. This is why, even in Dark Ages, there have been masters of perfection who witnessed the external condition while they, themselves, were not influenced at all. The peak of each Time-Cycle is higher than the previous peak of a similar Time-Cycle. Each Dark Age is less dark than the preceding Dark Age and each Golden Age is brighter than preceding Golden Ages. In this way, the world, over millions of years of repeating Time-Cycles, is transformed. This is the plan of God moving in the direction of transformation of planetary consciousness. According to the calculations of the seers, at least 2 billion years yet remain before this solar system is dissolved. The universe has a much longer life.

Students of esoteric sciences will be interested to know of Sri Yukteswar's conclusions regarding the reason why some teachers are of the mistaken opinion that the world is now in Kali Yuga or the Dark Age. As a result of deep study of the problem Sri Yukteswar found the reason for this error. Some writers claim that we are in the Dark Age period and will remain so for another 432,000 years. This error started about 700 B.C. during the reign of Raja Parikshit of India. During that time Maharaja Yudhisthira, noticing the evidence of the coming Dark Age, turned his throne over to his grandson and retired into the seclusion of the Himalayan mountains, taking with him his astronomers and astrologers. There were none left in the remaining court to correctly calculate the movements of the celestial bodies. The astronomers did not want to record the coming of the Dark Ages at all because they did not want to create fear in the public mind. So, they recorded the beginning of the Dark Age as being the beginning of the following Electrical Age. They wanted the public to believe that they were moving with an upward cycle instead of a downward one. However, about A.D. 499, the mistake in the almanac was found, but not the reason for it. The almanac recorded the length of the Dark Age as one period of 1,200 years, instead of two periods (1,200 descending and 1,200 ascending). So, the later astrologers assumed that the Dark Age years were not real solar years but, rather, were "Years of the Gods" with one year being a day and 1,200 years amounting to 432,000 solar years. Even when this information is explained, there are many who will refuse to accept it because they either cannot comprehend the process of world cycles or they prefer to remain secure among their peers who are likewise settled in a traditional pattern of thinking. An unfortunate result of this false teaching regarding the true status of our present Time-Cycle is that it serves to create a mood of pessimism among those who hear and believe it.

We are in the dawning of the true Age of Enlightenment: the Age that will fully emerge about 7700 A.D. Between now and then, however, the Electrical-Age and the Mental Ages will be experienced and, in comparison with the Dark Age recently past, these Ages will be occasions of greater Self-realization and increasing outer discovery.

The beginning of the descent of the last Golden Age has a correlation with the legend of the fall of that empire known as Atlantis. This process of decline began around 11,500 B.C., for reasons we have already explained. Plato, in the *Critias*, described the Golden Age condition of Atlantis. It was a philosophic democracy, the arts flourished and the sciences were cultivated in great universities. Man had no enemies and war was unknown. Gradually, because of electrical influences from space, men lost their spiritual awareness and with this their virtues. Personal ambition and corruption ensued. Atlantis fell and the fortunes of men on the planet declined. Atlantis was devastated by cataclysmic earthquakes around 10,184 B.C., approximately 1,316 years after the Golden Age began to dim. Some prophets would have us believe that civilization declined because men became evil. The causes of world trends is deeper than surface appearances. The light of Atlantis lingered on because poets and philosophers preserved the story in writings and transmitted it through oral teachings. The glory of later civilizations preceding the Dark Age was but the dying embers of a once great Cycle of Enlightenment.

Even in Dark Ages wisdom is never lost. It is carefully preserved by the masters of perfection and hidden from the eyes of the profane, veiled in symbolism, and guarded until the time is ripe for its re-emergence and acceptance. The only reason why subtle truths are hidden from unawakened man is so that information will not be abused and greater harm caused to the planet.

One tenth of the duration of each Age is a time of mutation and of overlapping of electric influences; at the end of one Age, the external evidence of the Age to follow becomes apparent. After entry into the next Age, remnants of the Age just passed remain for a short duration. About A.D. 1700 saw the end of the last Dark Age, but the influences of that Age continued to affect world consciousness. As of this writing (A.D. 1979), world consciousness has almost pulled free from Dark Age influences and Electrical Age influences are becoming predominant. The challenge of today is to remain current with new discoveries and to learn to make necessary adjustments in attitudes and relationships in order to keep pace with increased understanding and the obvious needs to respond to evolutionary challenge.

The Remaining Decade of the 20 Century: The "Hour of God" and the Unveiling of Truth Consciousness

It is a frequent refrain, among unenlightened doomsday prophets, that the years ahead are to be filled with severe hardships for the majority of people on the planet. Crisis after crisis seems to emerge to force self-confrontation. Nothing, it seems, about the relative world is stable. But, then, this is not new, for this teaching has been central to the message of the masters for thousands of years. Change is built into the fabric of the natural order. Conditions emerge, remain for a time in a seeming stable condition, and then dissolve. This is the way of nature; there is nothing to fear. We have explained the reasons for cycles and for the changes in the general condition of human consciousness. But what about the prophecies of disaster and what about our near and distant future experience on this earth?

We have said that we are pulling free from Dark Age influences and that we are more and more coming under the influence of the Ascending Cycle. This means drastic change as a result of mass awakening and a breaking from traditions no longer useful. There is even the possibility of changes in the planet itself, due to energy-influences and gravitational effects of planets and bodies in space which have a relationship with our planet. It is known that earthquakes are increasing in numbers. Variations in weather patterns are observed, and the effects on the planet of man's industrial pollution must be examined. But there is something to remember: God is equal to the world's needs. God works through cosmic electrical influences and God works through souls which are expressions of Himself. God is in command; we are but participants in the process. We can do the best of which we are capable to cooperate with world change and then leave the rest to God. In this manner we can live in this world without fear.

More than one spiritual teacher has said that the "Hour of God" is at hand. This means that the time has come, in our changing world, for a great spiritual awakening. The cause of this mass awakening is that the intellectual abilities of souls are being unveiled. The situation is encouraged as a result of the world's population having to handle the challenge of the need to change. Birth is not always comfortable. Awakening and the need to learn to relate in higher and better ways is often painful, but it is useful for us to rise to the challenge. Man is awakening from materialism to a sense of spiritual values and this is reflected on the world scene. The ideal is for us to face what is to come with courage and high anticipation. Fear leads only to despondency and mental and emotional paralysis. Have we not witnessed, in recent decades, strong evidence of mental and spiritual awakening? Of course we have. This is the pattern in this era before us.

I can see no reason for talk of gloom and world disaster. Some minor prophets have said that two-thirds of the world's population will be wiped out due to a global catastrophe. War is not mentioned as the cause of this happening. What *is* mentioned is the possibility of drastic earth changes: earthquakes, floods, and severe weather conditions. Also mentioned is the havoc to be wrought because of millions of people becoming self-destructive due to panic. That change will be experienced is certain, but for anyone to publicly declare that two-thirds of the world's population will be killed is certainly an extreme prediction. Such prediction is not even reasonable. It is interesting to note that some who make such dire statements serve to benefit as a result of attracting numbers of people to their personal utopian cause. Not a few of these prophets even declare that their special group, which will survive the catastrophe, will then go forth to lead the remnants of the world into a Golden Age. This theme has been enacted before and it is of interest to me to observe that, seldom among such groups, are there any truly enlightened people who are qualified to play a useful role in world regeneration! Fear of change, pessimism, and delusions of grandeur are not in harmony with the enlightened consciousness.

One can observe in those who are truly enlightened that there is a serenity, a radiance, a certainty about God's plan. There may be, with enlightened world teachers, a sense of mild urgency to get on with the world enlightenment process because it happens to be their personal destiny to participate in it and to encourage mankind to turn to the truth. The masters of whom I have knowledge are inwardly aware of the trend of the times and of the glorious destiny that awaits the world. We are in the dawning of the Age of Enlightenment; the new era is upon us and, from now onward, world conditions will improve with startling rapidity. Occasions of stress and challenge are opportunities to grow and times of great need are moments of invitations to positive action. Not all positive action is world-directed action; much of what is required is internal, as one engages in sincere self-examination and responds to the need for personal change in attitude and consciousness.

During Dark Age cycles the majority on the planet are spiritually unconscious. During the Electrical Age more people become spiritually conscious. During the Mental Age the greater percentage of the world's inhabitants are spiritually awake. During the Golden Age the majority on the planet are enlightened. The current Electrical Age started about A.D. 1700; the coming Mental Age will begin about the year A.D. 4100; the true Age of Enlightenment will begin about A.D. 7700; and the peak of that Age will be about A.D. 12,500. However, compared to past conditions that most people can recall, from now onward the planet's consciousness will seem to be in an enlightenment era. Also, no matter what the Time-Cycle in which the world exists, the individual can experience the Age of Enlightenment at any time as a result of Self-realization and God-consciousness. Just as cosmic events result in the unveiling of the intellectual capacities of the many, so individuals can experience rapid awakening as a result of attunement with God and the resultant unveiling of the soul's innate capacities. To think in terms of relating with mass awakening is to move with the general trend of events; to surrender to God is to become free of such dependency and to experience conscious freedom.

Many masters of perfection have been asked, at one time or another, about the possibilities of world changes and what the average person can do to best fit into the process. The answers are uniformly given: be self-disciplined, study about the nature of Consciousness, meditate, and learn to surrender to God's will. The only security is to be absorbed in God's will. The only true freedom is the result of world transcendence. We can live in the world while remaining inwardly established in God. There is no power for good or for evil in the world itself when we are anchored in God. One who is established in God sees only God expressing and there can be no judgment regarding right and wrong, goodness and non-goodness, or fear of what appears on the outer scene. God not only regulates the world-process but God *is* the world-process, and this is clearly understood when we are enlightened. When we are flowing with God's intentions we are free, just as God is free. God does not suffer; therefore there is no suffering in the world when we comprehend from the highest point of view. Pleasure and pain, loss and gain, success and failure are not a part of God's consciousness. There is, to God, only the orderly working out of a predestined plan. When we are awake in God we also see how this is so; therefore there can never be a personal problem for us when we are truly conscious.

Because of circumstances, the Light of Consciousness has flowed from East to West. During the last Dark Age cycle seers residing in and near the Himalayan mountains kept pure the most secret doctrines: secret, only because of the condition of mass consciousness, not because the masters were keeping information to themselves for private reasons. Who can tell where on earth the next abode of revealed truth will be preserved. This occurrence, however, is so far in the future that we need not even contemplate the matter now. God will arrange whatever conditions are needed in the most appropriate manner. Truth is what it is; *it* is all pervading and will emerge through whatever mental field it can. Because of cultural influence one may conclude that there is an Eastern teaching or a Western teaching, but that which is revealed, if it is the Truth, transcends geographical designations. God runs the universe. God regulates all natural conditions on planet Earth. God manifests as the worlds and as all forms. God is not at all concerned with man-made boundaries and temporary lines between peoples or places. There is only one God. All else is pictured in individual minds.

God Has a Plan for His World

Every world is God's world and God has a plan for each and every one of them. Most of us are attuned to this planet we know through present life experience. The masters of perfection sometimes speak of life on other planets of this solar system. The general instruction is that planet Earth is the only planet in our solar system with human beings. Humans represent the marriage of gods and men; therefore their physical forms offer the best possible opportunity for Self-realization because of the highly refined nervous system. Intelligent life on planets in our solar system other than Earth are not so refined, but life does manifest through organic forms on some planets. Beyond this solar system, in our known galaxy, there are millions of planets similar to the Earth environment and, so the masters teach, there are civilizations scattered throughout the galaxy which are more or less intellectually advanced. There are galaxies beyond our own, including many of which we have no knowledge at present, and God is expressing as God will in many of these distant places. There are also the astral realms and the more subtle causal realms where souls work out their salvation. Beyond these, there are the finer heavenly realms on the other side of maya. There is the material universe, so vast that the average mind cannot even envision it. There is also the inner spiritual universe which cannot be approached by one unless the soul's ability to directly cognize is readily available. All of these worlds and realms are but *shadows* in the mind of God. They are the material extensions of God's will. Approaching from the direction of understanding each level, sphere and plane at a time, we can become involved in an almost endless round of causes and effects. Looking at the process from the overview we can see the total picture at a glance. The former way is the way of working out our salvation; the latter way is the enlightenment experience which makes everything clear instantly.

Just as people and things in our environment influence us, so we influence people and things which are in proximity to us. What is not generally known is that we are influenced by energies which have their origins in distant space and we contribute our energy and our consciousness to every manifest aspect of the universe. Our state of consciousness, our awareness of Being, is important to the welfare of the whole. We speak here not only of the physical universe but also of the subtle worlds which coexist with it and of which we are a part. Our physical energy directly influences our physical environment as well as the subtle realms which are the cause and support of the physical universe. It is understood by the masters of perfection that a truly enlightened person, even if living in relative isolation, makes a superior contribution to the purification of planetary consciousness. Ramana Maharishi, who lived in a secluded ashram environment, was once asked, "With your spiritual attainment, why do you not move among the people in society and help them?" The sage quietly responded, "How do you know that I am not helping the world?" His unique contribution to the world was to remain firmly settle in true knowledge. A liberated person knows: "I do nothing at all. God does everything."

What are we to do to fit into the plan God has for the world? First, we must see to our own enlightenment because, unless we are truly conscious, most of our good intentions will be in vain. Second, we can be open to inner guidance and then respond to the impulse of the soul to do what seems to be the best to do in whatever moment and occasion presented. This is the teaching of the masters of perfection.

Text and Commentary on Self-Knowledge

The WISDOM YOGA
of SHANKARACHARYA

Shankara was born, so legend has it, in A.D. 788. He "with-drew" from this realm in the year A.D. 820, just thirty-two years old when he became invisible to mortal sight. He was a child prodigy and devoted himself to the practice of yoga and spiritual austerities at an early age. It was not long before his intellectual acumen was acknowledged by the leading philosophers of India. His mission was to reform the *sanatana Dharma*, The Eternal Religion, and with that end in view he wrote commentaries on the principle scriptures of the time: the *Bhagavad Gita*, the *Brahma-Sutras*, and the *Upanishads*. They are translated in many languages to this day and are considered to be the most accurate of all available renderings. *Acharya* means "the teacher who draws the student to the truth of the teaching" and *acharya* became affixed to Shankara's name. He was the "teacher of teachers." Of this, there can be no doubt. Traveling the length and breadth of India he bested all scholars and philosophers in the debates which were then popular. Before his final departure (it is not clear whether he retired into Himalayan solitude or actually left his body), he established Centers of learning in the major quarters of India. Even today these Centers are headed by highly intelligent and realized men who trace their spiritual lineage back to Shankara. These four are the spiritual leaders of millions of devout Hindus.

Shankara also reorganized the monastic order of swamis and

assigned to it the leadership of society. It was felt that daily living should not be separated from philosophical study and application, that the vitality of spiritual insight should run through the entire social organism. Shankara lived at a time when Buddhism was beginning to lose influence and the teachers extant were themselves not capable of knowing or teaching clear doctrine. Hinduism was beginning to reassert itself. Leadership was lacking and Shankara was a man for the times. Though he is often best known for such works as *Self-Knowledge*, he also wrote poems and hymns in praise of God so that people's faith could be stirred and their aspirations raised to new heights. One biographer describes him as the "unusual combination of philospher and poet, savant and saint, mystic and religious performer, debater of rare forensic power and passionate love of God."

It seems to me that Shankara must be considered as one of those rare beings who are sent to earth on a special mission. Perhaps he is an *immortal-mortal*, a forever-free soul whose destiny path is that of remaining in proximity to the mundane realms in order to radiate beneficial influences. The great siddha, Babaji, first in my line of gurus, has stated that he gave *Kriya Yoga* initiation to Shankara many centuries ago. In recent times Babaji's most publicly known disciple was the Bengali master, Lahiri Mahasaya, who revived *Kriya Yoga* after centuries of neglect on the part of the average man. Through Lahiri's disciple, Swami Sri Yukteswar, Paramahansa Yogananda was trained to bring yoga teachings to the West.

It is taught, in the great religious books of the world, that whenever mankind needs a spiritual infusion, then the Divine Power moves through a qualified and prepared person to restore the way of right living to the planet. Such persons are aware of their duty and desire nothing but to clear away the confusions which sometimes tend to settle in mass mind.

It is said that when Shankara was thirty-two years of age and his work was completed, he retired into the Himalayas and there meditated; "absorbing his gross vehicles into the Self" he passed from this world. This does not mean that he dematerialized the various sheaths of the soul, but that he withdrew identification from them in true yogic fashion and became firmly established in the realization of Supreme Consciousness.

The reader will notice that certain elements of style are different in this section, as compared to the pages preceding. The reason for this is that the following material was formerly published in book form as *The Path of Soul Liberation*. We have, therefore, chosen to leave the presentation as it was first published.

1. **I am composing this treatise on Self-Knowledge to serve the needs of those who have been purified through the practice of spiritual disciplines, who are peaceful in heart, free from (selfish) cravings and desirous of liberation.**

Knowledge of the Self, or Self-Realization, is the reason for our spiritual practices. The soul, it is taught, is an individualization of Pure Consciousess. Self-Knowledge is the clear self-awareness of the truth about our essential nature. We are not to think in terms of acquiring realization, but of awakening to it. We are not to think in terms of developing a state of soul consciousness or of building it up, but to clear away the obscuring matters which prevent natural and spontaneous recognition of the truth. Shankara states in this first verse that he is writing, not to the one in whom the impulse toward realization has not arisen, but to "those who have been purified through the practice of spiritual disciplines, who are peaceful in heart, free from (selfish) cravings and desirous of liberation." We are, therefore, addressing ourselves to those who are ripe for the enlightenment experience.

Six *treasures*, according to master-teachers, form the ethical foundation of a truly spiritual life. Their practice prepares the inner faculties for the cultivation of higher knowledge. They are: *calmness of mind and being; self-control and discipline of the senses; contentment as the result of being inwardly settled; patience, regardless of what transpires about us; proper contemplation on the nature of Reality; and pure faith in the Life Process once its nature has been understood.* In addition, we are counseled to use our powers of discrimination, be free of attachments and yearn for liberation of consciousness. If we are true to ourselves and, therefore, true to life, we will realize the goal in the most efficient manner. Discipline, for our purposes, means: to sunchronize thinking, feeling and intelligent action so as to be successful in our ventures with a minimum of wasted energy and time.

Unless one is sincere on the path, unless one is totally dedicated to the ideal of experiencing the highest realization, random attempts are practically useless. No real guru will spend precious time with a person who is not yet committed to the enlightenment experience.

2. **As fire (heat) is the direct cause of cooking, so knowledge, and not any other form of discipline, is the direct cause of liberation; for liberation cannot be attained without knowledge.**

If one's goal is to cook food, heat must be used, or something which results in the cooking process. Here, even though disciplines have been mentioned earlier, we are given the forthright information: "Liberation cannot be attained without knowledge"; knowledge, or full comprehension, about the nature of the Life Process Itself. Sages speak of higher knowledge and of lower knowledge. The former refers to comprehension of the subtle causes behind outer effects; the latter to comprehension of happenings in the relative worlds. To experience only, is not to have knowledge. One might taste food yet know not the real essence of the food, one might drive an automobile yet know not how it is manufactured, or even functions. One may feel an attunement with Life but not really know what Life is all about.

Knowledge is the result of the correct use of the faculty of intelligence; the ability to discriminate, or tell the difference between what is true about the object under analysis versus what we only assume to be true. The intuitive faculty is also useful, for it is the soul's way of knowing by knowing; no "reasons" need be present to support such knowing. Intuitive perception is always accurate, it is not like the vague assumptions, or convenient conclusions, at which we sometimes arrive to satisfy an emotional need.

The major point here set forth is that disciplines, while useful in clearing mind and emotional nature and in training us to use our abilities correctly, are not the cause of enlightenment. Enlightenment is the result of awakening to the realization of the truth about life. Hence, knowledge is automatic and liberation is spontaneous.

3. Action cannot destroy ignorance, for it is not in conflict with ignorance. Knowledge alone destroys ignorance, as light destroys dense darkness.

Ignorance, as used here, does not mean lack of education. It refers to our assuming that the world is real by itself, rather than a manifestation of the One Life. As long as we persist in operating from the level of understanding which assumes the world to be a mechanical multi-combination phenomenon and that we are but bodies moving through time and space, our actions, whatever they might be, are doomed to failure relative to our eventual experience of enlightenment. One who works from an understanding of causation and who thinks, "I am the doer," is self-deceived. It is only by moving into the transcendental level of awareness that one is able to see clearly and be possessed of perfect understanding.

4. It is only because of ignorance that the Supreme Consciousness appears as finite. When ignorance is destroyed, the Supreme Consciousness, which does not admit of any multiplicity whatsoever, truly reveals Itself by Itself, like the sun when the cloud is removed.

When one is deluded and does not clearly comprehend the nature of Life, from subtle to gross expression, only the finite aspect of creation is observed and believed to be real of itself. When, through discrimination and intuitive meditation practice, one trancends mental concepts one directly perceives the truth. Then Supreme Consciousness "reveals Itself by Itself." Consciousness is self-luminous and requires nothing external to Itself. It is "the light that lighteth every man" who comes into the world. This essential essence, the soul or Self, is referred to by members of the Christian faith as the indwelling Christ.

5. Through steady practice, knowledge purifies the embodied soul stained by ignorance, and then itself disappears, as a purifying agent disappears after it has cleansed the water.

Of course, the soul does not need to be purified. What is meant here is that the soul's coverings, or sheaths, are purified as one remains steady in Realization. In the early stages there is usually a taint of delusion remaining, so that one who intuitively realizes the truth about Life is still under the conviction that he is realizing; that is, "I am not Knowledge Itself, I am perceiving the truth about life." In the course of time, through "steady practice," energies flowing from the Transcendental Source infiltrate the mental field and the nervous system, resulting in cleansing and purification. Finally the consciousness *of* Knowledge disappears and only the Trancendental Existence remains. It just is; It does not enjoy Its beingness, for this would be evidence of duality, calling for yet more purification.

6. **The world, filled with attachments and aversions, and the rest, is like a dream: it appears to be real as long as one is ignorant but becomes unreal when one is awake.**

This is a classic explanation. Dreams are common to all of us and can be understood in this context. Our dreams are totally the product of our own mental processes. It has even been said that dreams are "memories" which become active and influenced by subconscious urges and impressions. Sometimes, dreams are creative but the dream-material is still of the mind. Mystics teach that the average person, even when awake to the sense-perceived world, is like one in a dream; he does not see clearly because he does not use his intellectual faculty correctly, and he "projects," or assumes, instead of getting to the truth. He is also at the mercy of inherited tendencies, early impressions, social conditioning and peer-group influence. Also, because he is not anchored in the Self he either tends to grasp at things or rejects them; thus, he is caught up in the seeming never-ending process of nature. The ebb and flow of energy, the setting and reaching of goals, the inter-relationships between things and other life-forms—these are natural to the relative plane of existence. The Sanskrit word for this phenomenon is *samsara*, and its natural trend is to continue. As long as one is identified with this trend, one is sure to continue in the waking-dream experience. But, when one awakens to the truth about Life and sees clearly the *why* and the *how* of it all, the relative world is no longer real in the sense of its having independent support.

7. **The world appears to be real as long as nondual Consciousness, which is the basis of all (manifestation), is not known. It is like any other illusion, having no basis of its own.**

Non-dual Consciousness is the true support of the phenomenal universe. When we conclude that the universe is without support and see only the various expressions of relative nature, we miss the point, or we draw a false conclusion. Seeing an inanimate object in the dark, for instance, we may assume it is something else. If the "something else" we assume it to be represents a threat to our well-being, we will react emotionally, even though no real threat exists. My guru, Paramahansa Yogananda, used to say, "The universe is God's dream; it is all taking place in God's mind." From the point of view of God's mind we can see that the universe, which seems so obvious to sense perceptions, is truly a dream-happening. Therefore, Supreme Consciousness is the primal cause, as well as the sole support of the universe. When we realize this, the universe will not truly vanish from our sight, but we will see it in a new and different light. It will no longer be the fearsome, or misunderstood, forever flowing happening we have heretofore presumed it to be. It will be Supreme Consciousness appearing *as* the world. Supreme Consciousness, through the process of self-modification, extends as the universes and all that inhabits them. The universe, then, is the result of the play of Consciousness.

8. **All the various forms exist in the imagination of the perceiver, the substratum (supporting principle) being the eternal and all-pervading Consciousness (in partial manifestation) whose nature is Existence and Intelligence. Names and forms are like rings and bracelets and Consciousness is like the gold from which they are formed.**

The meaning of "the various forms exist in the imagination of the perceiver" is that the names, or labels, we give to the various forms are ours and do not belong to the forms themselves. No matter what we elect to call a thing, it is we who have thus labeled it. The thing itself is a manifestation of Consciousness in Its temporary and relative form. Pure Consciousness is without attributes, but when moving in the direction outward manifestation, takes on characteristics and attributes. Existence there always is, the Intelligence is the aspect of Consciousness which directs the universal process. We refer to a piece of gold, used as a body ornament, as a ring, a bracelet, or whatever best describes its use; the names are ours, the object remains what it is, gold.

9. **As the all-pervading space appears to vary on account of its association with various forms (mental, electric, magnetic) which are different from each other, and (again) remains pure upon the destruction of the form-giving qualities, so also the omnipresent Lord (Consciousness as creative manifesting power) appears to be diverse on account of His association with various form-building qualities and remains pure and One upon the dissolution of these qualities.**

We can examine this verse on at least two different levels of understanding. Space is broken up, to our vision, by the various objects existing in a given space that is perceived. Yet, if the objects were to be removed, space would remain. Space is not *distance*, space is that in which things rest and happenings occur. Distance is a measurement from one point in space to another. Space is a field in which the universe happens. Time-sense is due to our changing our perspective. To some, time seems to flow; we have past, present and future. Time, space, light particles and energy make up the basic substance of which the manifest realms are expressed. The Sanskrit word for this basic substance, a modification of Consciousness, is maya. Maya is not an illusion: but our taking it to be real, that is, to have independent existence, constitutes for the sense of illusion. This is the basic cause of delusion, ignorance, or self-forgetfulness. When maya is dissolved, Consciousness will remain. This is the second level of understanding and is clearly realized when the transcendental level of Consciousness is realized. Even before realization is ours, we can use our intelligence, our faculty of discernment, to be reminded of the true nature of the Life Process.

10. **Owing to Its association with varous restricting qualities and attributes, such ideas as differences (between people), color, and social position are superimposed on Supreme Consciousness; as flavor, color, and worth are attributed to water.**

During deep meditation and when we are active in the world while remaining soul-conscious, we are above mundane concerns regarding other people: their personality, skin color, or social status. We know that all people are souls expressing through the various bodies and minds, which are themselves conditioned. The outer is conditioned, the inner is the same in all human beings. One of the characteristics of a saint, it is said, is that a saint will see all people as being expressions of Consciousness and will accord them equal respect. With understanding we can see that everyone has a place in the cosmic scheme and that what is needed is to encourage individuals to find their true place and work out their personal destiny in harmony with the whole. Society, like Nature, is a continuum, a series of connected parts, and the health and well-being of the total organism is dependent upon the health and well-being of the individual.

11. **The physical body, the medium through which the soul experiences pleasure and pain, is determined by past actions and formed out of the five great subtle elements, which become gross matter when one-half portion of one subtle element becomes united with one-eighth of each of the other four.**

Seers teach that the body is not fully the effect of the union of our parents; there is also the matter of the soul's desire for physical expression. This desire is due to need, or craving, for sense-oriented experience. The need is due to the accumulation of subconscious impressions, or karmic patterns, which supply the motive force.

The subtle elements, five in number, are at first pure and not yet involved with manifestation. They are in rudimentary form. However, when they mix, grosser elements are expressed, and involvement with and *as* nature is possible. The first element is said to be ether, the background of space, due to a mixture of Consciousness and Its modification, maya. From ether evolves air; from air, fire; from fire, water; from water, earth. Transmitted to the elements, from the Godhead, at the time of initial outflowing, are the three electric attributes which permeate all creation: *sattva, rajas,* and *tamas.* Simply, these terms mean: sattva, elevating and purifying attribute; rajas, neutralizing current, or attribute;

tamas, gravity, inertia, or heaviness. The first and last relate to the positive and negative polarities, the middle attribute is the current flowing between them, resulting in balance.

The subtle elements are untainted, then become mixed, resulting in gross compounds. Combinations of subtle elements, in specific proportions, result in the production of gross elements. The verse states that each gross element consists of one-half portion of its subtle counterpart and one-eighth each of the four remaining subtle elements. For instance: One-half subtle ether and four one-eighth parts (amounting to one-half) of the remaining subtle elements results in the appearance of gross ether. One half portion of subtle air and four one-eighth parts of the remaining subtle elements results in the appearance of gross water. And, so on.

12. The subtle body, the instrument of the soul's experience, consists of the five divisions of prana, the ten organs (those of perception and action), the mind and the faculty of intelligence: all formed from rudimentary elements before their subdivision and combination with one another.

Vital force, *prana*, is divided into five parts according to their respective functions in nature: that part which is the basis for the rest; that part which functions in the body, moves downward and expels unassimilated food; that part which pervades throughout the body; that part which ascends in the body, allowing regurgitation, and assists the soul to depart the body when the time arrives; that part which enables the body to digest food and convert it into needed nutritional mixtures. As the three electric attributes (see above) make up nature, so the five *pranas* are derived from the *rajasic*, or neutralizing parts of the five subtle elements.

The organs of perception are the ears, skin, eyes, tongue, and nose. The organs of action are the hands, feet, speech apparatus, and organs of evacuation and generation. The five organs of perception are said to be formed from the *sattvic*, or elevating parts of the subtle elements, because this attribute has the characteristic of brightness. The organs of action are believed to be formed of the *rajasic* parts of the subtle elements, because they are active and allow the embodied soul to reach goals, satisfy desires, and neutralize desire patterns.

Mind is considered to be produced from the sattvic parts of the five subtle elements and is that function which enables one to consider different viewpoints about a given subject. In modern metaphysical circles a definition of the human mind is: "an individualization of Cosmic Mind." Mind is considered to be the creative medium which makes possible the appearance of the world and the intentional modification of it. Another aspect of the mind is the *intellectual* faculty. This enables one to discern the true nature and character of an object analyzed. Another characteristic of the mind is that it tends to seek pleasurable experiences.This can have survival value as most survival activities (eating, sleeping, succeeding in ventures, communicating with others, etc.) are pleasurable. A problem can arise, however, if one seeks pleasure for the sake of pleasure, instead of merely enjoying pleasure as an adjunct to survival experience. One is likely to seek pleasure at the cost of health, social stability, or even peace of mind. The final characteristic of the mind is egoity, the sense of I-consciousness. When we understand what the "I" really is, we are enlightened; when we assume that the "I" is a separate and important (by itself) entity, we are in trouble.

13. Consciousness-maya (which is the cause of unknowing), indescribable and beginningless, is called the cause of restriction superimposed on Supreme Consciousness. Know for certain (however) that Supreme Consiousness is other than (and not really restricted by) the three vehicles of the soul (causal, astral and physical).

We cannot describe Consciousness as having a beginning because it is the root-cause of everything, the first cause, the only cause. We cannot fully describe It, however we may try, because the mind which perceives It is, itself, a product or an effect. The Self, the realized soul, can know the truth about Consciousness, but as long as the realized soul is working through a mind there must remain a thin veil of delusion. Maya, though a self-modification of Consciousness, veils the perception of ultimate truth from one involved with maya. This self-modification is essential to the purpose of creation, for without it, Consciousness could not become manifest and the world-process could not exist. Supreme

Consciousness, that aspect which is without modification or attributes, is other than the subtle vehicles of the soul and is not restricted by them at all.

The three vehicles of the soul here mentioned are: causal, astral, physical. The causal body is formed of the aforementioned divisions of prana, or vital force, and is possessed of the *inner organs*, of a subtle nature, which are later expressed through astral and physical forms. The astral body is made up of grosser energies and sustained by a "heart" which pumps vital force throughout. The astral eye is the *single eye* or the third eye. It is not an eye as we know a physical eye to be; it is a center of perception. It is also the distribution point through which down-flowing vital forces enter the astral and the physical bodies. Vital force flows down from the *crown chakra* in, and above, the higher brain area.

The Self, which is individualized Pure Consciousness, is likewise independent of the three bodies. Here is a subtle point; the Self is described as above, and is referred to as a soul only when identified with the mind and is, then, as a result, deluded. It is the soul-aspect of Consciousness which struggles, experiences in the world, and yearns for knowledge. The Self-aspect is ever free, even though individualized.

14. **On account of union with the five sheaths, the Supreme Consciousness appears to be like them, as is the case with a crystal, which appears to be endowed with such colors as blue or red (or any color, depending upon the color source) when in contact with a blue or red background.**

The author of this treatise stands firm in his exposition of eternal truths. Since Pure Consciousness is the cause of the subtle and gross elements, It cannot be them. Because of temporary identification it seems to reflect the characteristics of gross matter. The bodies, or vehicles, used by the Self, are sometimes referred to as *sheaths*; the Self uses the bodies, but wears them for a purpose. When a body ceases to function the Self continues to fulfill needed destiny.

15. **One should, through discrimination, separate the pure and inmost Consciousness from the sheaths by which It is covered, as one separates grain from the covering husk (or covering).**

There are several ways which are taught to seekers as possible ways to liberation of consciousness. *Hatha Yoga* practices insures health and correct body function and prepares one for the awakening and ascent of *kundalini*: the aspect of the vital force that usually resides in a dormant condition, until aroused, when it then ascends through the *chakra system* and becomes stabilized at the *crown chakra*. During this time-process internal changes are experienced, vital centers are quickened, the mind is made steady and eventually the transcendental experience is had. *Karma Yoga* is the way of selfless action; which insures that no more desires bind one to the future, presently active subconscious patterns can be handled and neutralized, and dormant ones dissolved. *Bhakti Yoga* is the way of personal surrender to God and the worship of God; which can lead to the transcendental experience. It can also lead to emotionalism and involvement in powerful feelings. *Raja Yoga* (the "royal" way) is the way of meditation; through mind regulation, concentration, and the transcendental experience. *Jnana Yoga* is the way of Self-Knowledge through the discernment process; it is the most subtle, but the safest way of all because it enables the practitioner to see clearly the nature of the Life process and does not accept any emotion, theory, or opinion which bars direct comprehension. There are other "yogas" but they are variations of these basic and traditional paths.

16. **Though all-pervading, Supreme Consciousness does not shine in everything; It is manifest only in the organ of intelligence, like a reflection in clear water, or in a stainless mirror.**

The *organ of intelligence* is almost clear, or translucent, and allows light to pass through. Because of this it is through the organ of intelligence that Supreme Consciousness is known. It is not clearly known through the other organs of the mind because the other organs serve other purposes and are not suitable for the transmission of Pure Knowledge. Supreme Consciousness pervades everything as the support and underlying being of all. Because the faculty of intelligence is an aspect of the mind and the mind is composed of "mixed" elements, when the Light of the Supreme is cognized through intelligence, then the one who is realizing the Supreme is defined as a soul.

17. Realize individualized Supreme Consciousness to be distinct from the body, sense organs, mind, intelligence and non-differentiated primal-nature. It is the witness of their func-ions and the ruler of them.

When resting in the full realization of our Real Nature, we know we are not any of the coverings, nor are we anything of a material nature. We use the term "material" to designate anything manifested, from subtle to gross levels; we use the term "physical" to mean the substance of the world we know through sense perception.

18. As the moon appears to be moving when the clouds move in the sky, so also, to the nondiscriminating, individualized Supreme Consciousness appears to be active when in reality only the senses are active.

Obviously, the impression that we sometimes have of the moon moving when only the clouds are moving, is due to faulty sense perception, however rational it may seem. Likewise, when the senses are active and we are caught up in the surge of feelings and thoughts, we assume the soul is restless and similarly caught up. We then say, "I am restless." "I am confused." Or, "I am sick." None of these can be really true of the Self, even if true of the body and mind. When we can rest in the conscious realization of our Real Nature, which is ever stable and bright, this realization can extend into the mental field and the physical body and healing is the effect.

19. The body, senses, mind and intelligence engage in their respec-tive activities with the help of Consciousness, which is inher-ent in the individualized Supreme Consciousness, just as men work with the help of the light inherent in the sun.

We are able to function and to operate through our bodies and sense organs because the light of Pure Consciousness infiltrates and nourishes. It would be foolish to state that without It we would not be able to function, *for without It we would would not exist.* It is wise for us to use our mind and body intelligently, but we

should never forget our basic nature as Consciousness and that
we are working *through* and not *as* a body, only.

20. **Foolish people, through nondiscrimination, superimpose upon
the stainless Supreme Consciousness which is Existence and
Consciousness Absolute, the characteristics and functions of
the body and senses, just as people attribute such traits as
blueness and the appearance of curved space to the sky.**

The author of these verses was skilled at debating with representatives of other philosophical schools and, therefore, is me-
thodical in his repeated emphasis concerning the nature of Supreme Consciousness as being clear and untouched by any of the
characteristics of nature. While this may seem repetitious to the
casual reader, let us be reminded that it can serve a purpose, and
tends to anticipate questions which might come from different
persons at different times. By "foolish" is meant being weak in
intellectual powers. One without the capaciy, or the inclination, to
correctly use the faculty of discernment is almost certain to draw
incorrect conclusions when examining any problem.

21. **As the movement that belongs to water is (sometimes) attributed, through ignorance, to the moon which is reflected in
it, so also, enjoyment and other limitations which belong to
the mind are falsely attributed to Supreme Consciousness.**

Here we touch on what is a sensitive subject to many people,
that of experiencing enjoyment. On the one hand a teacher will
be heard to say, "Self-Realization brings lasting joy and never-
ending bliss." On the other hand, teachers of liberation through
Self-Knowledge stress that enjoyment is made possible because
of the mind and ego-sense. A liberated person, to the eyes of one
who observes him, is happy and content, but notions of "how
good it feels" to be enlightened does not enter his mind. That is,
he is not motivated by the urge to enjoy, or the need to enjoy,
anymore than he is given to actions which will result in pain and
limitation. One who is established in the realization of the Self
experiences a bliss which is independent of sensory organs. In
many philosophical systems the mind is considered to be an extra-

sensory organ, because impressions are received by it and interpreted by it.

22. Attachment, desire, pleasure, pain and other misguiding urges and reactions are perceived to exist as long as intelligence and mind function. They are not perceived in deep sleep when the mind is no longer cognized. Therefore, they belong to the mind and not to Supreme Consciousness.

The first sentence of this verse refers to the ordinary waking state. It is true that we also experience a variety of feelings and urges during dreams. However, during dreamless sleep we identify more closely with the subtle vehicle of the soul and experience a detachment from the mental functions. This is why dreamless sleep is used as a crude comparison with the transcendental experience. Not that dreamless sleep, as a forever condition, is the ideal, only that one can analyze the condition and draw the conclusion that when attention is withdrawn from sensory organs and mental activities, a type of peace and serenity is realized. Also, at this time all problems vanish and all sense of difference recedes.

23. The nature of Supreme Consciousness is eternity, purity, reality, awareness and bliss, just as luminosity is the nature of the sun, coolness of water and heat of fire.

The natural condition of Pure Consciousness is as described and is not the result of qualities or imposed characteristics. When an enlightened person says, "My nature is bliss," he is stating a truth. He is not blissful because he has attained the spiritual heights, but because the nature of unrestricted awareness *is* bliss. Such bliss is not an emotion, or a feeling, in the common sense; it is the nature of Supreme Consciousness.

24. Such a notion as "I know" is produced by the union, due to nondiscrimination, of a modification of the mind with the two (manifest) aspects of Supreme Consciousness, namely existence and self-awareness.

It is taught that Supreme Consciousness remains ever un-attached to maya, the subtle fabric of the relative worlds, even though It works through it. The wave action of the mind is referred to as a modification. The memory of a past experience, or pre-viously observed object, as well as present perceptions, stimulates one or more of the electric attributes inherent in the mind. This starts a wave which gives rise to notions such as "I now know," or "I am happy." So it is not due to direct perception of the truth about Life that mental activity is initiated. To truly see life hap-penings as they are, is to be the thoughtless observer and to be content here and now. To be identified with memories, or overly involved with present happenings, is to be dependent upon exter-nals and to be open to such influences. This is why even-minded-ness is recommended as an essential for one seeking liberation. To have a mind which is even, in which waves do not interfere, is not to be uncaring; it is to be the observer, always balanced, always centered and composed.

25. Supreme Consciousness never undergoes change and the fac-ulty of intelligence is never endowed with consciousness (of its own). But man believes Supreme Consciousness to be iden-tical with the faculty of intelligence and falls under such delusions as that he is the seer and the knower.

Change is characteristic of the relative planes, not of the non-dual Pure Consciousness. The faculty of intelligence, being an organ of perception, is formed of the stuff of nature; it is not conscious, any more than the mind or body is conscious. It is Supreme Con-sciousness which shines through nature. It alone is conscious and as it expresses through nature we sometimes falsely assume that objects in nature have independent consciousness. Assumptions give rise to delusions.

26. The soul, regarding itself as an individualized living being, is overcome by fear, just like a man who regards a rope as a snake (when he sees it in a dim light). The soul regains fear-lessness by realizing it (the soul) is not an individualized entity but the Supreme Consciousness.

We have often stated that the soul *is* an individualization of Supreme Consciousness. This definition is given in general classes and books meant for wide readership because it comes close to the actual condition. The majority of seekers who are new on the path are not yet endowed with sufficient analytical powers to discern the true nature of things. In some scriptures soul is defined as "individualized Pure Consciousness which has become identified with nature." In other commentaries soul is defined as "the *reflection* of Pure Consciousness in the mind." In this latter definition one is asked to imagine a moon and its many reflections in many bodies of water. The reflections are not the moon itself, anymore than the reflection of Supreme Consciousness is Consciousness Itself.

Fears and all emotional reactions are due to our accepting the false notion that Life is not one, but many. In this verse the author is not suggesting that we not be observant concerning our relationships in the relative world, or that we not be practical. The rope-snake reference is used to point out how we often tend to react to what we think is before us instead of what is actually there. Due to the mixture of tendencies and attributes in nature and people, while we are functioning in the relative world we must use common sense. Wisdom should always take the upper hand in our relationships.

27. The mind, sense-organs and other body-parts are illumined by Supreme Consciousness alone, as a jar or a pot by a lamp (receives the light of the lamp). But these material objects cannot illumine themselves.

Again the point is made that it is the light of Supreme Consciousness that makes possible all seeming external lights. We might here consider the matter of liberation of consciousness. Liberation refers to freedom from bondage. As long as we are deluded into thinking that we are restricted, we are in need of liberation. Some schools teach that liberation is the result of a long difficult journey through various times and spaces, incarnation after incarnation. This is how it seems to be, to some. But, it is not essential that one look forward to "working out" his salvation by confronting karmic debts and building a spiritual consciousness. That we must be practical and learn to handle subconscious patterns is obvious. To think of building a spiritual consciousness is ignorance, for this implies further conditioning and further modification of the mental aspect of the body's nature. Spiritual consciousness is the result of awakening and knowledge; it is not the result of conditioning the mind. Liberation is possible only when Consciousness is detached from the mind, or when the point of view is changed from being a mind to resting in the awareness of the true Self. To an aware seeker who is intent upon liberation, any practice which does not result in freedom is to be avoided; any speculative philosophical systems that are offered to pacify the mind, or to settle the emotions by imparting false information, are a waste of time.

28. As a lighted lamp does not need another lamp to manifest its light, so the Supreme Consciousness does not need another instrument of consciousness to illumine Itself.

Supreme Consciousness is self-effulgent. It is the Light of lights. It is That by which all is made possible. It alone is Real (permanent and changeless); all else is unreal (subject to change). We are not here saying that sense-perceived objects are not discernible to the one who perceives them. They are "real" in that context. Seers speak of Consciousness as being Real and not in need of another support; all else we might observe is either a reflection, or an extension, of Consciousness.

29. By negating all restricting appearances through the help of scriptural statement, "It (Supreme Consciousness) is not this (the appearance), It is not this (whatever else might be perceived)," realize the oneness of the Self as Supreme Consciousness by means of the great affirmations and statements of the seers.

A scripture is not a mere book of philosophical speculation; it is revealed truth, given by enlightened sages who speak clearly of the essential nature of Life and the world. We are advised to counteract negative mental impressions and see through the appearances of the world by affirming that which is true. By affirmation we do not mean repetition of a formula, or phrase, to condition the mind; we mean to take a statement which contains the essence of what is true and dwell on it until our own realization is experienced. One way is to be reminded that no matter what we observe, from the vantage point of being an observer, cannot be our true nature. Nor can that which is observed be Supreme Consciousness, for It is experienced and not observed. The "help of a scriptural statement" is useful advice, for by contemplating the meaning behind such statements we are correctly instructed and our dormant awareness of the truth is awakened. This is why repeated study is recommended. A reader who scans this book once, or twice, and then moves on to one which is more "interesting" or "exciting" will be missing the point of the book's purpose. Not that several scriptures should not be studied, but they are to be carefully and repeatedly examined.

30. The body, mind and all modifications of them, created by Consciousness-*maya* and of the nature of objects, are perishable like bubbles. Realize through discrimination that you are the stainless Supreme Consciousness, completely apart from them.

All manifest things will one day pass away. As long as we persist in accepting ourselves as a thing, we will suffer pain and live in fear of eventual death. When we realize our nature to be Pure Consciousness, we can function in the world with understanding and in perfect peace. We *are*, already, Supreme Consciousness. This is our true nature, all the rest is the result of outer identification. When we affirm, with understanding, "This Self is Supreme Consciousness," we are not trying to take the place of God; we are merely affirming the truth. When we affirm that we are limited human beings we are affirming something which is false. In this philosophical presentation God is considered to be the Oversoul, or Cosmic Soul. Beyond God is Supreme Consciousness. To many, they are one and the same, and to follow this line of thought we could say, "All of nature and Supreme Consciousness are one and the same." Consciousness can produce nature out of Itself, but nature cannot produce Consciousness.

In some yoga systems it is taught that the goal is union with God. To come into a conscious working relationship with God is certainly not an inferior ideal. Those intent upon liberation through knowledge also want to realize the final truth about the nature of Consciousness. As the soul is Consciousness reflected in the mind, so the Godhead is Consciousness reflected in Universal Mind. It is further taught that if the soul does reach the level of "union with God," when the universes are dissolved, if liberation is not experienced, the soul may well be expelled into the new universal process when the process begins once more.

31. I am free of changes which are the inherent characteristics of matter; for I am other than the body. I am unattached to the sense-objects for I (Supreme Consciousness) am without sense organs.

It is obvious that one would not be able to make this statement without sense organs. When we express verbally we must use the organ of speech. Here, however, is a statement indicating high realization and one to be affirmed and contemplated. Contemplation is the act of flowing attention to a given object, or theme, in order to discern the truth inherent in it. This statement is not one to superficially repeat, but one to inwardly acknowledge.

32. I am free from sorrow, attachment, malice and fear; for I am other than the mind. "He (Supreme Consciousness) is without breath and without mind, pure, higher than the high and imperishable."

Since Supreme Consciousness is free of identification with mind, It is also free from all the tendencies to which the mind is an heir. In the affirmation, "He" refers to Supreme Consciousness. Of course, in the pure state such designations as "he," or "she," do not accurately apply. Here a relative reference is used. The male aspect, or positive polarity, impregnates the female aspect, or negative polarity. The male gives, the female receives. In Eastern scriptures First Cause is designated as male because It is the initial activating influence. Nature, or creation, is referred to as female because nature is receptive and responsive. These are convenient terms only. Since Pure Consciousness is not a person, no hint of supremacy relative to male, or female, characteristics is implied. "Higher than the high" refers to Supreme Consciousness as in contrast to It as manifesting as the Godhead. There is no great difference between Them; Supreme Consciousness is pure, or without attributes; the Godhead is Supreme Consciousness with attributes; therefore, dual expressions of the same Thing.

33. From Supreme Consciousness are born breath, mind and all organs of the senses, subtle matter, air, light, water and earth, and Supreme Consciousness supports them all.

From the true Source are born, or are projected, all modifications and forms in the universe. Everything emerges from that primal Something, for things cannot come out of nothing. A magnetic field is produced, then from the negative polarity there flows a current which modifies as it becomes more gross, until the physical realms are manifested. *Tamas guna*, the electric attribute of inertia, makes this possible. *Sattva guna* is the positive polarity which eventually redeems the worlds. *Rajas guna*, the neutralizing current, makes possible the activity in nature and the eventual balancing of the pairs of opposites.

34. I am without attributes and action, eternal and pure, free from stain and desire, changeless and formless and always free.

Though everything in manifestation is possessed of attributes and is in motion, Pure Consciousness rests serene and free from Its outer projection. The verse is ideal for contemplation and will lead one to the experience of the transcendental plane.

35. I fill all things, inside and out, like subtle matter-space. Changeless and the same in all, I am pure, unattached, stainless and immutable.

Pervading everything, similar to space which is material, but not qualified as space is, Supreme Consciousness is the support of all that appears. It is not "above" this material plane in the sense that *above* is a direction upward; It resides at the inmost center of everything, even within us, for we are advised by seers to "seek out the truth of existence in the heart." Heart here means the center, the core, the basis of things.

36. I am verily that Supreme Consciousness, which is eternal, stainless and free; which is One, indivisible and nondual; and which is of the nature of Bliss, Truth, Knowledge and Infinity.

One, in the sense that Supreme Consciousness is not related to anything else. It is the only Reality, Infinity, in that It is not identified with time. To paraphrase, one might say, "I will have no other Goal before me." Even when one is worshipping God, or an aspect of the Godhead, one can remember that behind the *form* is that which makes the form possible. Even though one listens, with respect, to one's teacher, or guru, one can remember that behind the form of the teacher, or guru, is that which makes them both possible.

37. The impression of "I am Supreme Consciousness," which comes as a result of uninterrupted reflection, destroys ignorance and its distractions, as a special medicine destroys disease.

The word "impression" is correct, for when one can state "I am Supreme Consciousness," it is the result of a mental impression even though realization is almost clear. If one were really nondual and transcendent one would not make the statement, one would merely *be*. Uninterrupted reflection, steady meditation and contemplation on the highest ideal, with devotion and yearning to know, has been extolled as the certain route to enlightenment. The "special medicine" referred to is an ancient concoction, a compound of mercury and sulphur thought to contain powerful cleansing and restorative influences.

38. Sitting in a solitary place, freeing the mind from desires, and controlling the senses, meditate with unswerving attention on the Infinite and Supreme Consciousness-Reality which is nondual.

Qualified yoga teachers do not discredit other forms of meditation, but the emphasis here is contemplation on the non-dual aspect of Consciousness, in order to rise free of all possible restricting influences. The suggestion here is to practice meditation as explained in the *Yoga Sutras* of Patanjali: to free the mind from desires by purposely withdrawing attention and vital force from the senses, which is the practice of pranayama (control of vital forces); to be restrained, so that no temptation to flow outward remains; to concentrate, or focus the attention at one point; to continue this flowing of attention, or to meditate; then, to finally transcend identification and experience Pure Consciousness. This is a scientific, practical and result-getting procedure.

In this meditation procedure we even rise free of the electric attributes in the mind and above the feeling nature; for as long as we retain identification with the electric attributes and the feeling nature, there is the possibility of mind-waves being generated. If we experience visions, strong feelings, or expanded states, we are still identified with the modifications of nature, no matter how "cosmic" the experience seems to be. So long as we retain identification with mind and feeling nature, whatever seems to be realization might well be an *impression* of realization; that is, we catch a glimpse of Truth but it then becomes reflected in the mind as an impression. We then tend to think in terms of partial-knowledge of the nature of Reality. This experience gives rise to the attitude expressed in the statement: "I feel I know the truth, but I am not sure I do."

39. **The wise person should intelligently merge the entire objective world in Supreme Consciousness alone and constantly think of that Reality as the stainless sky.**

Intelligently, that is with discernment, one should meditate and merge (dissolve) ideas of the world into the clear, non-dual aspect of Consciousness. As far as the eye can see, the clear sky has nothing which disturbs the perception; so one should consider Supreme Consciousness as being clear and without any pattern or form to obstruct It. This is known as meditating on the Absolute, or Pure Existence.

40. **He who has attained the Supreme Goal discards all such objects as name and form and dwells as the embodiment of Infinite Consciousness and bliss.**

To discard name and form does not mean, in our society, to

dramatize outer renunciation and cease to use names for things and to use objects without prudence; it means to see clearly, and forever realize, that names are for convenience and forms are to be wisely related to. To cease to be attached to things, even while functioning intelligently in the world, is to be a renunciate of the highest order.

41. The Supreme Consciousness, because Its nature is exceeding bliss, does not admit to any distinction of the knower, knowledge, or the object of knowledge. It alone shines.

Samadhi is a Sanskrit term meaning "to bring into even-ness." When the waves no longer arise in the mental field during meditation, the mind can be a clear reflector in which the Light of Consciousness can shine. As long as we are aware that we are experiencing, or that we know, we are still in a dualistic condition. This is the lower samadhi, or, *savikalpa* samadhi; it is samadhi with mental support, with a seed image in the mind. The higher experience is *nirvikalpa* samadhi: that which is without mental support. If one is not satisfied with the lower samadhi and continues to yearn for Knowledge, the mind will, in time, become purified and the higher samadhi will be experienced. Many meditators settle for less than the ultimate realization and are content to merge with an attribute of Consciousness; such as light, bliss, power, love, cosmic consciousness, and so on.

42. By constant meditation the flame of Pure Knowledge arises, which completely burns up the causes of ignorance.

The more we gain access to the realization of our true nature, the more we experience a transforming flow of energy, which has its origin in the transcendental field, and this neutralizes and burns out seeds of karma and all latent mental impressions which restrict clear realization. Every time we come out of meditation and retain the awareness of the experience, we open ourselves to this flow of high-frequency energy which has a cleansing and redemptive effect upon the organism. It is also likely that kundalini will awaken and, when it does, powerful upward surges will enliven the system, cleanse the nerves, calm the mind and make meditation easier.

Teachers of the way of Knowledge stress contemplation on the highest ideal, rather than over-emphasis upon the other basic yogic practices. They know that with awakening all will work out well, and the internal processes will be spontaneous. If we yearn to really know the truth about life, and contemplate Supreme Consciousness, we will be led into the path which is best for us and Innate Intelligence will be the true guide.

43. As the sun appears after the banishing of darkness by the coming of dawn, so Supreme Consciousness appears after the signs of ignorance have been dissolved by knowledge.

The "signs of ignorance" are the impressions and obstructions in the mental field. Pure Consciousness cannot be known as long as they remain, or until they are transcended in the quiet of meditation. Once steady realization of Pure Consciousness is a matter of course, delusion is banished entirely. There is then no danger of one ever falling back into unknowingness. However, as long as mental impressions remain, regardless of how high one might rise, there is the possibility of one's drifting from the former high resolve and becoming again entangled in the snare of the senses and in the confusion of thoughts. The positive impressions made on the mental field, by early intense practice of spiritual disciplines and meditations, will remain and eventually bring the person back on the path of conscious effort which can lead to realization. No gain is ever lost, no right attempt is ever wasted.

44. Though Supreme Consciousness is an ever-present reality, because of ignorance It is unrealized. When ignorance is dissolved then Supreme Consciousness is realized. Failure to realize Reality is often due to one's looking in the wrong place for it.

Even for one who is deluded and confused, the essential nature is always bright and shining, though not consciously realized. When one awakens from the "mortal dream," then Reality is known. One cannot realize the truth about Reality if one does not know where, or how, to look. The classic example given in this context is that of a woman who mistakenly thinks her necklace is lost and looks frantically for it, not knowing it hangs around her neck all the while. It is true that we go the route of study, counsel, trial and error, and association with teachers and a guru. The real search is within, but outer aids can be useful. Wise teachers suggest: the best study is that of scripture; the best counsel is taken from fully realized persons; the best association is with a teacher, or guru, who is firmly established in the highest realization.

45. **Supreme Consciousness appears to be a soul because of (temporary) forgetfulness (on the part of the soul). This sense of individuality is banished when the real nature of the soul is realized.**

When Supreme Consciousness is reflected in a mental field and one takes the reflection for the Real existence, then the Real existence is temporarily forgotten. "Temporarily," because reflections eventually cease to be reflections when the Source of the light is cognized. Steady reminding of one's self of the true nature, behind body and personality, results in Self-remembering. Hence the advice: "Remember how it was with you before you forgot." And the Zen master's request of the student: "Show me your original face." Our real nature, before forgetting, was Pure Consciousness with no delusion. Our *original face* is Pure Consciousness.

46. **The knowledge produced by the realization of the true nature of Reality destroys immediately the ignorance characterized by the notions of "I" and "mine," as the light of the sun solves problems regarding directions mistakenly taken in the dark.**

The notions of the ego-sense are caused, so sages declare, by the accumulation of subconscious impressions carried over from the past. Until these are worked out, or neutralized, as long as one is in the body one will notice some obstruction to the flow of Divine Power. Therefore, either at physical death, when the karmic patterns are exhausted (and we are absorbed in the contemplation of the Absolute) or before physical death if karma is neutralized, we will be stable in the highest realization. Some teach that final liberation is possible only after the body and the subtle sheaths are discarded. Yet, if Supreme Consciousness is obviously free of entanglements, even though projecting the worlds, why can we not rest in the realization of the truth about life and still function through a body in this world?

47. The liberated soul endowed with complete enlightenment sees, through the eye of pure knowledge, the entire universe in his own Self and regards everything as the Supreme Consciousness (in manifestation) and nothing else.

A truly liberated person has no entanglements with any aspect of nature, even though he works within the framework of natural happenings. To be endowed means, in this instance, to be in firm possession of Knowledge, without any conflicting concept or opinion. Knowing the Self, which is the only Reality, a liberated person sees Consciousness as everything and everyone. The whole of manifest creation is then cognized as the body of Consciousness.

48. The tangible universe is verily Supreme Consciousness in manifestation; nothing whatsoever exists that is other than Supreme Consciousness. As clay pots and jars cannot be anything but clay, so, to the enlightened person, all that is perceived is Pure Consciousness (in outward manifestation).

Supreme Consciousness is cause, and the universe is effect; the universe floats on a screen of consciousness and is said to be due to the imaginative intention of the Supreme. Just as cause and effect are one, so Supreme Consciousness and Its effect are one. Only the appearances and the names differ.

49. The liberated soul, endowed with knowledge of the Supreme Consciousness, gives up the traits of previous restricting characteristics. Because of his realization that he is of the nature of Existence-Knowledge-Bliss Absolute, he knows himself as Supeme Consciousness.

A person who is spiritually free while embodied, in possession of true Knowledge, ceases to identify with the traits characteristic of his prior limited lifestyle. He is no longer restrained by maya and lives under grace, always. When we are open to the flow of energy, and direction, which originates in the Transcendental Field, our life is lived not from an ego-sense but from the highest level. Here one can affirm, "I and Supreme Consciousness are one and the same." This does not mean that the embodied liberated person has control of the universal processes, but he knows he is a wave on the ocean, and the wave is the ocean *appearing as*.

50. A liberated soul, after crossing the ocean of delusion and rising above passion (and other feelings and urges which restrict), becomes one with peace and dwells in the bliss derived from the realization of Supreme Consciousness alone.

Since peace and bliss are innate with Supreme Consciousness, one who is settled in the highest realization quite naturally is the embodiment of peace and bliss. This peace is not the kind of temporary stillness resulting from holding tendencies and urges at bay; it is the peace that surpasses human understanding. We are to rise above passion and move in a new and transcendent state of consciousness. To suppress powerful urges can be psychologically destructive. To channel energies properly and to refine the sensibilities is the far more creative approach. Also, to the degree that the transcendental experience is had, the passions and urges are transmuted.

51. Relinquishing attachment to illusory external happiness, the Self-realized perfect being, satisfied with the bliss experienced in Supreme Consciousness, shines inwardly and thus illumines the world.

The average person is identified with sense-perceived things only, and his inner light flows out to cognize the world. A liberated person flows the searchlight of attention within and abides in the realization of the true nature. The worldly person's mind is darkened with sense impressions; the enlightened person's mind is illumined with the radiance of Consciousness. When, in the New Testament, we are admonished to, "Let that mind be in you which was in Christ Jesus," we are being invited to accept the power and the glory of Supreme Consciousness into our mental field, and very existence on earth. We can then know, "I am the light of the world." We do not speak of the personality, but of the manifesting Supreme Consciousness which is shining through the pure mental field of the master.

52. **Though associated with the restricting senses (and other aspects and attributes of nature), he, the contemplative one, is undefiled by their traits, clear like the sky, and he remains unmoved and unchanged under all conditions. He moves through life unattached.**

Even though associated with body, mind and senses, the liberated person views these from the vantage point of the witness. He is, therefore, not restricted or deceived. Even when the body undergoes changes common to nature, such as aging and adjustments in body chemistry, a liberated person's consciousness is untouched. Nothing stays him from his appointed course of responsible action He works always in harmony with natural laws and for the good of mankind and the world. Supreme Consciousness through him is able to carry out Its preordained plan of world enlightenment and planetary transformation. He dwells in the body for as long as the urgings of unspent karma demand; occasionally he will even remain longer, if work yet remains by an act of Divinely personalized will.

53. **Upon the dissolution of the restricting characteristics of the various bodies (sheaths) he, the contemplative one, is totally absorbed in Supreme Consciousness, which is all-pervading: like water in water, space in space and light in light.**

Without the suggestion of individuality, after the momentum of subconscious impressions have been exhausted, the liberated person drops the body and all subtle sheaths and is again Supreme Consciousness without restriction, as before self-forgetting. If water is sealed in a container and submerged in water, when the container is opened, or broken, there will no longer be any separation of the water. Leaving the physical body does not alone insure liberation; for the subtle sheaths and the mind can yet retain the soul's identification. But, when all "containers" are discarded, Supreme Consciousness is the Reality.

For a person to fear total awakening in Supreme Consciousness is as groundless as it is for a person who is dreaming, while asleep, to fear consciousness. It is not selfish of one to become Self-realized; it is the natural evolutionary trend. Some become Self-realized, and others do not. Some awaken partially and serve those who have yet to awaken, as guides and teachers of humanity. A few who are fully liberated remain in the body, not because of karma, but to do the will of God. That is, God works through available instruments and does as He wills to insure the orderly transformation of the world. A fully liberated soul, working on a God-sent mission, is referred to as an *avatara*, which means "the descent of divinity into flesh."

54. Realize that to be Supreme Consciousness, the attainment which leaves nothing more to be attained, the blessedness of which leaves no other bliss to be desired, and the knowledge of which, leaves nothing more to be known.

55. Realize that to be Supreme Consciousness which, when seen leaves nothing more to be seen, having become which one is not born again into the world of becoming, and which, when known, leaves nothing else to be known.

56. Realize that to be Supreme Consciousness which is Existence-Knowledge-Bliss Absolute, which is nondual and infinite, eternal and One, and which fills all the quarters: all that is above and below and all that exists in between.

57. Realize that to be Supreme Consciousness which is non-dual, indivisible, One, and blissful and which is indicated by the teachings of the seers as the irreducible substratum after the negation of all tangible objects.

In these verses the author affirms the highest truth in a manner which inspires and motivates. One feels an inner response to these affirmations because one *knows*, at the deepest level of being, that all that is affirmed is a certainty. Functioning at a level of

even partial unknowing, there is yet more to be seen; having realized the Supreme Reality, however, one has seen all there is to see.
The quest is at an end and one resides in Knowledge Itself. Having
experienced the Reality, in contrast to the *reflection*, one is no
longer born into the relative worlds; the worlds characterized by
the trends of time, or becoming. Some sages teach students on the
path: "God is ever-new, the realizations are never-ending." Yet,
upon experiencing Pure Consciousness, there is nothing more to
realize. Inherent in Pure Consciousness are bliss, timelessness and
being. Awakening to the awareness of our real nature we know
these to be our own essence. They are not modifications or characteristics, for Supreme Conscousness is without dualistic characteristics. This is incomprehensible to man, one who works through
mind, but is the nature of Pure Consciousness.

**58. Even the gods and goddesses taste only a particle of the un-
limited bliss of Supreme Consciousness and enjoy, in proportion to their purity, their shares of that segment of bliss.**

The "gods" and "goddesses" are said to be highly realized persons who have access to the *sphere of God*. This is the sphere of
Supreme Consciousness with attributes; therefore, the totality of
bliss is not "tasted" or enjoyed. We cannot divide Supreme Consciousness into segments, for it is indivisible, but to attempt an
explanation we say that a portion of Supreme Consciousness
manifests as the known universe, which is trillions of light years
across. By our measurements the universe is not endless, it is
bounded and space curves back upon itself. Yet, "outside" of
space Pure Consciousness remains, as it remains "inside" of space.
It is the basis, the substratum, the foundation of appearances;
that is, of subtle and gross modifications of nature, the causes and
the outer expression of forms.

The shining beings, even if without karma, are somewhat restricted by the modifications of their subtle vehicles: the causal
organs of perception and action. Therefore, they cannot know the
full Reality of Pure Consciousness. They are sometimes born into
lower realms such as causal, astral and (sometimes) physical
in order to continue their works and participate in the stream of
life.

59. All manifest objects are pervaded by Supreme Consciousness, all actions are possible because of It; therefore, Supreme Consciousness permeates everything but is not limited to the relationship.

The initial three aspects of Supreme Consciousness in manifestation are the triune characteristics of the Godhead: Existence; Consciousness-Intelligence; Energy flowing and cognized as Aum (Om, Amen), the Word, or Sound Current. At the positive pole of this initial magnetic field is the Existence aspect; God the Father, Brahma, or *Sat*. This aspect is stable and perfectly reflects Pure Consciousness and is known as the highest, or most pure, Truth. At the negative pole of this initial magnetic field is the Creative Energy: The Holy Spirit, *Shiva*, whose nature is bliss (*ananda*) and is discerned as the Sound Current. Between the poles is "the first begotten of the Father," or Consciousness-Intelligence, the Christ Consciousness, *Vishnu*. The Holy Spirit (*Shiva*) aspect makes possible the production of the worlds by flowing outward as almost-pure energy, then becoming modified as various planes and dimensions. This process is under the intelligent direction of Consciousness, the Christ aspect or essence. The Existence aspect is stable and maintains everything else, as well as eventually draws the universes back into the Godhead. There is creation, or manifestation, preservation and dissolution of the worlds. This takes place time and time again as part of the cosmic process. We are told that this is taking place in "other times and other spaces" also. All persons of realization have known of this process as a result of direct inner perception and have recorded their realizations which have become the great scriptures of the world. Seers and true prophets do not write to satisfy their own immature needs, for they have none; they write from inner realization. Therefore, such scriptures are said to be "revealed truth" and are not the product of anyone's imaginings.

60. Realize that to be Supreme Consciousness which is neither subtle nor gross; neither short nor long; without birth and change; without form, qualities or attributes.

61. Realize that to be Supreme Consciousness by the light of which

luminous orbs like the suns and moons are illumined, but which cannot be illumined by *their* light, but, instead, is that by which everything is illumined.

Since Pure Consciousness is without attributes It is impossible to fully describe. Therefore, one approach is to state what It is *not*. After negating, or setting aside, all that It cannot be, It remains. Here, "qualities" refer to the three electric attributes, or *gunas* which pervade nature. Even though the moon, in this world, is illumined by the sun and the sun, by relative standards, has its own light, the sun could not exist if it were not for Supreme Consciousness. Therefore, the *light* which makes possible all mundane lights is that of Pure Consciousness. No person has power of his own; his power has its origins in Pure Consciousness, flowing from the Godhead. This is why we say that there is One Power, One Presence, and One Being in the universe: God.

62. The Supreme Consciousness pervades the entire universe without and within and shines of Itself.

63. Supreme Consciousness is other than the manifest universe. There truly exists nothing that is not Supreme Consciousness. If any object appears to have independent reality it is an illusion, like a mirage reflected in heat waves.

This is the core of non-dualistic teaching. If this is understood, all else will be understood. One Thing exists: Supreme Consciousness. It is pure and it is impure; purity and impurity here do not relate to desirable or undesirable, good or bad, high or low, but to It being *without* attributes and *with* attributes. Without attributes It is Pure Supreme Consciousness; with attributes It is manifest as all that is. If we apply a name or label to an object and declare that it has independent existence, we are in error. The universe is not in error, it is not an illusion; *our faulty opinion of the universe is the basis for our own sense of illusion.* Therefore, like a mirage on a desert which is a reflection of something else, made possible by heat waves, what we see and touch is a reflection of something else, made possible by maya and our own faulty judgment. If we are not enlightened we tend to project, to assume, and draw conclusions based on faulty judgment and conditioned thought processes. The world we perceive is real in that it is Consciousness *appearing-as* we perceive it, but it is not what it seems to be to the ordinary sense perception.

64. All that is perceived, all that is heard, is Supreme Consciousness (in manifestation) and nothing else. Attaining the knowledge of Reality, one sees the universe as the non-dual Supreme Consciousness.

65. Though Supreme Consciousness is Reality and is ever present everywhere, It is perceived by the eye of wisdom alone. But one whose vision is obscured by ignorance (and false perception) does not see the radiant Reality, as the blind do not see the resplendent sun.

The truth about the Life Process cannot be totally known through the senses alone. One must use the "eye of wisdom," the faculty of discernment, if one is to know the truth. We might analyze the nature of the organic world and come to some understanding about the nature of the Life Process.We might turn within and perceive the subtle realms and, thereby, understand even more of the glory of creation. But this will still be the perception and apprehension of dualistic phenomena. Only when we see *through* the appearances to the Cause and Sustainer of it all, will we really be possessed of perfect knowledge. It is commonly believed that one can start where he is and gradually learn "more and more truth" until he works his way to final realization. Seers declare that it is possible for one to meditate correctly and discern the highest, or clearest, aspect of Life and, thereby, understand the entire cosmic process from the point of origin to the fullest outer expression. The *way of knowledge and wisdom* is not for the faint in heart, nor for the one lacking in courage. A seeker whose attitude is one of, "I will get there sometime," is not the ideal student to tread this path. There are other disciplines for those who are content to work in the realms of qualities and attributes, and they are useful as preparation: to attune the mind and clear the accumulation of obstructing impressions.

66. The Self-realized soul, being purified in the fires of knowledge (arrived at by discipline, study and meditation) shines
like gold.

The basic disciplines are for the purpose of clearing away obstructions of body and mind, transmuting energies into a more
subtle essence, and directing attention to useful goals. Ideal study
is that of contemplating the meaning behind the scriptures. One
can use reason, if all data is known and the mind is well-ordered,
or one can use the contemplative process to discern truth. When
unwanted matters are removed from gold, gold is then pure. When,
through the fires of discipline, the undesirable qualities are removed
from the consciousness of the seeker, he shines and is the visible
organ of the resplendent Light.

67. Supreme Consciousness, which is the sun of knowledge, arises
in the firmament of the heart and dissolves the darkness. The
Pervader of all and the Sustainer of all, It illumines all as well
as Itself.

The true Source of light is Supreme Consciousness and is referred to as "the sun of knowledge." It reflects (arises) in the intellectual organ of the mind (the firmament of the heart) and darkness is immediately eradicated.

68. He who, renouncing all (selfish) activites, worships in the sacred
and stainless shrine of Supreme Consciousness, which is independent of time, place and distance; which is present everywhere; which is the destroyer of heat and cold and the other
opposites; and which is the giver of eternal happiness, becomes
all-knowing and all-pervading and attains immortality.

The shrine of Supreme Consciousness is the organ of discernment; without using discernment one will not be able to tell the
difference between what is Real, versus what is the appearance.
It is possible that one might also "worship" in the crown chakra
and, thus, be swept into clear realization by the ascending energy
flows. Liberation is natural to one who worships Supreme Consciousness with surrendered yearning, clear mental powers and
total soul absorption.

Appendix

SUPPLEMENTAL NOTES
Chapter One

Truth, it is taught, has its origins in Pure Consciousness and not with any particular person or with any specific geographical location. For the past few thousand years, at least, the enlightenment teachings have traveled from East to West. This is because the East is the home of more ancient civilizations and there the science of soul discovery was carefully researched. The basic information we now possess has filtered down through the ages through several lines of illumined teachers known as the masters of perfection. Little is known concerning man on our planet before 4,000 B.C. We have legends, we have folk tales, and we have the traditions of various occult historians. Some evidence exists to indicate that human beings have been around on Earth for hundreds of thousands of years. Perhaps the rise and fall of civilization and occasional cataclysms explain long lapses in recorded history.

Scholars of the Vedas teach that their body of knowledge regarding the nature of the universe goes back through at least one hundred thousand years. Some of the most intricate explanations about the nature of Consciousness are to be found in Sanskrit texts. Both inner and outer, esoteric and exoteric, traditions have their roots in the Vedas. All great philosophical systems have been influential as essential streams of knowledge. The outer teachings deal with codes of human ethics, morality, and social convenience. The inner teachings reveal the purpose and intent of the creative urge of Life. Through history we see how Vedic influence illumined the fabric of philosophical teachings. We see a mingling of Platonism and the doctrines of the Essenes, resulting in the formation of esoteric Christianity and, then, to insure its survival in the Dark Age, the form given it by Constantine. The Egyptians, Persians, Chinese, and Jewish people owe their religious teachings to the lightbearers of the human race. Even the fraternities, such as the Freemasons, were offshoots of teachings of Vedic times. The esoteric schools grade their initiations to coincide with the steady realizations of the awakening soul on the spiritual path.

The world knows of a few superior types: Akhenaten, the restorer of the mystical tradition among the Egyptians; Hermes Trismegistus, the thrice-great master of the Alchemic and Hermetic Mysteries of Alexandria; Zoroaster, the sage of ancient Persia; Buddha, the great reformer of East Indian religion and one of the greatest philosophers of his time; Confucius, the practical moralist of China; Lao-Tse, whose metaphysical speculations constitute the deepest religious teachings of the Chinese; Orpheus, the Grecian lord of music and noble theologist; Jesus, around whose life and teachings the Christian faith has been integrated; Quetzalcoatl, who, it is said, brought the secrets of the Atlantean religion to the ancient peoples of America; Plato, a most powerful philosophical force in the western world; Mohammed, Prophet of Islam, who sought to restore basic religion to humanity; and there are others.

Vedic influence moved into many world cultures over the centuries, due to the travels of seekers and of certain teachers. The Eastern branch moved through Asia and the Western branch moved through Greece and was carried to the Near East by Moses, a priest of the Egyptians. Many of the philosophical giants of Greece were initiates of Vedic teachings. Pythagoras actually went to India to learn from the sages there. Plato tried to go but wars along the travel route prevented his journey. The early Christian Church, for instance, accepted the doctrine of reincarnation, which was taught by initiate-teachers. Clement of Alexandria, Origen, and St. Jerome expounded at length on the doctrine. It was in A.D. 553 that the doctrine of reincarnation was declared a heresy by the Second Council of Constantinople. This decision was not the result of any personal revelation, it was a matter of convenience. A vote was taken and the organization men won.

In his work *Mystic Masonry*, J.D. Buck, M.D., summarized the relationship between Vedic tradition and the descent of the Esoteric Schools. He refers to Vedic seers as the sublime lights of the Lodge and discusses the Adept tradition, explaining how the sages transmit, in ways most expedient, the truth about life. The exoteric schools, lodges, and fraternities are then but "fragments of a faith forgotten."

For reasons best known to themselves, many masters of per--fection have chosen retreat areas in the Himalayas. It is of no value for the average seeker to think of traveling to the abodes of the masters in the hope of receiving personal instruction. Before sitting at the feet of a perfect master most people are advised to attend to necessary preliminary disciplines and preparations. Sometimes, when the student is ready, such contact is possible, either on the inner planes or by personal contact. Apollonius of Tyana, it is written, traveled to India to spend four months with secluded sages. He revealed little of his experiences. In one written excerpt of his we learn: "I saw men dwelling on the earth and yet not of it; defended on all sides, yet without any defense, and yet possessed of nothing but all possess."

In Europe, during the Middle Ages, initiate-teachers were known only to each other because of the Dark Age ignorance which prevailed. They were, at times, able to advise political leaders and make such contributions through their writings and scientific "discoveries" as the general condition of consciousness would allow. Rather than arouse the opposition of the established church, these men worked quietly. The alchemists and other secret workers of that time-period emphasized that their teachers were the same as those once taught by the ancient sage Hermes Trismegistus, an Egyptian initiate, whom the Egyptians identified with Thoth, the scribe of the Gods. Among the Middle Age alchemists are Albertus Magnus, Roger Bacon, and Raymond Lully. The Masons were originally a group of adepts who studied the laws of geometry and proportion in order to build temples which would inspire and raise the consciousness of those who knew nothing of their secret purpose.

The early Rosicrucians and the Brotherhood of the Golden Cross specialized in the natural sciences and studied celestial movements and their effects (astrology), and also alchemy, or the composition of matter. The seventeenth century German alchemist Paracelsus worked to develop the concept of chemical specificity, a cornerstone of modern medicine. The Knights Templar channeled their energies into commerce and cultural exchange, bringing a wealth of material and scientific benefit to the West from Arabic and Greek lands.

Enlightened people are universal in their outlook and understanding. An ancient prayer is: "That which is called God by the Christians, Jehovah by the Jews, Ultimate Reality by the Hindus, the Buddhamind by Buddhists, Allah by Mohammedans, and which the Chinese call the Tao—that is the real Self and is all-pervading. May we experience that!"

The Flow of Virtue

In the *New Testament (St. Mark 5: 25-34)* the story is related of how a woman in need of healing walked close behind Jesus and touched his garment. So great was her faith and so immediate the outflow of healing current that she was instantaneously healed. Again, in the *New Testament (St. John 15: 5)* we read a most revealing verse: "I am the vine, ye are the branches: He that abideth in me, and I in him, the same bringeth forth much fruit: for without me ye can do nothing." Jesus was obviously speaking from the level of Christ Consciousness and clearly taught that people in human consciousness should awaken to the realization of their true spiritual connection with God.

Chapter Two

Enlightenment is more than a partial awakening. True enlightenment is total Self-understanding and comprehension of the nature of Consciousness. Enlightenment, Illumination, Cosmic Consciousness, and Revelation are just some of the terms used to describe the conscious knowing of the truth about life. People who have experienced illumination have often shared their perceptions. Richard Maurice Buck, M.D., in his classic *Cosmic Consciousness*, wrote of some of the characteristics which seem to accompany illumination. Among these characteristics is a marked intellectual acuteness. Also, moral elevation, an all-embracing optimism, and the sense of immortality. In our examination of enlightenment experiences we see that every awakened person, while feeling an attunement with cosmic forces, is made aware of the importance of using the new abilities for the benefit of the human race. Never do we find an enlightened person misusing his powers.

Sometimes dramatic happenings occur during times of mystic rapture. John Yepes (St. John of the Cross, 1542-1591) wrote: "After some time certain rays of light, comfort and divine sweetness scattered these mists and translated the soul of the servant of God into a paradise of interior delights and heavenly sweetness." It is also recorded of this mystic that others could observe brilliant light emanating from his body, especially after prayer or after performing a religious ritual at the altar.

Jacob Boehme (1575-1624) of Germany, also considered a case of illumination, wrote: "You are a little world formed out of the larger one, and your external light is a chaos of the sun and constellations of stars. If this were not so you would not be able to see by the light of the sun." Again, "Not I, the I that I am, knows these things: but God knows them in me."

William Blake (1757-1827) said: "The world of imagination is the world of eternity. It is the divine bosom into which we shall all go after the death of this vegetated body. This world of imagination is infinite and eternal, whereas the world of generation, of vegetation, is finite and temporal. There exists in that eternal world the permanent realities of everything which we see reflected in this vegetable glass of nature."

Honoré de Balzac, considered by some as the greatest name in the post-Revolutionary literature of France, once asked a friend: "Are you certain that your soul has had its full development? Do you breathe in air through every pore of it? Do your eyes see all they can see?"

Consider the words of Walt Whitman, as he tried to share his enlightenment experience: "Swiftly arose and spread around me the peace and joy and knowledge that pass all the art and argument of the earth; and I know that the hand of God is the elder hand of my own, and I know that the spirit of God is the eldest brother of my own . . . ."

Alfred Tennyson, in *Ancient Sage*, wrote: "More than once

when I sat all alone, revolving in myself the word that is the symbol of myself, the mortal limit of the Self was loosed, and passed into the nameless, as a cloud melts into heaven.''

What is it, we ask, which determines who shall experience enlightenment and who shall not? Obviously, it is the readiness of the soul for the experience which is the determining factor: this, plus the readiness of the brain and nervous system to handle the greater flow of fine energy. Mental unfoldment is a common result of enlightenment experiences as thought-transcending things are known through direct intuitive perception and the powers of the intellect become more evident. Frequently, the physical body also becomes transformed due to the influence of awakened vital forces. As energies flow upward into the brain the brain learns to adapt to the flow of force and becomes refined. All of the glands and systems of the body also work more efficiently when stress is removed and fine energies flow without disturbance.

The Nature of the Soul

Vedic seers explain that what we call the soul is *the light of Supreme Consciousness reflecting in the aspect of the mind known as the organ of intelligence.* That concise definition can be examined during occasions of contemplation with great benefit.

The masters teach that the major error of an unawakened person is to confuse soul with mind and body and to then think in terms of having a soul instead of being one. Seers such as Shankara wrote many treatises about the importance of calm Self-analysis with the end in view of experiencing the truth about life through the process of discernment. An example of this emphasis is to be found in the latter segment of this book, titled *The Wisdom Yoga of Shankaracharya.*

Purpose in Life

An essential aspect of our spiritual training lies in learning to be conscious of what is being experienced, always. My guru taught me to give attention to even routine activities in order to live in the moment and to experience to the fullest. He taught that when one gives full attention to what is being experienced, great powers of concentration are developed which can then be used with benefit during occasions of meditation and inner contemplation. When we are living with a sense of true purpose we are living as fully liberated beings. Many make the mistake of thinking that present work is going to result in future enlightenment. They do not realize that by living consciously in the moment, the purpose of spiritual training is fulfilled.

Chapter Three

Because of the combination of elements, frequencies of subtle nature which combine to form gross elements are referred to as subtle elements.

The elements referred to are: ether (subtle form of matter), air, fire, water, and earth (gross form of matter). In ancient texts of India, known as Ayurveda (The Science of Life), the matter of health and well-being is approached from a very subtle direction, based on an analysis of the influences of natural elements on the system. Everything is a manifestation of prana or life-force. We have said in an earlier lesson that this life-force appears as mind and extends as matter. Thus, we are dealing always with One Thing, even if It does change in frequency and mode of function. The approach here is to encourage the natural working of subtle elements in the system so that the gross or outer effects are ideal to health and to well-being. We even work at the level of ions (an electrically charged atom or group of atoms). Some components of ions making up compounds (salts, bases, acids) are thought to be held together by electrical attraction. In one of the old texts (*Taittiriya Upanishad*), we read: "The elements require food (work), and for this they take birth (come into involvement with gross matters), they live and strive. Secondly, the elements have vital air, and for this they take birth and live and strive. Thirdly, the elements have a mind, and for this they take birth and strive. Fourthly, the elements have consciousness, and for this they take birth, live and strive. Fifthly, the elements have a feeling (bliss), and for this they take birth, they live, and they strive." In other words, these elements, being rays of Supreme Consciousness, are endowed with the characteristics of Consciousness. This is the reason they can and do find their way to the part of the body in need of repair or balancing and do the needed work. The ion, it is taught, has the power (influence) of creation, maintenance, or destruction. If given the opportunity, these ions will create (build anew) and maintain the organism in a healthy condition.

In one approach, the healer examines the patient to see if the three influential elements of air, fire, and water are in a condition of imbalance. This is known as the "three-fault" (*tri*-three, *dosa*-fault) approach, seeing if any of the three elements, alone or in combination, are in a condition of imbalance. Then, therapy is prescribed to bring the system back into a natural state of balance.

In this system, the first element, *air*, refers to the nerve force and the vital power in the body. The second, *fire*, represents the circulatory system. The third, *water*, refers to the mucous surfaces of the body. If these three elements are in balance, health is likely, as all systems will function properly to handle food and needed chemical changes. It is not our purpose to prescribe here for special cases but to recommend balance in matters of health measures, diet, and attitude.

The Influence of Air Element

Air is represented throughout the body. It is a subtle and pervasive element. Air propels the elements of fire and water and is essential to their existence and function. Air as prana (vital force) has five subdivisions that perform the five different functions in the body.

1. *Vital* aspect (prana)—Centered strongly in the mouth cavity and near the heart. Is diffused throughout the system and enables one to swallow.

2. *Upward* aspect (udana)—Flows strongly in upper part of the body and throat. Makes speech possible and any action which brings things up and out.

3. *Even* aspect (samana)—Centered strongly in the stomach and region of intestines. Encourages digestion and separates waste from needed nutrients.

4. *Diffused* aspect (vyana)—Moves throughout the system. Circulates fluids such as blood and perspiration.

5. *Downward* aspect (apana)—Centered strongly in the lower intestines. Forces things out of the body through the lower extremities.

If any aspect of the air element is deranged, then a corresponding physical problem will result. When balance is regained, the problem will cease. This is the theory. The air element can be deranged as a result of faulty diet, incorrect breathing, storms and rains, excessive exercise, excessive worry, anxiety, shocks to the system, suppression of urine, gas, tears, stools, vomiting, or sneezing.

The Influence of Fire Element

Fire protects the body from cold and helps to keep the thermal balance of the system. It also contributes to proper function of eyesight, digestion, and radiance of the body. Again, there are said to be five divisions of the fire element.

1. *Digestive* aspect—Digests food and reduces it into nutrients and wastes. Also supplements the other divisions.
2. *Coloring* aspect—Said to be red in color. Most strongly influences liver and spleen.
3. *Fulfilling* aspect—Strongly influences the area near and in the heart. Said to dispel darkness (inertia) from the system and contribute to intellect and the fulfillment of one's desires.
4. *Seeing* aspect—Strongly influences vision, eyes.
5. *Shining* aspect—Influences the skin, imparting radiance and a glow.

When subtle aspects of the fire elements are deranged the following are said to result: (1) Deranged digestive fire producing indigestion, acidity, heartburn; (2) deranged color aspect affecting the liver and spleen; (3) deranged fulfilling aspect interfering with thinking, resulting in confusion and inertia; (4) deranged seeing aspect causing problems with vision; (5) deranged shining aspect producing skin problems.

The fire element in the body is believed to be aggravated by anger, fear, grief, excessive physical exertion, indigestion, and excessive sexual activity.

The Influence of Water Element

Water keeps fire in check, and both fire and water require air. Water acts as a lubricating agent. It generates new tissues and adds strength and firmness to the system. It is said to be located in the chest, stomach, head and joints, as well as in the fatty areas of the body. Here are the five subdivisions of water in the body.

1. *Moistening* aspect—Strong in the stomach and aids digestion.
2. *Supporting* aspect—Provides lubrication to joints and aids heart action.
3. *Feeling* aspect—In the throat and root of tongue, saliva. Imparts feeling and power of taste in the mouth.
4. *Easing* aspect—In the head, aids in the function of eyes, ears, and nose.
5. *Heavy* aspect—Or thick phlegm and mucus—also lubricates the joints.

Aggravated water element is said to contribute to loss of appetite, chills, drowsiness, heaviness, white coating on the tongue, excessive sleep, and overly sweet taste in the mouth. Loss of water results in dryness, burning sensations, thirst, and general weakness. Imbalance of the water element leads to loss of strength, indigestion, excessive fat, white urine, and stools.

When any of the elements (air, fire, water) are aggravated, foods should be eaten in opposition to that element in order to pacify it. When deficient, foods should be eaten to increase the activity of the element. In general, if foods are taken in balanced combination, no problems should arise, except in instances of mental or emotional stress or physical shock to the system. The body can also resist the invasion of any virus if all elements are in balance, one is rested and enjoys peace of mind and emotional balance.

Guide to Elements in Foods

For an easy guide, I will use the A, F, and W for Air, Fire, and Water elements in foods. Here are a few foods and their corresponding elements which, when eaten, influence like elements in the body.

1. *A (air) foods*: Apples, corn meal, lemons, parsley, salt, squash, tea, and yeast. They strengthen the nervous system but weakening the circulatory and mucous (water) systems.

2. *F (fire) foods*: Celery, coffee, curds, onions, peanuts, pickles, potatoes, legumes, soybeans, sunflower seeds, and raw sugar strengthen the circulatory system but weaken the nervous and water systems.

3. *W (water) foods*: Alfalfa, bottled milk, cauliflower, honey, lettuce, meat, rice, tomatoes (and other vegetables) strengthen the water system but weaken the nervous and circulatory systems.

4. *AF (air-fire) foods*: Sweets, refined sugar, etc., strengthen the nervous system and circulatory systems but weaken the water system and increase cold.

5. *AW (air-water) foods*: Bananas, beets, carrots, dates, eggs, grapes, oatmeal, and yellow corn strengthen the nervous and water systems but weaken the circulatory system and aggravate heat.

6. *AFW (air-fire-water) foods*: Only a few foods are designated in this system as having a perfect balance of all three element-influences. They are fresh cream, fresh milk, fresh fish, and black pepper. These are said to have the power to influence the corresponding elements in the body with their fifteen (five per element) principles. Remember, we are dealing here with the influence of electrically charged atoms (ions) in the system and are not referring to the other values of foods regarding vitamins, minerals, proteins, carbohydrates, and salts. There is no reason why one can not balance the diet, taking into consideration the ion value as well as the commonly known nutritional value.

In dealing with the ion value, we are suggesting modest food intake. It is well-known that most persons, to satisfy emotional rather than body needs, consume too much food. Common sense is the rule, always. As for taking black pepper, an easy way is to take five to seven black pepper corns, chew them, and then swallow some water. They are not "hot" to the taste, generally, and this minute quantity stimulates the corresponding three elements into balanced function and interplay.

As in most instances, different authorities have their personal opinions regarding the influence of foods on the body. On the following page will be found a list of common foods, with their element characteristics designated according to A, F, or W (air, fire, or water).

Apples	A5	Honey	W5
Banana	A5W5	Lemons	A5
Black olives	A5W5	Meat	W5
Cabbage	W5	Mushrooms	W5
Celery	F5	Onions	F5
Cloves	F5	Peanuts	F5
Artichoke	W5	Pepper (black)	A5, F5, W5
Beets	A5W5	Potatoes	F5
Bottled milk	W5	Rice	W5
Carrots	A5W5	Soybeans	F5
Chestnuts	A5W5	Tea	A5
Coffee	F5	Wheat	F5
Avocado	W5	Cream	A5, F5, W5,
Broccoli	A5	Endive	F5, W5
Cauliflower	W5	Grapefruit	W5
Dates	A5W5	Kelp	W5
Grapes	A5W5	Milk (fresh)	A5, F5, W5
Kolrabi	W5	Parsley	A5
Lettuce	W5	Pears	W5
Oatmeal	A5W5	Pulses (beans)	F5
Peas	F5	Salt	A5
Pickles	F5	Vinegar	F5
Squash	A5	Yellow Corn	A5, W5
Swiss Chard	W5	Walnuts	F5
Turnips	W5	Curds	F5
Corn Meal	A5	Fish (fresh)	A5, F5, W5
Eggs	A5W5		

A useful guide to nutrition is to eat a balanced diet, enough only to satisfy. Never overeat. It is also useful to see to body cleansing, as discussed in an earlier lesson. Sometimes the system is so clogged with waste that a specific program is required to cleanse it of impurities. We do not recommend drastic measures or extended fasts, if one is ill, without professional advice. Again, common sense is the rule. If the body is out of balance due to improper diet or mental and emotional unrest, it will take time for matters to be adjusted. One may notice almost immediate improvement, but the "cure" will take a few weeks or months before the system is stabilized and everything is once again in perfect balance and harmony. Then, one should earnestly be engaged in a program of correct diet, sufficient and correct exercise (for the person), mental and emotional health, and spiritual practices. Diet alone will not solve all problems . . . nor will mere positive thinking and exercise. A practical program will involve all aspects of living and being. Exponents of every therapeutic approach can claim cures for the patients: diet can cure; body manipulation can cure (chiropractic, foot reflexology, acupressure, etc.); mental and emotional clearing though counseling, prayer, and self-analysis can contribute to health. *In every case, it is the life-force which cures as a result of inhibiting factors being removed.* Color therapy and gem-metal therapy can be useful. This will be covered in a following lesson. If the soul consciousness is dominant, one will naturally follow through and be led to do whatever is best for the system, without having to be too conscious of methods and procedures. The process becomes spontaneous. But, how many are enlightened and in harmony with nature? Such persons have no need of this material.

Some foods and their characteristics in relationship to air, fire, and water follow below. The number 5 indicates full strength of the subtle aspects of each element. A stands for Air; F for fire; W for water.

Dietary Suggestions

Here is a guide to some common foods and their influence on the body, according to Ayurveda and to contemporary nutritionists. In general, it is believed that water moistens, salt liquifies, alkali digests, honey synthesizes, butter tends to be fattening and lubricating, fresh milk is life-giving, flesh strengthens, and excess alcohol causes senile degeneration. More details follow.

Grains

Wheat is sweet, nutritious, tonic, and nourishing. *Brown* rice is sweet, cooling to the system, and a slight stimulant to the air principle in the body. *Millet* is hot, dry, and tends to increase the fire principle in the body, but it is also a good tonic, strengthening and improving general health. *Buckwheat* is excellent in nutritional value.

Spices

Cumin seeds are light, dry, and hot to the system. They lower the air and water principles by increasing the fire principle. They are an appetizer, a digestive, a stimulant, a blood purifer, and also a diuretic. They are useful when there are diseases due to problems with excess water and air principles in the body.

Black pepper is a digestive and an appetizer, influencing the air principle as well as increasing the fire principle, containing a balance of water, air, and fire principles. Black pepper also improves the gastric fire and is a general tonic to the system.

Ginger is considered a cleanser and is one of the most common spices used by Ayurvedic therapists. Fresh ginger is preferred and need not be used in excess, as is the case with all spices.

Asafoetida is hot and light simultaneously. It should be used sparingly. It is a stimulant and is useful in correcting gastric troubles and in cleaning the intestinal tract.

Coriander tends to lessen or calm all three principles of air, fire and water in the system. It is a diuretic and stimulates the appetite.

Tumeric is dry, light, and tends to lower all principles in the body. It improves digestion and purifies the system.

Garlic is a potent food on the herbal medicine list. Used as a rejuvenator, it is also a blood cleanser and an antiseptic for the mucous linings of the body. Some find that one or two cloves of fresh garlic, finely chopped and swallowed with water once or twice daily, is useful in cleansing the system and warding off flu and cold viruses. One will want to eat a bit of dark bread or some raisins or dates, after taking garlic in this manner, to avoid the feeling of burning in the stomach. Garlic can also be used in salads and sautéed in butter or oil as a flavoring for other vegetables.

Cinnamon increases the fire principle in the body, cleans the throat, and is useful in mouth diseases, as well as being a general body cleanser.

Cardamom lessens all the elements in the body and is a useful tonic to the system.

Cloves lessen all three elements in the body and are useful as a general cleanser for the system.

Mint is useful in respiratory problems and in intestinal difficulties. It is a stimulant and can be taken as a tea.

Saffron is a stimulant and a rejuvenator. It lowers the fire and air principles and increases the water principle.

Tamarind adds a sour taste to cooked dishes and is considered a cleanser to the system. It should not be used in excess.

What to Drink?

As a general rule, drinking liquids with meals is not recommended because it dilutes the stomach juices and interferes with the process of digestion.

Pure Water is undoubtedly one of the best drinks. One should drink enough during the day and between meals to flush urea and salts from the system. It is recommended that persons living in areas where fresh water is not available (that is, good well water or spring water) obtain a device for distilling water, since chemicals and pollutants in city water are harmful to the system.

Milk should not be taken in excess and not at all in instances of problems with mucus. Goat's milk, superior to cow's milk, should be fresh and preferably not pasturized. An excellent way to take milk is in the form of yogurt. One can purchase a *starter* at a natural foods store and make yogurt at home. Here is a simple way to do it: obtain a wide-mouth quart thermos jug; bring milk to a boil and remove from heat, letting it cool down to a little over body temperature (be sure to use just a little less than one quart to allow room for the starter in the mix); when the milk is cooled to about 115 degrees, pour it into a thermos jug, add yogurt starter, stir, cap, and leave six to eight hours. Be sure to rinse the jug with hot water before adding milk, so that the inside of it will be warm and the temperature maintained. Check to see if the mixture is thick in about six hours. An easy way to make yogurt is to do it before going to bed and to check it first thing in the morning. To thicken it, add a cup of powdered milk to the mix before heating. Spoon yogurt into cups or large glasses, cover, and place in the refrigerator to chill. Reserve half a cup for the next batch. One can usually continue making yogurt for several weeks, even months, in this manner. Yogurt can be eaten straight from the jar, used as a fruit topping, or in salad dressings, whenever one would use sour cream or however one prefers to use it.

Coffee is usually not recommended. Unless advised otherwise by a physician, used in moderation, it will probably be harmless. Used in excess, it is definitely not useful to the system.

Tea can be used in moderation, in most instances. The more healthful herb teas are best, of course. Herb teas have various useful influences on the system, and, with the various publications available on the subject, one can easily find those teas which are beneficial. A visit to the local natural food store is always a useful idea.

Whenever a sweetener is desired for drinks or for fruit and cereals, honey is ideal. It should not be used in excess, however, A helpful drink is to mix apple cider vingegar and honey, in equal portions, and take a swallow two or three times a day before meals. This is useful in maintaining the alkaline-acid balance in the system. When fasting or for body cleansing during a diet routine, water and lemon juice into which some honey has been added is useful. Some prefer to make the lemonade with pure maple syrup instead of the honey. Processed sugar is not recommended in the human diet.

Fruits

In general, fruits should be eaten raw and chewed well. Some can be lightly cooked or steamed. They need not be eaten in excess, as they are potent sources of solar radiation and act as cleansers of the body. Fruits should be eaten between meals and not mixed with proteins, carbohydrates, or vegetables. When crisp and ripe, apples are an excellent fruit. The whole range of fruits can be eaten with benefit to most persons: oranges, bananas, strawberries and berries of all kinds, fresh coconut, dates, grapefruit, limes and lemons, pears, pineapple, and so on. If the skins are to be eaten, and they should be whenever possible, wash the fruit well before eating to remove dust and possible pesticide residue.

Almonds and nuts of all kinds are recommended. Some find that peanuts are hard to digest. Pumpkin and sunflower seeds, as well as other edible seeds, are rich in trace minerals and in proteins. Pumpkin seeds are rich in natural zinc. They are useful to men, because zinc is required by the male body to maintain the health of the reproductive system, especially the prostate gland.

Vegetables

A wide variety can be eaten, either raw when possible or cooked when needed. Never overcook. When boiling vegetables, retain the pot water to drink later or to use as soup stock, because this water retains many of the vitamins and minerals from the vegetables. Use the skins whenever possible, after scrubbing the vegetables well and discarding inedible parts. When making raw salads, use a variety of vegetables together. One can easily make a tasty salad dressing without resorting to commercial preparations. A basic one I use is really a modification of that used in the classic Caesar Salad: crush one or two garlic cloves in a wooden salad bowl and rub into the wood; either discard the residue or let it remain (according to personal taste); add a pinch of dry mustard, a pinch of salt, some ground black pepper, olive oil, and enough fresh lemon or lime juice to bring to an oily-tangy taste. One way is to start first with the juice-oil mixture, adding the other ingredients to taste. Mix the dressing in a cup or a bowl and pour on the salad just before serving. Toss lightly and serve. One can liven up the salad by tossing in some toasted bread squares.The dressing can be altered by adding a coddled egg to the dressing just before tossing. To do this, pour boiling water over an egg in a cup. Let it sit for a couple of minutes, then crack the egg into the dressing and stir well.

There is no problem with preparing vegetables as long as the ones that require cooking are not overdone and the raw ones are chewed well. Fruits are body cleansers, vegetables are body builders. Whole grain flours can be used for breads, for pie crusts, or whenever baking.

An excellent way to derive optimum benefits from seeds such as alfalfa, mung beans, and wheat is to learn to sprout them. Served in this manner, with salads or in sandwiches with avocados (or whatever is desired), sprouts offer enzymes, vitamins, and minerals in rich abundance.

To obtain both vegetable and fresh fruit juice, a juicer will be a good investment. The best kind will extract the pulp so that it can be crushed, thus obtaining full value from the vegetables or fruits used. Carrot juice is especially useful as a body builder and cleanser, and a pint a day can be taken as an afternoon drink or in place of lunch. Celery and parsley, in small amounts, can be added to the carrot juice and squeezed at the same time. If taking juices for a cleansing program, drink the fruit juice in the morning and the vegetable juice in the afternoon. Drink them slowly in order to mix saliva in the mouth with the juice for improved digestion.

General advice is for one to select foods which are agreeable to the system and to eat in "proper measure." Proper measure means in correct combinations. Heavy foods should be taken in smaller measure than light foods at a meal. Here is what an ancient text says: "The person whose gastric fire is well-tended, who feeds it with wholesome diet, who is given to daily meditation, charity, and the pursuit of spiritual salvation, and who takes food and drinks that are agreeable to him, will not fall victim to approaching diseases except for special reasons. The disciplined person who takes wholesome food lives for a period of one-hundred years, blessed by good men and devoid of disease."

Still another guideline to the taking of food and drink is the reaction we have to the food: whether it tastes sweet, sour, pungent, bitter, salty, or astringent. The tastes are said to act upon the body, in particular the three elements of air, fire, and water. Here is a guide:

Air Element is aggravated by astringent, bitter, and pungent tastes, and is lessened by sweet, sour, and salty tastes.

Fire Element is aggravated by bitter, sour, and salt tastes, and is lessened by astringent, sweet, and bitter tastes.

Water Element is aggravated by sweet, sour, and salt tastes, and is lessened by bitter, pungent, and astringent tastes.

If the system is balanced, one can follow natural inclinations regarding food selection. *Sweet* taste is usually a tonic, improves health, is good for the eyes, the blood, and general complexion. And overabundance in the system contributes to obesity, lassitude, excessive sleep, heaviness, coughs, colds, indigestion, constipation, vomiting, respiratory troubles, eye diseases, tumors, urine diseases, and headaches. *Sour* taste is an appetizer and increases the flow of saliva and gastric juices. An excess, however, contributes to thirst, bladder problems, inflammation, anemia, weak eye sight, and fever. It increases the impurities in the blood and infections and disease, due to extreme influences of fire and water in the system. *Salty* taste increases appetite and digestion and aids in the circulation of fluids in the body, by diluting the water element. In excess, it causes problems with teeth and gums, hyperacidity, blood problems, and general inflammation. *Pungent* taste cleans the mouth and improves digestion and assimilation of food. In excess, it dries up the water element and cuts down the flow of breast milk in mothers and the natural fluids useful to the system. *Bitter* taste dries up fevers and fluids. It also imbalances air element in the system. *Astringent* taste lowers the water and the fire element and dries up the fluids in the body. It purifies the blood. In excess, it causes pains in the chest cavity, dryness in the mouth, gas in the intestines, constipation, and interferes with the circulation of fluids in the system.

Attention to diet is recommended by all practical truth teachers, so that body and mind might be nourished and the soul consciousness able to express fully in this world. The food we eat is converted into blood, flesh, nerves, fat, skin, bones, bone marrow, and sexual fluid. Excess food energy is converted then to subtle energy, which is stored in the pituitary gland and used to regulate the body functions. Meditation and prayer also convert gross energy into subtle energy, which is used for the development of the brain and the nervous system.

An Ancient Rejuvenation Method

In the literature of India there are stories about sages who live many years beyond the average lifespans of ordinary people. Some accomplish this, for reasons known only to themselves, through the sheer power of superior realization. That is, they are so Soul-conscious that they see the body as a mere extension of the mind and they can, therefore, see to it that the body is nourished from within and that the process of decay is neutralized. Some masters also possess a knowledge of how to use certain herbs for the purpose of cleansing and strengthening the systems of the body. One extreme rejuvenation method is known and practiced by a few who learn it from another who understands the process. The purpose of extending the number of years in the body is either for allowing more time for spiritual practices or to maintain the body for service to humanity.

I have read an account and have seen photographs to support the story of a master in India who three times underwent a special rejuvenation process. The first time, when he was in his eighth decade and his body was failing him, he went through the process for a year. It involved purification of the body through removal of toxic matters and then an extended period of rest and special foods. This man was attended by an expert in the science of rejuvenation as well as by two disciples who saw to his every need. After initial purification of the body, the master went into seclusion in a special house built of thick walls, which rendered the interior absolutely quiet and devoid of sound-intrusions. For the duration of the program, except for occasional use of candlelight at meal times, the room was dark. In fact, the environment was planned so that no outside influence could invade the mind and consciousness of the person experiencing the process.

A regular schedule was maintained to insure the body an opportunity to get into a needed self-renewing routine. The theory behind this program is that the body, under the influence of the intelligence of the soul, will renew itself if given the opportunity. What often destroys the body is the accumulation of stress and the retention of toxic waste matter. While there are a few masters who sleep not at all, and there are some people who require but a few hours of sleep, many people require about eight hours of restful sleep in order to compensate for the accumulation of stress experienced during the other sixteen hours of the day. The average person, by obtaining sufficient sleep on a regular basis, is able to somewhat compensate for the general daily challenge to the body but is not able to overcome the gradual low-level accumulation of stress, toxic build-up, and gradual destruction of body cells. The ordinary person, through sleep and observance of the basic laws of natural living, is able to almost keep up (but not quite) with the slowing down of the body processes. The result is decay of the body and transition within the time-frame of those in mortal consciousness.

However, during the rejuvenation process now under discussion, the subject is given the opportunity for complete seclusion for as long as the process takes. There is a brief occasion every day for bathroom needs, mild exercise, and the taking of a special "food" for the body. Usually the diet will consist only of milk and a special mixture of herbs. One experiencing this process does not talk, ever, during the experience. The reason for this is two-fold: one, no outside data must intrude into the mental field of the subject; two, the subject is usually engaged in prayer and meditation and must not be asked to "come out" from this practice.

The person to whom I refer, who experienced this special renewal process three times during his 180 years on the planet, shared a very interesting insight after one of his programs. He said that body cleansing was useful, the special diet was useful, but the most important ingredient in the process was meditation and absorption in God! Clearly, then, what this process allows is for the body to be self-healing while the soul is resting consciously in God during undisturbed meditation. When the sage emerged from seclusion he did not appear to be in his eighties, he appeared as one twenty years younger. An interesting item to here observe is that when he began the process his hair was gray and he was almost without teeth. When he emerged his hair was black and he had grown new teeth to replace the ones which he had lost.

Stories were also shared concerning his many mystical experiences which were experienced during that time of self-imposed seclusion from worldly influences. He told of perceptions which enabled him to see into the very heart of nature and of great sages who came to him in luminous form to instruct and give their blessings. He mentioned that many times, during such visitations, Babaji and those closely attuned to him were present.

Experiments have been written about, in recent years, regarding personal experiences of people who have voluntarily put themselves into an isolation situation: in a dark room without sound-interference; a special environment of heavy salt water (also dark and impervious to sound); or just going off to the mountains or staying a few days in a motel room with no disturbance. Reports are interesting. Most tell of mind-transcending happenings. These are due to the simple fact that when no outside influence is allowed to invade the mind, the mind surrenders and soul influence takes over.

Chapter Four

Creation is sent forth as the inner urge of God and results in *movement*. The outflowing force, on the negative pole, carries creation into full manifestation. The Darkness is everywhere present but not yet formed.

When this is completed, the action of the positive pole, the Magnetic Attraction, begins to influence creation. Light particles are brought together and take ethereal, gaseous, fiery, liquid, and solid forms. In this way the suns, planets, and moons appear.

In due time, because of the influence of this Magnetic Attraction, sometimes referred to as Divine Love, the outer coatings of Spirit are withdrawn. With the partial withdrawal of the first covering, the vegetable kingdom appears. Life and vitality begin to manifest. A partial withdrawal of the next covering results in the appearance of the animal kingdom. When the coverings are withdrawn sufficiently so that the body of intelligence is revealed, the soul gains conscious ability to know right from wrong; it develops discrimination. Hence, rational man comes on the scene. When the next to the last covering is withdrawn, man becomes aware of the existence of his Divine Nature. *When the final covering is withdrawn, man realizes himself as Spirit and remembers his nature as a Son of God.* Entering into the ocean of Light, he becomes eternally free.

> "In the beginning God created the heaven and the earth. And the earth was without form and void; and Darkness was upon the face of the deep. And the Spirit of God moved upon the face of the waters. And God said, Let there be light; and there was light. And God saw the light, that it was good; and God divided the light from the Darkness." Genesis 1: 1-4;

First came the Darkness or the full projection of the fabric of nature. Then, Magnetic Attraction began to influence this formless void and light appeared. Elements refer to the components of the Darkness from which things were formed. The dual flow of electric currents appeared as heaven—the World of Reality; the earth—Darkness or the form building medium. But, at this stage the Darkness had no form. It was ready for the creative act. With the influence of the Magnetic Attraction, the process of creation began. Spirit and Nature, Light and Darkness interact, and the invisible begins to become visible.

"And God called the light day, and the darkness he called night. And the evening and the morning were the first day."   1: 5.

The Light is the Eternal Day which forever shines. It is the realm to which we all aspire. The Darkness or first subtle expression of nature is night, or delusion. Here the dual aspects of Spirit set the stage for what is to come. The unfoldment of creation takes place in *time*: and time is one of the four basic units of the Darkness. Divided by segments each stage took millions of years to unfold.

"And God said, Let there be firmament in the midst of the waters and let it divide the waters from the waters. And God made the firmament, and divided the waters which were under the firmament from the waters which were above the firmament, and it was so. And God called the firmament heaven. And the evening and the morning were the second day."   1: 6-8;

This marked the completion of the building of the inner, subtle realms. Definite lines of division were laid out as magnetic fields, marking off planes and spheres. Waters means various manifestations of Consciousness.

"And God said, let the waters under the heavens be gathered together unto one place, and let dry land appear: and it was so. And God called the dry land earth; and the gathering together of the waters he called sea: and God saw that it was good. And God said, let the earth bring forth grass, the herb yielding seed, and the fruit tree yielding fruit after his kind, whose seed is in itself, after his kind: and God saw that it was good. And the evening and the morning were the third day."   1: 9-13

The concealed vitality began to come forth as the vegetable kingdom. Definite images in Cosmic Mind began to emerge as the different kinds of plants, capable of reproducing their kind.

"And God said, Let there be lights in the firmament of the heaven to divide the day from the night; and let them be for signs and seasons, and for days and years: And let them be for lights in the firmament of heaven to give light upon the earth: and it was so. And God made two great lights; the greater to rule the day and the lesser light to rule the night: he made the stars also. And God set them in the firmament of the heaven to give light upon the earth. And to rule over the day and over the night, to divide the light from the darkness: and God saw that it was good. And the evening and the morning were the fourth day."   1: 14-19.

During this day or cycle, order was established in the solar system. The planets settled into movements in relationship to each other. All of nature, from the lowest to the highest, works together for good so that the Divine Plan might unfold. As we go along we shall see how man himself is attuned to all of nature, due to the electrical activity in the universe.

"And God said, Let the waters bring forth abundantly the moving creature that hath life, and the fowl that may fly above the earth in the open firmament of heaven. And God created great whales, and every living creature that moveth, which the waters of the earth brought forth abundantly, after their own kind, and every winged fowl after his kind: and God saw that it was good. And God blessed them saying, Be fruitful and multiply, and fill the waters of the sea, and let the fowl multiply in the earth. And the evening and the morning were the fifth day."   1: 20-23.

Due to the Magnetic Attraction, the organs of sense were revealed resulting in the appearance of living forms. The redemption of the worlds began with the appearance of the planets because this was when the Attracting Force began to pull the gross Darkness back to Itself: to the original condition, as it was before the initial act of creation. Redemption started then, eons ago, and has been continuing ever since.

"And God said, Let the earth bring forth the living creature after his kind, the cattle, and the creeping things, the beast of the earth, after his kind: and it was so. And God made the beast of the earth, after his kind, the cattle after his kind, and everything that creepeth upon the earth after his kind: and God saw that it was good.
                                                        1: 24-25.

The animals appeared and learned to adapt to their environment. The inner urge to survive resulted in a modification of the species, but the species were determined from the beginning. They brought forth after their kind. There is no evidence that there was a change from one species to another. The seed-ideas or blueprints existed from the beginning and made their appearance when conditions were suitable.

In plants we see the capacity to trap energy by the process of photosynthesis and in animals we see a further evolution in that they, unlike plants, can move from point-to-point in space. Animals eat plants which have trapped the energy and take energy into their bodies in this manner. Some animals devour other animals. Animals live by instinct and their subconscious minds are programmed as a result of their efforts to adapt to their environment. Animals might be termed "energy-converters" of plants or animals, and thus the energy is transferred. They learn by experience to survive, and these instinctive survival patterns are transmitted to their offspring.

"So God created man in his own image, in the image of God created he him; male and female created he them. And God blessed them, and God said unto them, Be fruitful and multiply and replenish the earth, and subdue it; and have dominion over the fish of the sea, and over the fowl of the air, and over every living thing that moveth upon the face of the earth. And God said, Behold I have given you every herb bearing seed, which is upon the face of the earth, and every tree, in which is the fruit of the tree yielding seed; to you it shall be for meat. And to every beast of the earth, and to every fowl of the air, and to everything that creepeth upon the earth, wherein there is life, I have given green herbs for meat: and it was so. And God saw everything that he had made, and, behold, it was very good. And the evening and the morning were the sixth day."   1: 27-31.

Now we see the stage being set for the appearance of man on the planet. You will notice that in every step of the process, that which was necessary for the maintenance of life for higher forms, when they came on the scene, was provided before they appeared. First came vegetation: food for animals. The Divine Plan always works things out in orderly sequence. At this stage the pattern for man was set in Divine Mind, ready to emerge. And, true to the pattern, man was created as male and female, positive and negative, according to the dual flow of force.

CHART ACCORDING TO VEDIC SEERS SHOWING ORDER OF COSMIC MANIFESTATION

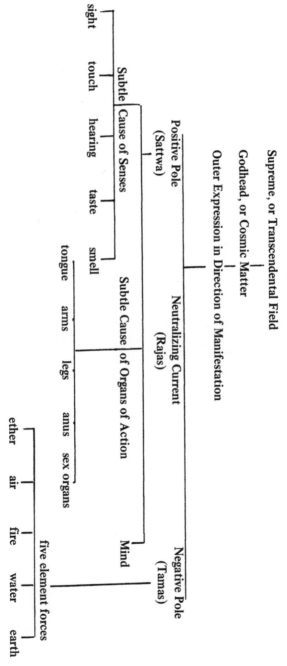

Supreme, or Transcendental Field

Godhead, or Cosmic Matter

Outer Expression in Direction of Manifestation

Positive Pole
(Sattwa)

Neutralizing Current
(Rajas)

Negative Pole
(Tamas)

Subtle Cause of Senses

Subtle Cause of Organs of Action

Mind

sight   touch   hearing   taste   smell

tongue   arms   legs   anus   sex organs

five element forces

ether   air   fire   water   earth

This shows how the One Current changes in frequency, influenced by the three electric attributes (positive and negative
. . . and neutralizing); then produces the "organs of sense, organs of action and appears as the nourishing forces.

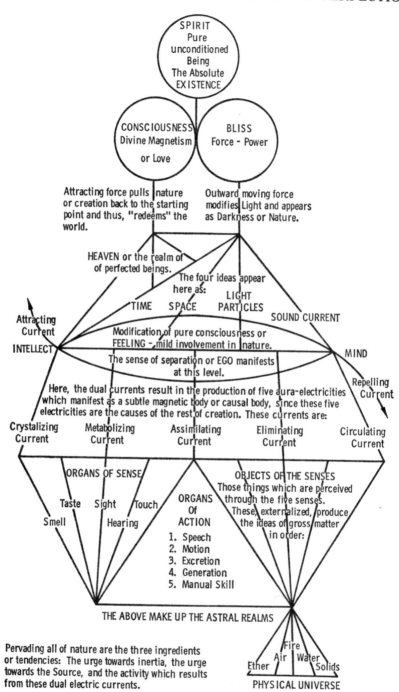

"Thus the heavens and the earth were finished, and all the host of them. And on the seventh day God ended his work which he had made; and he rested on the seventh day for all his work which he had made."   2: 1-2.

The time had come for the emergence of human beings. This point is critical to us as it marks the beginning of the most important step in the creative process.

"But there went up a mist from the earth, and watered the whole face of the ground. And the Lord God formed man of the dust of the ground, and breathed into his nostrils the breath of life: and man became a living soul. And the Lord God planted a garden eastward in Eden: and there he put the man whom he had formed."   2: 6-8.

In ancient occult history we read of the time when man was new on the planet and the planet was covered with a mist or fog. Where did man come from? How was it possible for him to appear?

Man appeared quite naturally as a result of the pull of the powerful Magnetic Attraction. Just as when the veil is lifted a bit, exposing the organs of action, plants emerge; and as the exposure of the organs of sense results in the appearance of animals; so, *the unveiling of the covering of intelligence results in the appearance of man.* Man, because he can discriminate, because he is self-conscious, can determine the course of his own evolution. He can decide to work in harmony with the laws of the universe which leads to freedom or he can decide to continue in an endless round of unreasoned activity. He has a choice to make.

Chapter Five

Opening of the Inner Eye

When, during meditation, the physical body is relaxed and attention flows from the senses to the source of vitality in the brain, many subtle perceptions are possible. The door to the inner realms is the spiritual eye, the third eye, or eye of wisdom. Knowledge of subtle internal processes is acquired as a result of spiritual eye perception. Through inner vision one can see into the heart of an atom, peer into astral and subtle realms, and explore aspects of the physical universe far removed from one's place of meditation. One who works from this level is not restricted to agreed-upon limitations of the universe.

Many yogis and mystics experience what is mentioned in the opening verses of the last Book of the *New Testament.* Let us examine the account given us by St. John in *The Revelation.*

"I was in the Spirit on the Lord's Day, and heard behind me a great voice, as of a trumpet."

Revelation 1: 10.

Having his attention turned within, St. John intuitively perceived the Aum vibration. It was *behind* him, flowing from Divine realms, from a source beyond the ego sense. Being in tune with the Magnetic Attracting Power, his attention was drawn to the Source. Surrendering to this pull, his inner vision opened and he saw, with the eye of intuition, both his physical and astral vehicles.

"And I turned to see the voice that spake with me. And being turned, I saw seven golden candlesticks;

And in the midst of the seven candlesticks one like unto the Son of Man, clothed with a garment down to his foot, and girt about the breasts with a golden girdle.

His head and his hairs were white like wool, as white as snow: and his eyes were as a flame of fire;

And his feet like unto fine brass, as if they burned in a furnace; and his voice as the sound of many waters.

And he had in his right hand seven stars; and out of his mouth went a sharp two edged sword; and his countenance was as the sun shineth in his strength.

And when I saw him, I fell at his feet as dead. And he laid his right hand upon me, saying unto me, Fear not; I am the first and the last:

I am he that liveth, and was dead, and behold, I am alive for evermore. Amen; and I have the keys of hell and death."

1: 12-18.

Seeing his own astral vehicle floating over the prostrate form of his physical body, St. John also saw the centers of vital force in the spinal passageway and the halo of light surrounding the form. The astral vehicle appeared to be formed much like the physical body, the Son of Man. The brain of the astral body was brilliant white and the third eye center, where positive and negative flows emerge, was a single flame of fire. A golden aura encircled the form, becoming darker at the feet.

This was the perception of the spiritual body, the astral-causal vehicle which is not dependent upon the physical body, though the physical body is dependent upon it. A sense of immortal life pervaded St. John's consciousness as he was rapt in this inner experience. That he correctly perceived the seven vital places and their energies is clearly revealed in the following:

> "The mystery of the seven stars which thou sawest in my right hand, and the seven golden candlesticks. The seven stars are the angels of the seven churches: and the seven candlesticks which thou sawest are the seven churches."   1: 20.

The *angels* are the controlling life currents which flow through the established centers to sustain the bodies. As these centers are opened, man's consciousness becomes ever more clear and he is able to understand the seven levels of soul unfoldment and the seven planes of Consciousness. This has been termed the ladder of self-realization which man climbs, step by step, from bondage to liberation.

Located throughout the cerebro-spinal nervous system, the vital centers serve as distribution points for the down-flowing life currents. Their locations are: upper cerebrum, body battery of main center of force; third eye center, the point where life forces are distributed through the medulla; cervical center; dorsal center; lumbar center; sacral center; and coccygeal center.

There is no need for us to try to awaken these centers by concentration, for as we learn to dwell in the realization of the Presence at all times, the vital forces automatically become activated. There has been much false information published about these vital centers and their corresponding effect on man's consciousness. The most common falsehood is that premature awakening of the vital force leads to sexual excess and emotional imbalance. What happens as a result of the awakening of vital forces in the body is not a negative phenomenon, but rather, some people who have never really been alive before do not know how to handle their feelings. If we remain steady on the spiritual path, living always in the awareness of our God-nature, there will never be any problems of any kind for any reason whatsoever.

Due to the movement of vital forces through the system, the contents of the unconscious sometimes float to the surface, giving rise to visions or hallucinations. This is why the master teachers stress the importance of Self-realization as the goal, rather than for a person to become intrigued by illusory inner expriences. All perceptions, except the clear awarness of Being, are to be considered as illusory by the sincere seeker of Truth.

St. John, continuing his meditation, going beyond the vision of his lower vehicles, is able to transcend the lesser realms and enter the *door* to the inner kingdoms:

"After this I looked, and behold, a door was opened in heaven; and the first voice which I heard was as it were of a trumpet talking with me; which said, Come up hither and I will shew thee things which must be heareafter.

And immediately I was in the spirit; and, behold, a throne was set in heaven, and one sat on the throne.

And he that sat was to look upon like a jasper and a sardine stone; and there was a rainbow round about the throne, in sight like unto an emerald.

And round about the throne were four and twenty seats: and upon the seats I saw four and twenty elders sitting clothed in white raiment; and they had on their heads crowns of gold.

And out of the thrones proceeded lightnings and thunderings and voices; and there were seven lamps of fire burning before the throne, which are the seven Spirits of God.

And before the throne was a sea of glass like unto crystal: and in the midst of the throne and round about the throne, were four beasts, full of eyes, before and behind."   4: 1-6.

Passing beyond the levels of material creation, St. John moved in awareness through the *door*, being summoned by the Attracting Current and hearing the Aum continuously. In his awareness as an individualization of Spirit, he perceived the *inner workings* of

God. Beholding the true Source, he also perceived the outward radiating flows of force; including the twenty-four active principles of Spirit; which are perceived as the fifteen subtle electricities; five gross elements; plus feeling, ego, mind, and intelligence. The soul, detached from creation, can clearly see all forces of which creation is formed.

St. John also perceived the seven major divisions of God involved with creation, as the *Spirits before the throne*, which are responsible for the seven levels of creation. He also understood the nature of the Darkness, the fabric of creation, and the *four beasts*; termed thus because man identified with them, instead of with his true nature, is barred from spiritual perception. These four components are, as you will recall: energy, time, space, and light particles.

This experience is the true spiritual baptism of man. The Son of Man is the soul identified with these four component parts of the Darkness. The Son of Man is the offspring of the Darkness or the four *origins*. When man's attention is fully interiorized, in deep meditation, he realizes the true Source and Reality of all outer appearances and is at peace within himself, requiring nothing of the outside world for satisfaction or happiness. All of this can be realized while embodied when the doors of perception are cleansed. This is why the spiritual body of man with its electricities and dual poles has been described as a sealed casket of knowledge.

> "And I saw in the right hand of him that sat on the throne a book written within and on the backside, sealed with seven seals."   5: 1.

Chapter Six

Patanjali mentions sleep as a modification of the mind. There are stories of many yogis who no longer require sleep because they are so totally conscious and open to the flow of deeper currents that the body and nervous system do not tire and get into a condition where repair of the systems is required. Of course, many of these people sit for long hours daily in deep meditation, and this is even more restful than ordinary sleep. A news item was circulated some years ago telling of a man who had been involved in an accident and had received an injury to the head. Thereafter, he never slept and seemed healthy and well in spite of the condition. His major problem was what to do with his extra time.

For the majority of people sleep is essential to health, but the experience can be utilized as an opportunity to explore deeper levels of awareness. One technique, often taught by the masters, is to practice being conscious while going to sleep. In time, one can observe the usual slowing down of the body's rhythms so that one appears to be asleep, yet there remains inner awareness akin to profound meditation. The process is more successful if one is willing to be conscious. Many people look forward to the occasion of sleep as an escape from problems and boredom.

Through regular practice one can be conscious during occasions of dreaming and use the dream state to explore the way the mind works. While dreaming we can create new and novel worlds, we can walk through walls, we can fly, and we commune with those who have left this world and who now dwell in astral spheres. While dreaming we can commune with illumined seers and we can visit distant places. We can learn to create dreams of our own choosing and we can learn to awaken from a dream at will, retaining the memory of all that transpired.

A brother disciple of mine who is highly advanced spiritually told me, years ago, that he no longer slept in the conventional manner. At bedtime he would meditate and flow his attention into the crown chakra and then rest the night through in the conscious experience of clear light. Satya Sai Baba has said on occasion that he does not sleep. He uses the night hours to be alone in his room for the purpose of working with devotees on the inner planes. During dream-like conditions I have had what seemed to be conscious communication with such persons as Sri Yukteswar, Yogananda, Joel Goldsmith, Father Divine, Swami Sivananda, Satya Sai Baba, and many others. On some occasions these dream communications were prior to my actually meeting a person, and sometimes it has been after they have left this world for more subtle realms.

Meditation on the Word

The Word of God is the sound current, and this energy-frequency can be heard when we are very still and attentive. To meditate on this sound current one settles into a meditation position and turns attention to the third eye center or the crown chakra. Being surrendered to the focus of attention, one will soon hear a subtle inner sound. By giving into it completely the attention will be led from gross to subtle levels of sound, until one transcends the sound and experiences Being. In some teaching traditions this is the only meditation method taught, as it is considered to be the most direct and easiest to practice. The secret to success with this process is not to allow the attention to become fixed on phenomenal perceptions which might be experienced. Whatever is perceived, renounce it and flow past it to the source of the sound.

Control of Vital Forces
Through Special Breathing

A useful exercise for the regulation of vital forces in the system (pranayama) is this: just before meditation begins, practice alternate nostril breathing. Hold the right nostril closed with the thumb and inhale through the left nostril easily and completely. Hold for a moment, then close the left nostril and easily exhale through the right nostril. Then, inhale through the right nostril, hold, and exhale through the left one. Repeat ten to twenty times in the early stages. This exercise will harmonize the flows of vital force in the right and left sides of the body and will calm the mind. It will also cleanse the nervous system and remove stress.

In deep meditation and at other times when we are relaxed and inwardly balanced, we can be aware of flows of vital force through the central spinal channel. Yogis call this sushumna breathing. When this occurs there is no outward evidence of violence during breathing because the major activity takes place within. Sushumna breathing activates kundalini and maintains constant activity of creative energies in the system.

The saint known as Shivapuri Baba (because he lived in the Shivapuri forest in Nepal) explained to his disciples that one could extend life in the body for up to one thousand years through slow and controlled breathing. Before he retired to the forest this illumined master traveled the world for forty years to give intimate and private advice and counsel to many world leaders. While doing his public work, he was known by other names to various people with whom he came in contact. His major message was that one should love God totally and serve humanity.

Chapter Seven

The science of Kriya Yoga has been known and practiced for centuries. Even during Dark Age cycles, when the majority of people on the planet were not receptive to advanced spiritual instruction and training, qualified seekers were intuitively led to a master of this science. It was Mahavatar Babaji who, in the middle of the last century, began to initiate disciples into the Kriya Yoga process with the intention of having them share it with those among the general population who were ready to understand and receive it. While there still exist special training centers in out of the way places, it was Babaji's guidance that many spiritually aware people in the mainstream of society were ready for Kriya Yoga teachings. One of his advanced disciples who was sent into the world to teach was Lahiri Mahasaya, a family man with business responsibilities.

Lahiri initiated thousands of disciples in India but did not build any organization, as he felt the time premature to do so. It was his disciple, Swami Sri Yukteswar, who started an organizational vehicle for the propagation of the message. A major contribution of Sri Yuktwswar's was the training of his disciple, Paramahansa Yogananda, who came to America in 1920 to bring Kriya Yoga to the West. I met Yoganandaji in 1949 and was initiated by him into this sacred science.

Kriya Yoga Meditation Techniques

I have explained in this chapter the philosophy and purpose of Kriya Yoga. Here I will explain a little more about the Kriya Yoga meditation methods and techniques. Kriya Yoga embraces the useful aspects of all of the Yogas, but the meditation approach is of special interest. In this tradition the new student is first taught a mantra as a meditation tool. After some progress has been experienced the student is then taught how to meditate with sound and light. Finally, Kriya Yoga Pranayama is taught during a special initiation ceremony.

This special exercise enables one to activate and direct vital forces in the system. A unique aspect of the initiation process is an infusion of energy into the disciple which results in the eventual awakening of kundalini. Once this process begins, if it is nourished, inner purification and transformation is possible. During the practice of Kriya Yoga Pranayama the blood is cleansed of carbon and is recharged with oxygen. The atoms of extra oxygen are transmuted into vital force to purify and rejuvenate the brain, spinal centers, and nervous system. Advanced yogis experience perfection of the body through this process because tissue decay is prevented. A few masters of perfection were so advanced through the use of this process that they were able to materialize and dematerialize the physical body. The immediate practical benefits of correct Kriya Yoga practice are deep relaxation, improved concentration during meditation, and a powerful circulation of vital energies throughout the system. As these vital energies flow brain-ward, the brain adapts and becomes more refined. Also, when the upward flow of current becomes spontaneous, one's attention is carried effortlessly into the finer realms of Consciousness. The process must be learned from one who is skilled in the practice and who is a responsible representative of the teaching tradition. Kriya Yoga meditation techniques are graded in progressive levels, with the advanced techniques given only after suitable progress has been made with the use of preliminary methods.

One of the Kriya Yoga meditation techniques enables the meditator to consciously ascend the sushumna and leave the body easily at the time of transition. By drawing all of the vital forces to the crown chakra with unwavering attention, while contemplating Pure Consciousness, the meditator leaves this world and becomes immediately established in the Transcendental Field, if this is his destiny. Some advanced yogis leave the body by this process but retain a subtle form and remain involved with earth destiny for a duration. Others move consciously into astral spheres to there continue their spiritual practices or to teach others who reside there and who are in need of instruction.

Siddha Yoga:
The Path of the Perfect Masters

In the Siddha Yoga tradition, while instruction is given and meditation methods are taught, the most important ingredient in the relationship is the disciple's attunement with the guru. By living in harmony with the guru the disciple remains open to all beneficial influences flowing from God through the guru. In this tradition it is taught that the grace of God is the most powerful and influential aspect of the process. A siddha guru is one in whom subtle forces have full and unrestricted play; therefore, the disciple can receive an infusion of these energies which will awaken his own kundalini and propel him on the spiritual path. Being prejudiced and lacking in powers of discernment, the new disciple cannot see God in his fellow human beings. He can see the radiance of God in the illumined guru and he can trust and respect that manifestation. By serving, without question or argument, the guru's cause, the disciple learns to surrender personal ego and becomes attuned to God's enlightenment plan for mankind. The true guru, being devoid of ego, has no ulterior motive for maintaining a relationship with disciples. His only purpose is to share his knowledge and his presence with those who are open and receptive. A perfect master instantly recognizes his chosen disciples and invites them into his spiritual environment. Jesus, we will recall, called forth some of the most unlikely prospects for discipleship and, through them, God's power did mighty works.

Not only does a perfect master awaken dormant forces in disciples, he also chooses, from among his disciples, the ones most worthy to represent the tradition and conveys to them a larger portion of creative force, so that they will be able to continue the teaching emphasis. The ones chosen in this manner are never among those who want the responsibility, they are the ones who are destined and who have renounced personal desire. They, then, continue the teaching tradition from a sense of duty and not because of any compulsion. Those who are chosen to represent the siddha tradition may yet have personal problems with which to deal and they may sometimes falter along the way, but they can never fail because they are living channels through which a great purpose is being fulfilled. Sometimes the teaching becomes diluted because of the imperfect realization of a few teachers; sometimes the chosen representatives do not agree upon the most useful way to share the message; however, all who are chosen fulfill a unique purpose in the overall plan of world redemption.

In the Kriya Yoga tradition kundalini activity is natural and spontaneous. This is why it is in harmony with the needs of men and women who live with family and community responsibilities. In the Christian tradition the influence of the Holy Spirit is acknowledged. This is the identical process as kundalini; only the terms differ. A few people, whose nervous system has not been fully prepared, experience dramatic emotions and body movements when kundalini begins to stir the vital energies in the system. This should not be anticipated because it does not occur with everyone. In one who is relaxed and prepared, kundalini movement will only result in calmness, contentment, optimism, deeper meditation experiences, and increased vitality. In one who is not relaxed and prepared, should kundalini be awakened, there may be a period of emotional confusion, body tremors, and even pain in the spine and head. Should the latter be experienced, the advice is to experience it and surrender totally to God, never to dramatize what is happening and never to talk about it except with the guru. The guru's advice will usually be, "God is being good to you. Love Him more and surrender your ego." During my first year with my guru, I experienced mild emotional challenges and occasional pain and unexpected body movements during meditation. I never told anyone about it, not even Yoganandaji. He observed, however, and gave quiet advice which was useful and helpful.

During my first few years with my guru, he disciplined me gently, always pointing out what was necessary for me to know and do. I think he liked the fact that I was quiet and observant. He only had to tell me something once and I got the message. I loved him with a love that was personal but not human and I still do. I anticipated his spiritual grace but I wanted nothing except God-realization. He occasionally said to disciples, "If you will allow me to, I will reveal God to you." One of his favorite *Bible* quotations is taken from *The Gospel According to St. John,* 1: 12: "But as many as received him, to them gave he power to become sons of God, even to them that believe on his name." This is a perfect explanation of the siddha tradition.

Electric Characteristics in the Mind

In verse fifteen in this chapter the *electric characteristics* are mentioned. The author here refers to the triple aspects which run through all of nature, from the Godhead to material manifestation. The Sanskrit term for these characteristics, influences, or aspects is *guna* (see glossary for this and any term used in the text which is not understood). The explanation is easy to grasp and tells much about that which takes place in our universe. In the verse under discussion it is said that even if mental impressions are controlled there can be disturbance in the mental field due to electric influences. These influences can be tendencies in the direction of clear knowing, the direction of confusion, or in the direction of inertia or unconsciousness. From the *Bhagavad Gita* (Chapter 14: 5-19) we receive clear instruction: "The three tendencies in nature bind the soul to the body. Of these three, the elevating tendency causes health and eventual illumination of consciousness. However, it too binds the soul which seeks happiness and personal fulfillment. The activating tendency binds the soul by causing it to seek sense-gratification and purposeless activity. The tendency towards heaviness (inertia) causes the soul to be negligent, lazy, and seek escape through too much sleep. The elevating tendency will eventually prevail over restless action and the desire to sleep (be deluded). When dissolution of the worlds happens, the soul which is identified with the uplifting tendency will obtain liberation (merge in the Light). Souls who are identified with the tendency to perform purposeless action or who are identified with inertia, at the time of the dissolution of the worlds (after millions of years of rest) then incarnate among other souls like themselves (either sense-bound or deluded). The results of good action (identified with the elevating tendency) are pure and in the nature of blessings; those who are active only, because they seek sensation, eventually experience frustration and pain; those who are identified with inertia only find greater dullness and ignorance as the result of whatever they do or think. However, when a soul perceives That which is beyond the tendencies in nature he attains objectivity and freedom. When he completely detaches himself from all activities of nature he is free."

Chapter Eight

It is a common experience with beginning meditators that they try too hard to attain a degree of success in their practice. Once the body has relaxed and one's attention has been directed to the meditation ideal, the process becomes effortless. When one is surrendered to God, God's magnetic attraction unveils the faculties of perfection so that knowledge can be experienced.

Profound absorption in Soul Consciousness results in the mental field becoming calm and clear as conflicting thought patterns become neutralized. Early samadhi experiences are but the beginning of a longer purification process. In the first stages there is soul awareness mixed with mental processes. In time the tendencies of the mind are restrained by superior superconscious influences, and, finally, these tendencies are neutralized or removed. One may experience conscious identification with the object of meditation, such as light or sound. One may then feel, "I am light, or I am sound." But, as useful as these experiences might be, they are not representative of the pure experience of Being. When we are aware of feeling that we are anything other than Being we have not yet experienced the highest samadhi. These early stages are referred to as samadhi with support of an object. The higher experience is samadhi without support, the awareness of unconditioned and independent Being. Many yogis and mystics experience lower samadhi regularly but still retain psychological problems. They may even be proud of their attainment, with a zeal bordering on arrogance. Only when mental tendencies and instinctual drives are exhausted and only when the contents of the unconscious level of mind have been cleared can one be said to be truly liberated.

Scientists and the Masters on a Common Quest

Albert Einstein opened the door to a fuller understanding of nature's laws when, in 1905, his *Theory of Special Relativity* was first published. Then, for the last twenty-five years of his life, he worked on a problem for which he intuitively felt there must be a solution. This was his *Unified Field Theory*, which attempted to set forth in one series of mutually consistent equations the physical laws governing two of the fundamental forces of the universe, gravitation and electromagnetism. Most of the pheomena of our external world seems to be produced by these two primordial forces. Experiments by Oersted and Faraday in the nineteenth century showed that a current of electricity is always surrounded by a magnetic field and, under certain conditions, magnetic forces can induce electrical currents. From these experiments came the discovery of the electromagnetic field through which light waves, radio waves, and other electromagnetic disturbances are spread in space. Electricity and magnetism can be considered as aspects of a single force. Other forces there are, too, such as gravitation, but the former two forces are obviously influential. The interplay of matter is possible because atoms are composed of electrical particles.

Without benefit of any modern laboratory there are, in certain parts of the world, masters of a secret science which has emerged as a result of their deep analysis of the characteristics of matter. They know that all matter is capable of being changed from one form to another. Mass converts to energy and energy converts to mass: they are interchangeable. Knowing this the master can, through mantra, visualization, or an act of will, easily manipulate the appearance of matter. I am aware of research now being done, by advanced meditators in Europe and America, in the direction of scientifically proving what has been taught by esoteric orders for centuries.

It is essential that such research be done only by those with a highly developed moral sense because knowledge of this magnitude should not be shared with men whose values are selfish and materialistic. Masters who possess the knowledge of how the universe works are careful not to reveal the secrets to the ill-prepared or unworthy. It is not an idle game they play; they are concerned about the welfare of humanity.

Inner and Outer Spiritual Missions

While a few liberated masters remain in seclusion for their private purposes, they often have representatives who are active in the public field. Paramahansa Yogananda told us that when he was a small boy he had visions of the Himalayan masters who guided him on the inner planes. Babaji told Lahiri Mahasaya that he,

Lahiri, had been with him in a prior incarnation and had been born in the nineteenth century to fulfill a special mission. Yogananda was told by his guru that the masters had prepared him to bring Yoga to the West. Many masters have said that during times of meditation they inwardly communicate with their spiritual teachers and plan for mankind's highest good.

Cosmic Influences

Astrology, along with medicine, mathematics, music and architecture, was one of the great sciences of the ancient world. We know that this science was known to the Chaldeans and also practiced by the Egyptians, Hindus, Chinese, Persians, and the leaders of the great civilizations of the Americas. Astrology is divisible into two distinct phases. The esoteric science deals with the mysteries of the cosmos, the spiritual, intellectual, moral, and physical chemistry of the world. It reveals the anatomy and psychology of God. It sets forth an explanation of existence and a moral relationship between things. It reveals the mathematical pattern of creation. It is really a study of celestial dynamics. Exoteric astrology, on the other hand, is the predictive aspect. In this text I am dealing with esoteric, or inner astrology.

We know that man is composed of two parts: the Spirit which animates the body and the body itself. In order to properly understand astrology, we must understand the nature of man. We must understand the whole of creation, both visible and invisible, that which is seen and that which is unseen.

In space there are stars and each star is a sun, and these suns are manifestors of pure energy which sustains the world. Each of the suns has its planets which are reflectors of its energies. These planets not only reflect but they distribute the energies radiating from the suns. Channeled through the planets, the energy is converted into positive and negative qualities.

So-called material bodies are composed of energy which has a certain emanational power. The physical energies of these elements are referred to as force, and force exercises an influence upon structures which are in proximity to that force. Man on earth receives three kinds of energy: spiritual energy from the planets, physical energy reflected from the planets, and elementary energy from the earth on which he resides. Superior forces influence inferior forces. Therefore, lesser forces are acted upon by greater force.

The appearance of plants and organisms was the result of the upward movement of force, as explained earlier. And this force, within the forms of earth, is also acted upon from without. Spiritual force works through inert material forms and activity results from the interplay of Attractive Force and inertia (gravity). Theologians refer to this activity as the struggle between good and evil.

God regulates all of creation through these streams of force. The One Life flows through the suns and is converted and channeled through the planets. Over a period of time, as the result of inner revelation and outer investigation, ancient seers were able to discover the quality of force emanating from certain suns, modified by specific planets. Then they were able to recognize the relationship of these forces to the behavior of man, as well as to other living things.

The planet earth consists of a physical body with a series of electric and magnetic fields. We are bound to the sun by subtle cords, or lines of force. It is thought that the earth contains seven electric zones and, therefore, seven degrees of density. The number seven is an oft-mentioned number in occult literature; we read of seven continents, seven races, seven great orders of life, seven steps to liberation, and so on. The magnetic field of the earth is nourished by the sun. The entire solar system pulsates and forces circulate, not unlike the circulation in the physical body. We are linked, through the sun, to the rest of the cosmos.

The study of correspondences reveals the great truth that all living things are part of one magnificent pattern. This is the greatest lesson we can learn from the study of astrology. With proper study, the intellect and intuition become blended in a natural, harmonious manner, and man becomes a *sage*, one who sees clearly.

The ancients studied man. The human organism, so wonderfully complex, yet harmonious in all its parts, became their architectural design upon which they constructed the Grand Man of the Starry Heavens. The twelve signs of the celestial zodiac were divided into sections of the human frame, so that the entire zodiacal belt was symbolized as a man bent round in the form of a circle, with the soles of his feet placed against the back of his head. Each of the twelve signs of the zodiac contains 30 degrees of space, making 360 degrees of a circle.

More depends upon the position, aspect, and power of the sun and moon at birth than upon the other planets of the solar system. The sun and the moon are transmitters of stellar forces. They act as mediums and cast their gathered or reflected powers into our magnetic atmosphere, harmoniously or discordantly according to how they are aspected by the rays of the major planets.

Man has five positive points of projection and four positive centers of energy. The head, hands, and feet are the five points of projection. These are symbolized by the five pointed star. The positive centers within the body are the brain, spleen, heart, and generative organs. The great reception center of the body is the solar plexus. The astral system of a human body, with six (twelve by polarity) inner spinal centers, is inter-related with the physical sun and the twelve zodiacal signs. Thus is man affected by his inner and outer universe. The forces of nature, as well as the inner impulse to know Truth, work to refine and condition the body so it can be a fit instrument through which clear Soul Consciousness can filter and function.

The Possible Useful Influences of Gems and Metals

Much of what is contained here is the result of research done through the study of various books purporting to impart information on the subject. This research has not yet been exhaustive, by any means. I share the data here for the interest that readers might have in this theme.

As with our discussion on foods in an earlier chapter, here we are examining the characteristics of manifest things as they are influenced by subtle energies and by frequency changes. In relationship to the influences of gems and metals on the system, we are considering the three basic element-characteristics in the body: air, fire, and water. You will recall the basic elements making up the universe as ether, air, fire, water, and earth. According to this thesis, when the water and earth elements combine, the water influence is manifest in the system. When the fire and earth elements combine, the fire influence is manifest in the system. When the ether and air elements combine, the air influence is manifest in the system. Water cools, fire heats, and air is the vital force flowing through the nervous system.

It is suggested that the three systems can be maintained in a condition of balance, providing appropriate stimulation to them as a result of correct breathing, correct diet, correct mental attitude, and Soul-realization. Another way to maintain balance is by encouraging the systems through the use of color and subtle radiations from gems and metals.

Occult teachers have taught that all objects (things) emit a characteristic radiation; that is, energy locked within the object is steadily streaming off into surrounding space. The objects are slowly disintegrating. This is the way of nature, as energy changes from one form to another. Energy forms as things, and things eventually flow back to free energy status. Energy has specific frequency, according to how it is modified and to how it is controlled or directed by the Intelligence that arranges conditions.

Gem or metal radiation is believed to be received into the body through the skin, if worn on the skin as a ring, a bracelet, or as a necklace. Ayurveda specialists teach that the radiation is taken in through the skin, transferred to the lymphatic fluids, and then to the blood plasma, which contains conductive chemicals called "electrolytes" in solution. These electrical charges are said to promote the natural flow of body currents and to affect body function.

Ancient teachers taught that gems and metals are formed in the planet earth as a result of planetary radiations from space acting upon the *crystalizing* prana (vital force) of earth. We have learned that, according to this philosophical teaching, the One Current from the Source, when coming into manifestation as the world process, changes to five different frequencies in order to do so . . . and to perform needed functions: crystalizing, metabolizing, assimilating, circulating, and eliminating. Planets in our solar system emanate energy which flows into space and influences that with which it comes into contact. The universe is an electrical phenomenon in which flows interact, causing events to transpire. The *Rig-Veda*, one of the oldest scriptures known, informs us that gems are products of the action of intense heat and fire. Gems and metals are believed to represent the crystallization of ions of elements and elemental compounds. As essential forms of matter are purified by heat, gems are formed.

Vedic sources indicate that gems and metals have five primary qualities: the state, or effect; the particular attribute (whether the influence is positive, negative, or neutral); power to interact; the interaction itself; and the result of the interaction. Colors as well as chemical composition are considered. The gems are thought to be not only the result of planetary influence but also to attract radiation from the specific planet assigned as its ruler.

We use, always, natural stones and not synthetics or man-made ones. We want to be sure the planetary energy influence is present, and for this natural gems must be used.

How Gems are Recommended

There are a number of ways to determine which gem to use for an influential purpose. One popular way is to select a gem with the planetary rulership of the ascendant or rising sign, as calculated by sidereal astrology. That approach considers the actual placement of the planets in the constellations. This method was the one used as the basis for study of the applications of gems and metals to the human organism. One simply knows the ascendant, examines the chart to see which gem agrees with the sign, and wears that gem on a regular basis. Since the ascendant is a powerful influence, this gem should assure strong radiation of that influence.

Another way to arrive at the solution is to calculate the gem use according to signs of the zodiac. In the system now under discussion we use the Ayurvedic method, which was researched several thousand years ago before all of the now-known planets were discovered.

For the radiation benefits, it is recommended that the gems be set in an open-backed setting, so that the stone touches the skin.

Sometimes specific metals are recommended to go with gems, along with instructions for wearing them on specific fingers. Then the radiation flows along lines of force in order to influence intended parts of the body. General influence will be had simply by wearing the gem; specific influence will be a matter of certain need.

Zodiac Sign	Gemstone	Planetary Influence	Carats
Aries	Coral	Mars	9, 11 or 12
Taurus	Diamond	Venus	2 carats min. or wear zircon
Gemini	Emerald	Mercury	3, 5, 7 or 10 or wear Aquamarine
Cancer	Pearl	Moon	2, 4 or 6
Leo	Ruby	Sun	or use garnet 3 carats
Virgo	Emerald	Mercury	see Gemini
Libra	Diamond	Venus	see Taurus
Scorpio	Coral	Mars	9, 11 or 12
Sagittarius	Topaz	Jupiter	7 or 12
Capricorn	Sapphire	Saturn	5 or 7
Aquarius	Onyx (Gomed)	Uranus	6, 11 or 13
Pisces	Cat's Eye	Neptune	3, 5 or 7

There is yet another way to decide upon the wearing of gems and metals: by doing an astrological horoscope to find which planetary influences are weak, strong, or disturbed. Then, if one wanted to bolster a weak influence, one would wear a gem giving that particular radiation. If one wanted to neutralize a strong influence, one would wear a gem that would neutralize it. If one wanted to harmonize a disturbed influence, he would wear the gem (or gems) that created harmony in the matter. This takes careful analysis on the part of the astrologer.

I feel that food selection and working with mind and consciousness is a more direct route to balancing the system, but gem-metal therapy has been used with beneficial results.

Colors are felt to influence the human senses according to the applied frequency of vital force, as well as to the movement and the activity of the subtle vital forces themselves.

Five Subtle Senses	*Five Aspects of Vital Force*
Sight—Red	Vital (prana)—Green
Smell—Green	Upward (udana)—Violet
Touch—Violet	Even (samana)—Red & Yellow
Sound—Blue	Diffused (vyana)—Blue
Taste—Orange	Downward (apana)—Orange & Indigo

Colors taken in through the optic nerve, as well as gems or color frequencies taken in through food and breathing, will influence the chakras and harmonize the system. Also, the natural circulation of vital force through Kriya Yoga practice and the spontaneous flows in meditation will harmonize the chakras, the activity of glands, and will tend to balance the three element systems: air, fire, and water.

These three systems are also influenced by the times of the day. From 6 a.m. to 10 a.m. the water element in the body is more active; hence, the time is ideal for elimination of wastes from the body. From 10 a.m. to 2 p.m. the fire element is more active; thus, this is a useful time to eat food, particularly just before noon. From 2 p.m. until 6 p.m. the air element is more active, and nerve force is stronger. The times preceding and following dawn and dusk are times when the body elements are at

CHAKRA	PLANET	GEM	COLOR	ELEMENT (3 Basics)	POLARITY	INFLUENCE	TASTE
Crown	Mercury	Emerald	Green	Water	Positive	Hot	All tastes
Third Eye	Jupiter	Topaz & Moonstone	Blue	Air	Neutral	Hot	Sweet
Cervical Throat	Venus	Diamond	Indigo	Water	Positive	Cold	Sour
Thoracic Heart	Saturn	Sapphire	Violet	Air	Neutral	Cold	Saline
Lumbar Solar Plexus	Sun	Ruby	Red	Fire	Negative	Hot	Pungent
Sacrum	Moon	Pearl	Orange	Water	Positive	Cold	Astringent
Base Chakra	Mars	Coral	Yellow	Fire	Negative	Hot	Bitter

Note: In the above chart the Chakras (distribution points through which life-force flows) are listed first for simplicity's sake, for those who calculate from above-down; the 2nd column shows the planetary rulership for the gems . . . and from there . . : over to the right . . . are the colors, subtle-element characteristics, polarity influences . . . heat & cold influences . . . and "taste" of the frequencies as observed on the tongue when these influences are evident. The astral-physical chemical condition pervades the system and certain signs can be discerned; through color-sense, feel, energy input . . . and taste. All of the ordinary senses can be reflected in the subtle senses, so that one can discern color, sound, smell, taste and feeling for all influences in the environment regardless of whether the signs are outer or inner.

rest and meditation is easy. A natural calm is experienced by persons (and animals and plants) during these occasions.

It is advisable to acquire an over-view of the process of how Cosmic Current flows into manifestation. An understanding of this process enables a person to live in harmony with nature and even to gain control of inner and outer forces, if the constructive need should arise. While the chart shows the flow from above-- downward, it should be considered from within—outward, as manifestation flows from inner space or the Transcendental Field.

Metals & Their Influences

Metals are living things. The oxidation of metals is similar to the breathing process of the body in its metabolic change and reaction to the air principle of nature. Metals also show wear, fatigue, stress, and strain. It has been said that cutting tools, if given a "rest" after long use, will again hold a sharp edge. Research with pyramid energies and the effects of moonlight on razors indicates that metals respond to outside energy influences. Metals crystallize with age, wear, crumble, and break.

Gold, silver, copper, iron, lead, and mercury have been used for therapeutic purposes. Mercury is used in a refined state for body cleansing and for the eradication of disease. This refining process is unknown today to the western world; it requires heat and a mixture of sulfur and certain herbs.

Gold has the sun influence: it heats and expands. *Silver* is ruled by the moon: it cools and contracts. *Copper* is ruled by Venus and has a cleansing effect upon the system, especially in cases of arthritis and rheumatism. A recent test conducted by doctors at a university revealed that aspirin, infused with copper and given to subjects who did not know of the test, yielded superior results over aspirin given without the copper infusion. Many persons (myself included) wear a general purpose bracelet made of twisted strands of copper, silver, and gold. This was a common suggestion given by Swami Sri Yukteswar. I cannot tell if the bracelet is useful. I wear it for sentimental reasons, since it attunes me to the wave-length of my guru-line when I become aware of it. It, thus, has value as an amulet or a talisman, as it carries with it a "message" to be received by the mind.

ing of a specific mantra (related to the planetary intelligence which controls the energy of the planet). This refers, not to the actual intelligence of the planet, but to the aspect of Universal Intelligence expressed as that energy frequency. Also, certain rings, for specific purposes, are to be manufactured by one who is of high (clear) consciousness, with definite intent and during the time when the planets involved are ideally aspected. In this way, a powerful infusion of energies is contributed to the ring or talisman.

Other Items of Interest

Some yogis recommend that one sit on a wool blanket when meditating, to insulate the body from magnetic earth currents. Energies can then more easily be raised up the spinal pathway and retained in the body during meditation. Some wrap the body in a wool blanket. Silk is also said to be ideal for this purpose, and some occultists (those who work with finer forces) wear silk garments and use silk bedsheets.

Sleeping with the head toward the north causes energies of the body to be pulled upward in the body and contributes to an easier passing at the time of transition. Sleeping with the head to the south results in body currents being pulled down into the body (toward north) and allows the currents to work to insure health and function. Sleeping with the head toward the west is said to contribute to dreams; with the head eastward, to meditative sleep.

It is not our intention to emphasize reliance upon external aids. We merely examine the characteristics of energies as they manifest in nature and try to understand their influence. If we can utilize them, so much the better. Sri Yukteswar once said: "A wise person rests in the Infinite and makes intelligent use of any natural law which can contribute to his well-being." We were born with certain subconscious characteristics (karmic patterns) and we are influenced at birth by energy flows in nature. We are not "fated" to live out our lives in an extension of the way things were at the time of physical birth. Through self-analysis, right mental attitude, prayer and meditation, diet, and any useful thing we are led to do, we can neutralize negative tendencies and learn to work in conscious harmony with nature.

Chapter Nine

As a result of deeper meditation experiences the soul learns to know that it is independently self-sufficient. That is, the soul exists prior to identification with the mind and it exists after transcending mental identification. The masters teach that it is only through experience that one knows the final truth about life. One can acquire an intellectual grasp of the workings of Consciousness, but only direct experience of the nature of Being will result in one's mastery over the senses and other material influences.

Among the many who are actively involved in some routine of spiritual practice, only a few are really involved with useful inner change which alone can allow enlightenment. Realization should infiltrate the mental field, the nervous system, the body, and the surrounding environment so that transformation is effected. Living the ideal life fully is the only way to truly know about the nature of life. "Working at" spiritual practices can never take the place of letting God "work through" us. The reader must have, by now, come to understand that the teachings of the masters aims at the ultimate removal of all that prevents one from expressing as a completely free being.

Some people in today's society delude themselves into believing they are free if they are no longer bound by traditional social conventions when, in fact, they remain slaves to their own misguided whims. There are many who think they know the truth about life when, in fact, they only know a small part of the whole. They may be free from former limitations, but they are not liberated in the sense of which the masters speak.

While one does not have to outwardly dramatize his spiritual intentions in order to attract attention, one should inwardly realize that for the true spiritual life there must be a radical difference between how one thinks, feels, and acts as compared to how one thought, felt, and acted when in mortal consciousness. We cannot say that we truly love God if we resent our fellow beings, we cannot say that we truly trust if we are greedy and manipulative, we cannot say we are in tune with nature if we are overstressed. Spiritual consciousness cannot be contained in a mind which retains negative and destructive tendencies, and the ideal life cannot be lived if we are in conflict with the flow of nature.

We recall the mention made earlier regarding the effects upon us of electric influences. The Sanskrit word *guna* means rope. A rope can be used to bind. The electric influences bind subtle matter and make possible all alterations in matter and mind. For instance, if one is sincerely striving for enlightenment while yet retaining an environmental situation which is not compatible with the ideal, one is not providing the best atmosphere in which awakening can occur. If we pray and meditate on a regular basis but continue to socialize with negative and restless people, our efforts are neutralized. Our environment influences us and we influence our environment. If we create an orderly and harmonious environment for ourselves, if we eat live foods, if we think uplifting thoughts and engage in useful action, we are then providing the best advantage for spiritual unfoldment. Thoughts, actions, and conditions are not "spiritual" in themselves, but if we enter into a relationship with that which is uplifting, then the tendencies within us which contribute to inertia and restlessness will be neutralized. While some seekers have found it useful to live in secluded areas, removed from the chaos of public places, in order to contemplate life's mysteries, it is quite possible for one to create the ideal environment in his own community so that progress can be experienced.

It is certainly not a sign of weakness for one to choose where and how he will live and with whom he will relate. We have freedom of choice and we need not fall victim to believing that where we are, if it is an environment of poor quality, is where God wants us to be. Where we are is the result of our mental attitude and self-image. It is a sign of wisdom for one to create as ideal an environment as possible to further his personal and spiritual goals.

GLOSSARY

The following one hundred Sanskrit words are ones which are commonly used in Yoga books and philosophical texts. An understanding of their meanings will help the student to derive greater insight into various works studied. Other Sanskrit words and terms will be found explained in the text matter of this book.

Advaita—Non-duality: the teaching that God, soul and the universe are One. Known as *Vedanta*, the final summation of the *Vedas.*

ahamkara—The ego, or "I" consciousness.

ajna—The "plexus of command" or third eye center.

ajnana—Meaning either individual or cosmic ignorance. This alone is said to be the cause of false perception and delusion.

akasa—Often spelled "Akasha"; the first of five material elements making up nature; sometimes translated as *ether.*

ananda—Bliss; often used as part of a monastic name of swamis. For instance, Yogananda: "bliss through Yoga or divine union."

anandamayakosa—The initial subtle sheath of the soul.

annamayakosa—The "food sheath" or physical body.

antahkarana—The inner organ of the soul's perception when operating in space and time; comprised of mind, intellect, ego-sense and feeling.

ashram—A secluded place for the practice of yogic disciplines or spiritual training.

Atman—A ray of Supreme Consciousness shining in the organ of the intellect of the mind. A particularization of Supreme Consciousness.

avadhuta—A supremely Self-Realized soul who functions through a mind and body but whose consciousness extends to the Infinite.

avatara—The "descent" of Divinity into a human form; a Divine Incarnation; A Savior or World Redeemer.

avidya—Meaning "Not knowledge"; lack of understanding of the nature of Consciousness and Its manifestations.

Ayurveda—Science of Life; an ancient Indian science of medicine and health principles.

Bhagavan—Lord; literally one endowed with with the six attributes: infinite spiritual power, righteousness, glory, splendor, knowledge and renunciation. Used in reference to a fully Self-realized person.

Bhagavad-Gita—An eighteen chapter work: "The Song of God." One of the central yogic scriptures setting forth the conversation between Krishna (an Incarnation of God) and Arjuna (the seeker on the path of Yoga.)

Bhakti—Devotion; intense love for God.

Brahma—The first person in the Trinity in Hindu thought; the same as "God the Father" of the Christian tradition.

Brahmachari—A self-disciplined student who devotes himself to spiritual practices under a guru.

Brahmaloka—The abode of God; corresponding to the highest plane of heaven this side of the Transcendental Field.

Brahman—The Supreme Reality; the Absolute, without attributes or characteristics.

Brahma-Sutras—Also known as the *Vedanta-Sutras*; a treatise on high philosophical views and a central scripture for students whose quest is the path of knowledge.

Brahmavidya—The knowledge of Supreme Consciousness.

buddhi—The faculty of discernment or determination; sometimes defined as "intellect," that which makes decisions.

chakra—A subtle center for psychic energy in the central pathway of the spinal cord; also the distribution center through which energies flow. The word means "wheel."

Chiti—The Absolute in its creative and dynamic aspect as power.

chitta—The individual consciousness which perceives differences in Universal Being; it meditates between the inner and the outer realms.

deva—A "god" or shining one. Gods and goddesses (*devis*) dwell in subtle realms.

dhyana—Flowing the attention to one point during meditation; the sixth state in Raja Yoga practice. Next comes *dharana*, pure meditation, followed by *samadhi* or the peak experience.

diksha—Yogic initiation, during which time instruction is given in a precise meditation method and the guru transmits his *shakti* into the disciple.

Govinda—One of the names for Krishna.

guna—The qualities or electric attributes in nature. *Tamas guna* stands for inertia or heaviness; *rajas guna* is the neutralizing current, sometimes referred to as the active quality; *sattva guna* promotes righteousness and spiritual enlightenment.

Guru—Literally "darkness" and "light"; that which dispels the darkness from the mind and consciousness of the seeker. The *Guru* is considered as God in human form Who comes for the welfare of the disciple on the path.

Gurukripa—The grace of God flowing through the *Guru.*

Guruseva—Service to the *Guru* is considered service to God. Through attunement with the *Guru* one identifies with his consciousness and experiences liberation.

ida—Left *nadi* or channel through which vital current flows; the moon current or negative polarity.

Isvara—Or "Iswara," the personal aspect of God which governs and controls the universe. Supreme Consciousness *as* the ruler of the manifest worlds.

japa—Repetition of any of the names of God for the purpose of meditation and concentration.

Jivanmukta—A free soul; one who is liberated while yet working through the body. Remaining *karma* may still persist but the person is inwardly free.

jnana—*Jnana Yoga* is the way to freedom through discernment. The word means "knowledge" of that contemplated.

jnani—One who is possessed of highest knowledge.

karma—Action; sometimes translated as "duty"; for instance, "It is my *karma* to do this work." Also, used in the explanation of cause and effect in the phenomenal universe.

Khechari Mudra—The state in which one is free to roam in the spaces in consciousness; also the physical act where the tongue is drawn up into the nasal pharynx, stimulating a discharge of fluids from the cranial region.

Kriya Yoga—Yogic *kriyas* are spontaneous purification actions on subtle levels which take place when *kundalini* is awakened. *Kriya Yoga* also refers to the precise system of meditation techniques taught by my line of gurus as advised by Mahavatar Babaji.

kundalini—Dormant, static, vital force resting in Nature; when it awakens in nature, then life emerges on the planet. When it awakens in man, then the soul begins its journey through inner space in the direction of Self-realization.

Maha—Literally means "great," such as in *Mahatma* or "great soul."

Mahadeva—"Great god," often used in reference to *Shiva.*

mahasamadhi—The final conscious departure of a *yogi* from his physical form. Also, used in reference to the shrine which is erected over the body after transition.

manas—The aspect of the mind which is the seat or root of the five senses. When the soul identifies with *manas*, it is described as "man."

manomayakosa—The sheath or covering of the mind.

mantra—Sound used for its specific influence on its environment: physical, mental or more subtle. Can be intoned audibly, mentally recited or listened to in deep meditation.

maya—Sometimes referred to as the "stuff" of which the worlds are formed; the cause of illusion. Made up of time, space, light particles and the primal energy of OM. *Maya* has two characteristics: it forms as the world, and it veils truth from the soul.

moksha—Liberation or freedom from *maya.*

mudra—A symbolic pose or gesture; a "seal"; a yogic practice used to awaken *kundalini* and to gain control over vital processes.

nada—Different inner sounds heard during meditation which are variations of the primal sound of Om. *Nadayoga* is the science of sound.

nadi—A channel through which prana flows in the psychic system.

nadi-shuddhi—Purification of the nerves and subtle channels due to the active flowing of *shakti* after *kundalini* is awakened.

Nirguna Brahman—Supreme Consciousness without attributes or qualities.

Nirvana—To "blow out" or to eradicate from the mind all that prevents the clear perception of Reality. To attain *nirvana* is to be liberated as a result of all subtle impressions of the mind having been erased.

Nirvikalpa Samadhi—The experience of Pure Consciousness without mental or conceptual support. This *samadhi* is not pure or permanent, according to some, unless all latent impressions of the mind are removed.

OM—The primal sound from which all outer appearances manifest. The *Pranava, Aum* or *Amen.*

Paramahansa—The highest title for a Self-realized *Yogi.* One who rests in God-realization and is not touched by the world process.

pingala—Right spinal pathway for flowing *prana.* The "sun" current, as opposed to the "moon" current of *ida.* The positive flow of current in the system. When both currents are neutralized, then *kundalini* can ascend.

Prakriti—The material realms (nature) consisting of the elements and electric attributes or qualities.

prana—Vital force animating the universe and all forms. All *pranas* are divisions of the Sound Current.

pranayama—Regulation of vital forces, usually through conscious regulation of breathing and specific *mudras.*

pranamayakosa—The vital body or astral sheath of the soul.

prarabdha karma—Subconscious impressions now beginning to manifest or to be worked out in this incarnation.

Purusha—Conscious Principle, which unites with subtle elements in nature to form the material realms.

rajas—The principle of activity or neutralization.

rasa-lila—The eternal "dance" taking place between the Lord of the universe and individual souls.

rishi—A seer; one who reveals the wisdom of the scriptures.

sadhana—Spiritual disciplines of *Yoga.*

Saguna Brahman—Supreme Consciousness with attributes; the Godhead, with three aspects: Existence, Intelligence and Creative Energy.

sahasrara—The center of consciousness in the cerebrum; the highest of the seven *chakras* and the one which is superior to them all.

samadhi—When the waves of the mind cease and "oneness" is experienced. Lower *samadhi* is oneness with an object (saguna); higher *samadhi* is without any object (Nirguna).

samasara—The "forever becomingness" of the world process. One who is deluded and identified with change is sure to suffer from unwanted change of circumstances and relationships. To identify with the world process is to be bound to the "wheel of rebirth" and to rise above identification is to be free.

Sanatana Dharma—The Eternal Religion or the eternal way of righteousness. Can be traced to pre-*Vedic* times and is said to be without origin, having always been known to a few initiates.

sannyasin—A renunciate who has taken holy vows (*sannyasa*) for the purpose of devoting all energies to Self-realization and world service.

sattva—The elevating attribute of nature, that which leads one to *Sat*, the pure truth.

Shakti—The cosmic energy which forms the worlds and maintains them; the energy awakened in one who receives *kundalini* initiation.

Shaktipat—The infusion of energy from *guru* to disciple which can take place during initiation or spontaneously when the disciple is receptive to the experience.

Shambhavi mudra—When the attention is focused spontaneously and one's attention is flowing to the Divine nature, whether the eyes or open or closed. When the attention does not flutter.

Shiva—Third person in the Hindu Trinity; the aspect of the Godhead which sends forth Creative Energy and then dissolves It. *Shiva* is the patron diety of *Yoga*.

Siddha—A "perfect being" who is accomplished in *Yoga*. A true Master who can awaken *shakti* and lead the disciple to liberation of consciousness.

siddhis—Powers of perfection as a result of soul awakening.

sushumna—Central pathway through which *kundalini* ascends to the crown *chakra*, resulting in evolutionary transformation of the system and the highest *samadhi*.

tattva—The true or inner essence of a thing. The essence of the senses are the roots of the senses on the subtle level. The essence of the worlds is God, the Light behind the "darkness" of outer manifestation. The essence of a thing is known only when one turns the attention to the source of the appearance.

Turiya—The "fourth" state of consciousness; transcending the three states of waking, dream and deep sleep.

Upanishads—A section of the *Vedas*, which are considered an important collection of scripture. These scriptures were taught in the oral tradition, by word of mouth, for hundreds of years before being written in Sanskrit.

Vedanta—The summing up of the wisdom of the *Vedas*. The usual declaration regarding the nature of a person or any appearance is: *Tat Twam Asi*—"That Thou Art!" Supreme Consciousness is the cause and support of all that appears.

Vishnu—The second person in the Trinity. The aspect of the Godhead which maintains order and preserves the universe.

viveka—Discrimination between the changeless and the transitory.

Vyasa—A sage who is believed to have arranged the *Vedas* in their present form. Legend has it that the name refers to several sages who worked on the project over a period of time.

Yoga—To "yoke" or join together. The complete system of various compatible disciplines which enable one to harmonize conflicting and active currents in the system so that the light of the soul can be directly cognized.

The offering on the next three pages was written by the author as an exercise in the examination of essential principles relative to God, the nature of the world process, and the experience of soul awakening.

Review it at any time but especially before or after meditation. Daily contemplation of *The Realization of Spiritual Perfection* can only result in deeper understanding.

The REALIZATION of
SPIRITUAL PERFECTION

The realization of spiritual perfection is easy and natural. Easy, because we have only to turn our attention away from untruth and flow it to truth. Natural, because at the very center of our being we are already enlightened.

Truth is *that which is so* about life. Not what one thinks is so, nor what one concludes to be so, but that which *is* so.

Knowing the truth frees the mind from bondage and from dependence upon externals. Knowing the truth results in liberation of consciousness.

The realm of fulfillment exists now and all can have access to it. We can live in the material world and still be aware of heaven. Heaven extends to all aspects and all levels of material manifestation.

There is a pure realm, a non-dual realm, which remains ever the same. This pure realm is the cause and support of all outer manifestation. Extending Itself as the Cosmic Soul, Life appears as a Self-involved electrical field with full awareness. The Cosmic Soul is innately possessed of eternal being, total intelligent consciousness, and endless power.

The tendencies toward brightness, activity, and gravity exist in the Cosmic Soul and make possible the manifestation of the universes, the movements leading to evolutionary change, and final world redemption.

The Holy Spirit, the directing force of God, shines on the *moving creative energy of God* and the *Word, (Amen, Aum)* of God is made manifest. The Word emerges from God, the Word is God, the Word extends as all material manifestation.

The substance of the manifest worlds is made up of creative energy, light particles, space, and time. God, as this primal fabric, extends as the worlds. Behind this substance of which forms are made is the realm of the gods, the shining beings. Coming through this primal substance, the gods are known as man. Awakening from material identification man knows once again the pure nature, and thus is experienced the realization of spiritual perfection.

There is no independent universe, and there is no individual person. The universe is an extension of primal substance, the result of outflowing force acted upon by the intelligence of God. The seeming individual person is but a viewpoint of God. God appears on the surface of manifest nature as waves appear on the surface of the ocean. God is both the wave and the ocean; the soul and the Cosmic Soul.

Mind pervades the material universe. There is but one Mind; that which appears as individual mind is but a particularization of the one Mind. Through this particularization of Mind, used by a world-identified being, full conscious cooperation between man and God is possible. A viewpoint of God, identified with mind, assuming itself to be mind, is known as man. The sense of individual existence is the result of temporary self-forgetfulness.

Subtle aura-electricities are the causes of material appearances. Interacting, they manifest as the electric realm or astral realm. More fully extending they appear as the physical universe. The universe, on all levels, from subtle to material, is really a play of light and shadows, a forever occurring drama against the screen of time and space.

As God is superior to the one Mind and, through the one Mind, superior to universal manifestation . . . so God, as the viewpoint known as the soul, is superior to particularized mind and to personal environment. The universe is a reflection of inner causes and material bodies are reflections of inner causes and states. There is, therefore, no clear line to be drawn between mind and body.

By altering states of consciousness and mental attitudes, man can live creatively and freely in any universe. By awakening from the dream of mortality the soul consciously experiences its real nature. This is enlightenment. With the enlightenment experience the light of the soul floods mind and body with cleansing influence. The experience of heaven on earth is then natural and effortless.

By clearly understanding that only one Life exists, we can flow with natural trends and live by grace. By such understanding and by such experience we are in harmony with a supportive universe and every person and every living thing is friendly.

The soul is already healthy and prosperous. It is the nature of the soul to thrive, to flourish and to experience fulfillment, just as it is the nature of God to thrive, to flourish and to fulfill intended purposes. A conscious being does not need to try to be happy, healthy, and prosperous because happiness, health, and prosperity are completely natural. Unhappiness, sickness, and limitation are evidence of lack of true soul awareness.

The fulfillment of soul destiny is assured just as the fulfillment of God's plan for the universe is assured. There is nothing to fear; all things work together in perfect harmony.

The *seeming* stages of soul unfoldment are but degrees of natural soul awakening. One does not develop a spiritual consciousness; one awakens to the realization of spiritual perfection.

The force that consciously powers the universe can be known and experienced as a benevolent, supportive urge in the direction of completion. This is the assurance of fulfillment in all spheres, dimensions, and realms.

Behind the manifest realm is that pure essence which remains *ever the same.* Behind man's feeling nature and behind the processes of thought is that pure essence which remains *ever the same.* This pure essence is known during settled contemplation and during occasions of clear self-awareness. As a result of clear self-awareness, one knows inner causes and outer effects, one is possessed of inner knowledge and the understanding of the world drama.

Firm in the realization of spiritual perfection, one is forever at peace.

Guidelines

**GUIDELINES to PERSONAL
STUDY and MEDITATION**

We have two major purposes in life. First, we are here to consciously realize our divine potential. Second, we are to flow in harmony with God's plan and participate in the process of world regeneration. These purposes can be fulfilled concurrently because greater soul awareness will inspire us to world service and active participation in this direction, according to our highest guidance, will accelerate spiritual unfoldment. If we think we can enlighten others without an inner personal relationship with God, we are in error. If we assume that we must experience final liberation of consciousness before becoming involved in constructive and useful work, we have missed the point. Here are some suggestions for steady and realistic participation and experience.

*For a Personal Relationship with God
Acknowledge Him and Do These Things*

Moment to moment inner acknowledgement of the reality of God keeps us attuned to His purpose and influence. We may contemplate the nature of God from time to time. We may meditate for a personal experience of God from time to time. We may practice the awareness of the presence of God from time to time. But it is the ever-awareness of the reality of God which will maintain an open and responsive relationship between the inner realms the the outer world.

311

Pray to God — We can talk with God anytime and anywhere we choose. The inward mental conversation with God assures attunement with the Source. Prayer does not always have to be in words or thoughts, it can be a surrendered inclination in the direction of God and an open attitude to God's impulse from within our very depths. Prayer can precede meditation. We seek first an intimate relationship with God, and, when prayer has cleared the mental field, meditation proceeds easily. Pray to God simply and directly. Pray to God in any form or aspect to which you can relate. All sincere prayers flow to the Source, regardless of the aspect visualized. Pray in your own words and in your own way because prayer is between soul and God. The attitude should be, "God, I surrender thoughts, feelings, and the sense of personal self to you." Such prayer awakens the soul nature and banishes the clouds of confusion from the mind.

Meditate Regularly — Regular meditation will transform one's life. Whatever method or approach is used, let it be natural. Flow attention to the Source of life within you and there rest. Conscious meditation allows direct soul experience and results in superconscious forces flowing into the mental field, nervous system and physical body, cleansing and regenerating. Correct meditation practice drains tension from the system and allows the vital forces to circulate without restriction. Meditating with others can sometimes be useful but one's decision to practice is a personal matter. If you cannot relax during the early stages of meditation, practice exercises to induce relaxation or pray until meditation begins naturally.

After meditation rest in the stillness and acknowledge God as your very life. Acknowledge that you are, as a soul, an extension of the Cosmic Soul. Accept full responsibility for your mental attitude, your thoughts, your feelings, and your response to all that unfolds in your world. Remain centered, clear, and aware of your real nature and your relationship with God.

Study Correctly — Read the writings of the masters and the enlightened seers of the ages. Study the nature of God and the world. Examine carefully the total process of cosmic manifestation and derive inspiration and motivation on the path. Study with keen discernment and with intuition alert for insight. At the deepest soul level you already know the truth about life. This is why you recognize truth when it is presented to you through the written or spoken word. There is a deeper and more subtle influence to be experienced as a result of correct study. The written and spoken words of enlightened teachers are infused with their own spiritual realizations. Such words, therefore, are vehicles for the transmission of spiritual energy which enters the mind and consciousness of the seekers. When we study with surrendered anticipation we can receive subtle spiritual energy and we can become attuned to clear levels of awareness. Just as we are influenced by the characteristics and tendencies of people with whom we live on a daily basis, so we are influenced by the characteristics and tendencies of God-conscious souls when we live with them on the mental and spiritual plane.

Put Your Environment in Order — If there are any unresolved problems in your life, clear them through intelligent actions and wise decisions. Problems drag us down into inertia and conditioned mental states. To the best of your ability put your life in order. Even if facing a difficult task, be reminded, "With God I Can!" See to spiritual health, mental and emotional health, physical health, health in human relationships, and health in relationship to the world in which we live. Overcome inertia by being involved with purpose. Purify your activities by allowing the light of the soul to influence your decisions and actions. In all things put God first in your life. Because we are influenced by environmental radiations, see to it that your environment is harmonious, clean, and elevating.

Make a Useful Contribution to Your World — Whatever your vocation, if you feel it to be useful and constructive, enter into it with full awareness and perform as well as you can. Conscious living is a very useful spiritual exercise and soul freedom can be experienced as a result of intelligent fulfillment of personal duty. Your state of *being* is the most influential contribution to your world because this is shared silently with other people, the collective mental condition of the planet, and the very energies of nature. God is awakening souls and transforming matter (as energy), but God also expresses through us when we are open to the flow.

We have many levels of responsibility while we are involved with the creative process. We have a responsibility to ourselves to see that we are possessed of correct understanding and that we are attuned to God. We have a responsibility to members of our family and to those in our community. We have the responsibility of contributing to the general health and well-being of society. We have a responsibility to contribute, according to guidance, to the spiritual welfare of all people. The spiritual path is not a life of escapism during which we withdraw and refuse to play our destined role. It is not a matter of sitting back and letting other people do the work that is ours to do. As long as we are involved with relative matters, so long do we have a responsibility to render useful service to the extent of our means and capacity. It is by living fully in harmony with natural principles that we experience the truth. When we are Self-actualized, soul influence is blended harmoniously with mental and emotional processes, physical processes and personal interaction with people and our world.

Careful attention to the essentials will, in the long run, result in full realization and final completion.

ABOUT THE AUTHOR

Roy Eugene Davis has been teaching since his ordination into the ministry by Paramahansa Yogananda in 1951. He is the Director of Center for Spiritual Awareness, editor-publisher of *Truth Journal* magazine and a widely traveled speaker. Lectures and seminars have been given in the major cities of the United States, Canada, Europe and Japan. Several of his books are published in German, Japanese and Portuguese languages.

At the retreat center in Lakemont, Georgia Mr. Davis supervises seminars and classes for the hundreds of people who come from all parts of the world. His teaching emphasis is that there is a Power which runs our universe and we can learn to cooperate with it. Correct understanding results in personal fulfillment.

BOOKS BY ROY EUGENE DAVIS

An Easy Guide to Meditation
WITH GOD We CAN!
Conscious Immortality
Darshan: The Vision of Light
The Bhagavad Gita
The Technique of Creative Imagination
Yoga-Darsana
Miracle Man of Japan
Health, Healing & Total Living
Studies in Truth